Arkansas/Arkansaw

Arkansas/Arkansaw

*How Bear Hunters, Hillbillies,
and Good Ol' Boys Defined a State*

Brooks Blevins

The University of Arkansas Press
Fayetteville ❖ 2009

ISBN-10: 1-55728-905-0
ISBN-13: 978-1-55728-905-6

13   12   11   10   09   1   2   3   4   5

Text design by Ellen Beeler

⊗ The paper used in this publication meets the minimum requirements
of the American National Standard for Permanence of Paper for Printed
Library Materials Z39.48-1984.

Library of Congress Cataloging-in-Publication Data

Blevins, Brooks, 1969-
    Arkansas/Arkansaw : how bear hunters, hillbillies, and good ol' boys
    defined a state / Brooks Blevins.
        p. cm.
    Includes bibliographical references and index.
    ISBN 978-1-55728-905-6 (cloth : alk. paper)
    1. Arkansas—History. 2. Arkansas—Public opinion. 3. Arkansas—
    Social life and customs. 4. Bear hunting—Arkansas—History.
    5. Mountain people—Arkansas—History. 6. Rednecks—Arkansas—
    History. 7. Arkansas—Biography. I. Title.
    F411.B695 2009
    976.7—dc22

                                                            2009018510

Publication of this book was supported by the Old State House
Museum in Little Rock, Arkansas, whose exhibit on "Arkansas,
Arkansaw" was curated by the author.

For Annie

Contents

Acknowledgments

This is not a book about the state of Arkansas so much as it is about the idea of Arkansas. That is not to say that it is in some sense not *Arkansas history*. As most any native or resident of Arkansas knows, our state's image has long been critical to its history and development. The stereotypes and image problems of Arkansas have for many years occupied the attention of a variety of people in the state, from business-minded boosters to historians. This is the first book-length telling of an integral part of the Arkansas story—the creation and evolution of *Arkansaw*. I am first and foremost indebted to the work of many scholars and writers without whom this book would have been impossible, among them James R. Masterson, C. Fred Williams, Michael B. Dougan, Morris Arnold, Foy Lisenby, Lee A. Dew, E. E. Dale, William Shea, Ben Johnson, and Bob Lancaster.

This is also a book written for Arkansas people, Arkansawyers and Arkansans, natives and newcomers. Not that I'm asking you to shut it up and put it away if you don't claim to be either. Group image construction and identity can be a slippery subject. Confronting stereotypes and images can be painful; it can also be instructive and empowering. This particular piece of geopolitical angst, and the exhibit it will for a time accompany, grew out of an idea Larry Ahart had for an Old State House Museum exhibit on Arkansas's hillbilly image. As these things so often do, the breadth and depth of the research involved expanded far beyond anything that Larry and I first discussed in the spring of 2002. To Bill Gatewood, Larry Ahart, Jo Ellen Mack, Gail Moore, Amy Peck, and the rest of the staff at the Old State House I offer my thanks. Many thanks as well to Debbie Self and to Larry Malley, Julie Watkins, Katy Henrikson, and the rest of the staff at the University of Arkansas Press for their fine work.

I have received assistance and advice from a great many of you Arkansawyers and Arkansans. I wrote this book while on the faculty of Lyon College in Batesville, Arkansas, and I extend my appreciation to many people currently and formerly affiliated with that institution. Kathy Whittenton, Lyon College's interlibrary loan librarian, was my link to the world of research libraries, as were her summer replacements Marjorie Seasholtz and Deanna Devall. I also appreciate the various kinds of assistance offered by library director Dean Covington and his other staff members, Camille Beary, Judy Blackwell, and Brenda Lindsey. I received valuable assistance from a trio of work-study students at Lyon, Kim Halpain, Melissa Harrison, and John Dudley. I also thank former students Julie Sandy and Blake Perkins and former Lyon colleague John Weinzierl for their contributions.

Realizing that I will unintentionally leave someone unmentioned who should be mentioned, I acknowledge the following for their assistance: Jimmy Bryant and the staff at the University of Central Arkansas Archives; Wendy Richter, Russell Baker, Lynn Ewbank, Jane Hooker, Jane Wilkerson, and the rest of the staff at the Arkansas History Commission; Tom Dillard, Andrea Cantrell, Geoffery Stark, and the staff at the University of Arkansas Special Collections in Fayetteville; David Stricklin, Brian Robertson, and the staff at the Butler Center for Arkansas Studies; the staff of the Archives and Special Collections at the University of Arkansas at Little Rock; Mike Polston and Mike Keckhaver of the Encyclopedia of Arkansas; Tim Hollis of the National Lum and Abner Society; Maxine Whittaker of the History Museum of Springfield-Greene County; and Tricia Hearn, formerly of the now-defunct Ozark Cultural Resource Center at the Ozark Folk Center. Robert Cochran's critique of the manuscript was excellent and invaluable, as was Lynn Morrow's. Among the many who have offered valuable advice and information during the research and writing of this book are George Lankford, Susan Young, Jo Blatti, John Hensley, James Johnston, Michael Luster, Anthony Harkins, Stephen A. Smith, Tommy Hancock, Craig Ogilvie, Elizabeth Jacoway, Jeffrey Johnson, Laura Bowles, Marcia Camp, and the late W. K. McNeil. I am grateful for the many stimulating discussions I participated in during the Appalachia Up Close NEH institute at Ferrum College in the summer of 2004, and I thank Pete Crow, Dan Woods, Susan Mead, and my fellow participants. I take full credit for any valuable insights gained from conversations and correspondence with any of the people named above and stand ready to blame them for any shortcomings.

Arkansas/Arkansaw

Introduction

There's an old joke that most any Arkansas native has heard and that many have told in a variety of forms. One version goes something like this:

> An Arkansas family was on the way to California in the heart of the depression when their truck (and here we all envision something akin to the Joads' jalopy or the Clampettmobile) began to overheat. Pulling up to a filling station, the Arkansas father went inside to borrow a bucket of water. The attendant, by now no stranger to such beleaguered travelers, wryly asked, "Where you from, mister?" to which the Arkansawyer replied, "Arkansas. Now laugh, damn you!"

Other permutations find the defensive Arkie in modern-day Manhattan or on a nineteenth-century wagon trek or in a wartime boot camp, but the reaction, and the message, is always the same. Every Arkansas hearer or teller of the joke can empathize.

My grandpa certainly could have. Like many Arkies in the post–World War II era, my grandparents found financial salvation (at least of the temporary variety) on the migrant labor trails that snaked their way out of the Land of Opportunity in almost every direction. They often encountered voices of derision and looks of condescension for their trouble. Years later my aunt recalled an episode from one of the family's seasonal journeys, a trifle of a scene that flashed through my mind from time to time as I wrote this book. The setting was Yakima, Washington, in the latter half of the 1940s. After a grueling week of work in the hops vineyards that rose green toward the heavens in the Yakima River Valley, my grandparents dressed the kids up and took them into the city for the rare treat of popcorn and a coke. The teenager running the popcorn machine at the five and dime had seen enough of her little world to know a bunch of itinerant workers when she saw them, clean duds or no, and my grandpa's request for "two pokes o' corn" sealed the deal. "Let me guess," the girl said, her tinny voice fortified with sarcasm and exasperation. "You're from Arkansas." Only it wasn't really a guess, more of an accusation, as if these paying customers were guilty of a crime and should feel ashamed for trying to hide it. My grandpa, by now no stranger to Arkie bashing but nevertheless caught off guard by the girl's brazenness, fired back without hesitation. "Why, no, we're from Texas!"

In my aunt's memory, my grandpa's denial of his home state was motivated by embarrassment and anger. It wasn't that he was ashamed to be

3

from Arkansas. Perhaps he had just had his fill of condescension. He was a proud man, a farm owner back home in the Ozarks, and, besides, what business was it of some Yakima popcorn popper where they were from anyhow? But my grandpa was also known to have a little fun with people, and it is quite possible that his claiming Texas was a studied response he'd concocted to use on all the smart-alecks and uppity folks he had encountered on the laborer's trail. Whatever it was flashing through the mind of Bryan Blevins that August day some two thousand miles from home, the scene itself has played out innumerable times. Those of us who have ventured very far beyond our state's confines have almost certainly found ourselves playing Arkansas Peter at least once—tempted on the one hand to deny our benighted state of origin or residence, on the other to lop off the ear of her detractor. That last reaction, I assume and hope, is only figurative. If you have sliced off the ear of a New Yorker or Californian who would defame the old Bear State, well, then bully for you; but, as we shall see, you were simply satisfying one of our oldest stereotypes and thus cutting off an ear to spite your face, so to speak.

The joke and anecdote point toward a few of the central concepts of this book. The first, probably more of a conceit than a concept, is that Arkansas has for one reason or another undergone more caricaturing and stereotyping in the American imagination than has just about any other state. Arkansas has, of course, not stood alone as a bastion of backwoodsiness. Davy Crockett called Tennessee home; Georgia lays claim to Sut Lovingood, Jeeter Lester, and the mountain menagerie from *Deliverance;* and every other state south of the Mason-Dixon line and east of the Pecos has at one time or another been noted for its overabundance of rednecks, hillbillies, and good old boys. New Yorkers have had their fun at the expense of New Jersey's honor for as long as anyone can remember; Kansas has taken it on the chin more than once; and Montana has in recent years emerged as a haven for renegades, unibombers, and anyone else claiming an arsenal larger than that of most third-world armies. So Arkansas isn't the only state that has been maligned for being, or at least appearing to be, out of step with mainstream American society. There seems to be no scientific way to quantify the level of stereotyping to which Arkansas has been subjected in comparison with other states, southern and nonsouthern, but the general consensus around the Natural State is that Arkansas was at some point in the murky past singled out and given a special place in the American consciousness. And it's a specialness that many in the state would just as soon do without. In a 1954 magazine essay, Eugene Newsom expressed the opinion of many in his native state: "It is safe to say, I believe, that Arkansas has been the butt of more jokes running from raillery to ridicule than any other political entity in the country." As recently as the Reagan era, a book on the fifty states portrayed Arkansas as having been "touched less by ways of industrialized society than any of its neighbors . . . It was an island set apart, a civilization primitive and poor."[1]

Little wonder then that the collective population of Arkansas, according to a 1942 *Time* article, "developed a mass inferiority complex unique in American history."[2] This concept is just as crucial to our story. Arkansas's "special" place in the American consciousness contributed to the Yakima popcorn girl's derision, just as the collective inferiority complex influenced my grandpa's reaction. The writer for *Time* was on to something, for defensiveness is a part of our cultural inheritance. At some point in an Arkansan's development—somewhere between the age of accountability and the first hangover—we realize that the old Wonder State is the butt of a perpetual national joke. Developmental psychologists refer to this experience as the "yee-haw moment"—the level of consciousness one must achieve to understand one should be offended by *The Beverly Hillbillies,* even though one may not be. Arkansas natives come to this heightened sense of self-awareness at widely varying stages in life, and some, thankfully, never advance, or perhaps devolve, to this state, and thus are spared the angst that emerges from the recesses of the progressive Arkansas imagination.

Whether you've spent a lifetime denying or defending the old Wonder State, the impact of the Arkansaw image on Arkansas and Arkansawyers today is no laughing matter—and yet it very much is. This Arkansaw image—with all the many visions that little dubya in place of the "s" inspires—is as old as this place I call home. And, like it or not, it's not going away anytime soon. As we will see, the defenders of Arkansas's honor are without a doubt the funniest characters in this saga, and the vociferousness with which they have given voice to that collective inferiority complex has served as a catalyst for further caricaturing and stereotyping. Arkansans' defensive reactions to their state's genuine image problems have had the effect of water on a grease fire, intensifying rather than subduing the stereotyping.

It is fitting that the state's image and defensiveness have often worked in tandem, because another of the book's concepts focuses on the duality of the Arkansaw image. You will notice that I utilize this spelling—Arkansaw —when referring to the state's image and when invoking the mythical place conjured by the various stereotypes and caricatures. This is not to suggest that Arkansaw represents some bizarro-world mirror image, an antithesis to the *real* Arkansas, but that Arkansaw stands for the complex mixture of fact, legend, and stereotype that is summoned from the depths of the American consciousness at the mention of the word Arkansas. You will also notice that I use both of the terms describing an Arkansas inhabitant, the widely accepted Arkansan as well as Arkansawyer, once the most common title used by natives but now reduced to the status of an embarrassing country cousin. I do this throughout the book to highlight the socioeconomic implications inherent in the Arkansaw image and to illustrate the different reactions Arkansas people have to the Arkansaw image. In other words, I try to label as an Arkansan anyone who would choke on his roast beef if called an Arkansawyer.

And while on the subject of vocabulary, I should also mention that I have chosen to use the term "image," which I would describe in this context as an iconic representation of the state and its people in the national consciousness, instead of "identity," which seems to suggest a sort of active participation in the process of defining the description by which one is known. In giving the nod to the more passive and perhaps amorphous of the two related terms, I am not suggesting that the people of Arkansas had no role in the construction and evolution of the Arkansaw image. Certainly Arkansas natives from Bob Burns and Orval Faubus to Donald Harington and Bill Clinton have played some part in the development of this image. What I am suggesting is that the Arkansaw of literature and popular culture was primarily the creation of a cadre of outside observers in the nineteenth century—whether they be travelers, writers of humorous tales, Civil War soldiers, or any number of others who shared their observations of the state and its inhabitants—and that much of what would pass for image-building and evolution in the twentieth century was little more than variations on a theme already well entrenched in the American imagination. Thus, rather than creating the Arkansaw image, Arkansawyers and Arkansans more often played such roles as unconscious model for the Arkansaw image, conscious tweaker of and sometime contributor to and capitalizer on the image, and occasional defensive reactor to the image.

In addition to the Arkansan/Arkansawyer identification duel and the Arkansas/Arkansaw divide, there are other dualities or multiplicities involved in this study. The defenders of Arkansas have not surprisingly reacted most strongly to the many negative products of the Arkansaw image, ironically generating even more bad publicity, but there has always been a more positive side to the state's image. Practically any one of us, Arkie or non-Arkie, can spout off the list of characteristics that contribute to the backwoods Arkansaw image—violence, ignorance, shiftlessness, laziness, with generous doses of racism, moonshining, clannishness, inbreeding, barefootedness, floppyhatedness, and general cussedness. But those are just the bad ones— that is, if you count moonshining as a negative. It is our defensive nature, I suppose, to jump to the conclusion that all Arkansas stereotypes are bad ones, but that is far from the case. Arkansawyers have from time to time been credited as independent, resourceful, nonconformist, close to nature, unpretentious, generous, and nonmaterialistic. The prevalence of these good characteristics in fictional and nonfictional accounts of Arkansas and Arkansawyers will probably surprise you. The Arkansaw image, almost from the beginning, has been at the very least a dual one, if not downright multifaceted. Time and time again the Arkansawyer has been portrayed as a back-woods buffoon or a rugged individualist or some combination thereof. In the following pages I will occasionally refer to the Janus-faced Arkansaw image, one that contains good and bad elements simultaneously. I will also on occasion discuss Arkansaw in terms of its gestalt capacity, whereby the positive and negative portrayals constitute in totality the Arkansas image, though the observer's interpretation depends as much as anything on his own perspective. In an overly simplistic yet useful dichotomy, these per-spectives might be described as romantic versus progressive, with the for-mer often cherishing the very Arkansaw characteristics condemned by the latter.

It is my contention that the portrayals of the Arkansawyer, romantic or fantastic they may be, have been positive ones as often as not.[3] For many a romantic or radical observer, as we shall see, Arkansaw has provided an antithesis to a variety of American illusions: the idea of American excep-tionalism, the blind faith in "progress," America's starring role in some cosmic, providential plan. In this rendering of the Arkansaw image, the Arkansawyer becomes a nonconformist who consciously or unconsciously rejects the tenets of an American narrative found in the Puritan-through-Progressive continuum. Like C. Vann Woodward's post–Civil War south-erners, who "learned to live for long decades in quite un-American poverty, and . . . learned the equally un-American lesson of submission," the Arkan-sawyer is one possessed of an ironic appreciation for America's "perpetua-tion of infant illusions of innocence and virtue."[4] Perhaps he lacks the level of self-consciousness necessary to articulate his skepticism, but the Arkansawyer has inherited enough of the Calvinist's abject humility and experienced enough of the southern frontier's poverty to develop a healthy distrust of anything half as postmillennial as the blueprint of a New England mugwump.

But if all we had to talk about were rather positive images of Arkansas—even ones embedded in the language of romanticism or radicalism—you can bet that this book would never have been written. The Arkansas inferi-ority complex, which flows from the same wellsprings that have nourished the Arkansaw image, and the hyper-defensiveness it breeds have caused us to seize upon the arrows of opprobrium flung our way by those assumed to be our betters. We have for generations magnified our defamations and overreacted to the ribbing of our detractors, all the while ignoring or mis-reading the pronouncements of those enamored of the Arkansawyer.

By "we" I don't mean all people in Arkansas. There is a socioeconomic element to this issue that we are not always cognizant of. Although swaths of Arkansas have often been seen as bastions of egalitarianism, the state has not been without class divisions, and such stratification has played a central role in the story of the Arkansaw image. The stereotyping of Arkansas, whether perpetrated by the romantics or the progressives, has focused on the habits and lifestyles and prejudices of the poor, and in this sense the condemnations of outsiders have often paralleled the attitudes of Arkansas's better sort toward their backwoods neighbors. But it has been the better sort, or at least the social climbers, the post–Civil War era's version of the nouveau riche "cotton snobs" and the Yankee-emulating New South boosters, who have most often gotten their backs up over the slights, both real and perceived, against their state.[5] They have represented the forces of "progress" in Arkansas, the middling classes, folks looking to stake their claim on the American dream and resentful of stereotypes that tend to lump them with common briarhoppers, ridgerunners, and peckerwoods. In Arkansas, this least aristocratic commonwealth of the Old South, a land of mudsills not masters, none of us needs scale too many branches of the family tree to find bare plainness, and those who've fought tooth and nail to trade rickets for Rotary have been acutely sensitive to this historic progression. Motivated by their own progressive impulses and perhaps by the hayseeds too recently combed from their hair, they have rejected both the romantic's embrace of the Arkansawyer's eccentricity and cussed traditionalism and the outsider's reductionist tendencies to identify all people of Arkansas with the Arkansawyer.

Again, not all of us are burdened with this inferiority complex. Many of the people whose lifestyles have inspired and continue to inspire the Arkansaw image, both the good and bad of it, probably lose little sleep fretting over what some writer in New York or filmmaker in Los Angeles thinks about them. Would Pete Whetstone and Jed Clampett and Gator McCluskey worry themselves with stereotypes and cultural denigration? A fundamental characteristic of the Arkansaw image has been the Arkansawyer's (not the Arkansan's) obliviousness to outside influence or his cussed resistance to an economic reform or philosophy imposed by someone who ought not be imposing.

Though class is the more active ingredient in this Arkansaw concoction, race plays its role. It is, in fact, conspicuous by its near complete absence in the evolution of the Arkansaw image. The Arkansaw image has been almost exclusively derived from and applied to the state's white inhabitants, especially those of the whitest regions of Arkansas, the Ouachitas and the Ozarks. The state's black citizens, almost one-quarter of the population until World War II, have historically been excluded from Arkansas's identity, just as African Americans in the South have been, in the words of historian James C. Cobb, "'othered' out of the construction" of southern identity.[6] As we shall see, the circumstances in which this "othering out" has occurred offer insights into the evolution of the Arkansaw image.

It is also apparent that many of the characteristics of the Arkansaw image are found in other regional stereotypes and images. Just about all of the stereotypes associated with the Arkansas image are also used to characterize southerners, or at least white southerners, many of them specifically geared toward the inhabitants of the highland South. At different times over the past two centuries, the Arkansaw image has been in many ways indistinguishable from concurrent stereotypes of backwoods southerners or of southern mountaineers and hillbillies. In some instances of media representations, Arkansas becomes the South or the southern mountains writ large and thus an Arkansas setting or origination has little bearing on the study of the *Arkansaw* image. Examples of this would be southern-themed movies that just happen to be set in Arkansas, such as Martin Scorsese's 1972 film *Boxcar Bertha,* and Arkansas-born or -raised country and western musicians. In fact, though the book contains observations on song lyrics specific to Arkansas, I have included here no discussion of the pre–World War II hillbilly music craze or of commercial country music in general because these phenomena have rarely contributed directly to the Arkansaw image, at least in a discernible way that has not also contributed to some sort of Alabama image or Oklahoma image.

If, as seems to be the case, many of the characteristics and stereotypes considered *Arkansaw* are only extensions of broader regional and cultural images, it might seem odd that a book like this would exist, that the ongoing image, and image problems, of a state would merit such a study. If you're from Arkansas, however, this probably will not seem at all out of the ordinary. Arkansas has as firm a claim as any of the fifty commonwealths on the title of most caricatured state. When it comes to the hillbilly stereotype, the historical record and modern evidence suggest that Arkansas is second to none, a claim we've generally made only for equally dubious or embarrassing categories such as strokes and pullets. A 2007 internet survey revealed that Arkansas was more closely associated with the words "hillbilly" and "hillbillies" than was any other state in the union.[7] Something to consider the next time the general assembly debates a new state nickname. So perhaps the reason that people in Arkansas are convinced that other people are making fun of them is because other people really are.

Regardless, Arkansas has a long history of fretting over its image, and this book is in some sense a culmination of the many years of derision and defensiveness. We all maintain a variety of identities based on such variables as religion, occupation, language, and family, and for many of us our identity as a citizen of or native of a particular state ranks near the top of our chart of self-definition. This may be especially true of those of us from small and seemingly inconsequential states like Arkansas. Our third-rate status in some ways alienates us from claims to some sort of generic Americanism at the same time that it saddles us or blesses us with an aura of otherness. And this pervasive otherness, this recognition that the sidelines were made for such as us, often manifests itself in intensive and sometimes myopic self-scrutiny. The mere fact that this book exists says something about the insecurities of being poor, of looking in from the outside, and of just knowing that whoever's on the inside, wherever that may be, is looking down their nose at you.

Whether you are a defensive Arkansan or a crotchety Arkansawyer, chances are that you know little more about the origination of this charming bundle of Arkansaw traits than you do about your family's propensity for violence against another family who shall remain nameless. This book is an attempt to identify the origination and trace the evolution of the Arkansaw image over the past two centuries. Some of these characters— Lum and Abner, the Clampetts—you will undoubtedly be familiar with. Others—the Weaver Brothers and Elviry, Pete Whetstone, Thomas J. Jackson —you likely have never heard of. Perhaps by the time we make it through almost two hundred years of caricatures, besmirches, ridicules, and condescensions, we'll at least have a start toward answering the question so many of us have asked through the years: Why Arkansas? It is my hope that you'll at least consider my jug-half-full interpretation of almost two centuries of the Arkansaw image; if you're not convinced then you can go back to being a sore-tailed cat. And even if we don't get to the very bottom of this, perhaps we'll be better able to laugh at ourselves—or at least more skilled in lopping off the ears of those who laugh at us. At the very least, you found a friend to read this book to you, and I found a friend to write it. Yee-haw, indeed.

✧ CHAPTER ONE ✧

Creating the Bear State

"In manners, morals, customs, dress, contempt of labour and hospitality, the state of society is not essentially different from that which exists among the savages. Schools, religion, and learning are alike unknown."[1] No ringing endorsement for life on the Arkansas and Ozark frontier. Instead, what we find in the account of Henry Rowe Schoolcraft's 1818 encounter with a family of Arkansas pioneers are the unmistakable elements of what would in the twentieth century come to be known as the hillbilly stereotype. The Wells family on Bennett's Bayou in modern-day Baxter County lived in a simple cabin whose "interior would disappoint any person who has never had an opportunity of witnessing the abode of man beyond the pale of the civilized world. Nothing could be more remote from the ideas we have attached to domestic comfort, neatness, or conveniency, without allusion to cleanliness, order, and the concomitant train of household attributes, which make up the sum of human felicity in refined society."[2] Schoolcraft was not the first to express disappointment over the style of living he found in Arkansas, and he certainly would not be the last.

It is fitting that we start our search for the origination of the Arkansaw image with a traveler's impressions of the inhabitants of the hills of northern Arkansas, for the dominant geographic influence on the Arkansaw image has been a highland one. For much of the state's history, in fact, the Arkansaw image has been in effect synonymous with the Ozark image. Until recently scholars suggested that cultural backwardness might come with the territory, for the Bluff-dwellers and subsequent native inhabitants of the Ozark plateau seemed to have lagged behind their Mississippi River Valley neighbors to the east. Isolation, largely terrain-induced, limited the contacts and trade activities of these early Ozarkers, according to the "Ozark marginality" thesis, creating a cultural and economic backwater in the hills.[3] In other words, if the riverine peoples of prehistoric Arkansas and Missouri would have had *Esquire,* the Native Americans of the Ozarks would have been cartoon fodder. Perhaps there was a Native American version of the Arkansas Traveler legend. We'll probably never know. But tracing the Ozark and Arkansaw image back to a people incapable of defending themselves against our modern connection games and only able to communicate with us through a few shards and spear points is most unfair. Besides, the whole exercise smacks of geographic determinism, which the Waltons and Tysons have been busy the past half century disproving. So we'll start with a different era in the history of the Ozarks and of Arkansas, with the early days of Euro-American settlement and the often-caustic quills of weary visitors.

Reconnoitering Arkansaw

Though most of our attention here will be paid to the accounts of visitors to Arkansas who followed, temporally and/or physically, in Schoolcraft's footsteps, the land known as Arkansas had generations earlier earned a sullied reputation among the Gallic and Iberian masters of the Mississippi Valley. The commoners of Arkansas Post in the eighteenth and early nineteenth centuries seemed content with their lives of hunting and trapping and periodic bursts of bacchanalia, but the educated and cultured who ventured among them were rarely impressed. According to historian Morris S. Arnold, one Frenchman occupying a Spanish colonial post in Louisiana accused the hunters of Arkansas of being "murderers, rapists, and fugitives from justice" and of inciting the Osage to steal horses, women, and children from other American Indians.[4] On the eve of the Louisiana purchase, François Marie Perrin du Lac denounced the social habits of the residents of Arkansas Post and attributed their cultural decline to the natives in their midst. "They pass their time playing games, dancing, drinking, or doing nothing, similar in this as in other things to the savage peoples with whom they pass the greater part of their lives." A decade and a half earlier a resident of a Spanish post at modern Monroe, Louisiana, had condemned his neighbors to the north more thoroughly. "These men," wrote Juan Fihliol, "consist of scum of all kinds of nationals . . . who . . . have become stuck here through their fondness for idleness and independence . . . Hardly do they know whether they are Christians. They excel in all the vices and their kind of life is a real scandal." Even the "savages . . . hold them in contempt," gasped Fihliol, and "[t]he women are as vicious as the men."[5] In general, Arnold has observed, the more respectable members of colonial and territorial society in the lower Mississippi Valley viewed these early Arkies as "for the most part lazy and shiftless, given to excess drinking and libertinage, and irredeemably lawless and amoral."[6] The influx of Anglo-American settlers in the early nine-teenth century would not noticeably alter this estimation, as the accounts of travelers would soon prove.

The Arkansaw image has been largely derived from and most closely associated with this Anglo-American population, and thus its origins lie in the cauldron of settlement, frontier survival, and violence that was territo-rial Arkansas. Our earliest literary peek into that Arkansas is available in a couple of travel accounts, most valuable for our purposes the journal of a young New Yorker with whom we have already become acquainted, one Henry Rowe Schoolcraft. More interested in minerals than men, Schoolcraft passed most of the winter of 1818–1819 traipsing through the hills and hollows of the Arkansas Ozarks (still part of Missouri Territory at the time), studying the natural phenomena of this rugged, sparsely settled region. The accounts of his encounters with terrain, beast, and man, published a couple of years later, suggest that the budding scientist may have been intrigued by geological peculiarities of the Ozarks but that he was gener-ally disgusted with the region's human oddities. In committing to paper his candid observations on the nadir of human civilization—of the reduc-tion of white Americans to semi-, if not full-blown, savagery—Schoolcraft joined the age-old crowd of sophisticates who sneer at the cultural short-comings of those who exist on the geographic and economic fringes of the civilized world. But he also, more crucially for our story, helped lay the foun-dation for the Arkansaw image.

Although Schoolcraft's accounts of early-day Anglo settlers in Arkansas could range from mild bemusement to grudging admiration, he reserved his most vitriolic rebuke for the unfortunate family whose description opened this chapter, the Wellses. The Wells children were dressed in "abun-dantly greasy and dirty" buckskin clothing; not a person in the family was literate. The hunt was the nexus around which the household revolved. The interior walls of the grimy cabin were festooned with deer antlers and buffalo horns, rifles, shot pouches, dried meat, and skins. The family, mother and children included, "could only talk of bears, hunting, and the like. The rude pursuits, and the coarse enjoyments of the hunter state, were all they knew." "Their manner and conversation were altogether rough and obscene, . . . characterized in partaking of whatever was disgusting, terrific, rude, and outré in all."[7] The fact that the Wellses fed and sheltered the traveler—whose own journal entries unwittingly reveal Schoolcraft as a greenhorn who managed to kill his horse and almost himself—seems not to have softened his opinions. The fact that Mr. Wells—perhaps the first but certainly not the last Ozark hillman to empty the pockets of a wide-eyed "tourist"—proceeded to overcharge his visitor for sorely needed sup-plies almost certainly influenced Schoolcraft's portrait.

Fortunately for the young traveler, and perhaps for us as well, Schoolcraft did not find all his Arkansas hosts as appalling as the Wellses. The M'Gary (McGarrah) family of modern-day Marion County received a better review. Their cornfield and livestock suggested at least an effort toward domestication, and a smattering of books and some factory-made clothing "bore some evidence that the [McGarrahs] had once resided in civilized society."[8] The McGarrah family's generosity—free food for the road—may have ensured their rosy reputation for posterity. If Mr. Wells had only known what the stranger's sharpened feather was used for. But even those in the Wells family, "rude in appearance" and clearly beneath Schoolcraft's social station, were not totally without utility. They and their neighbors in the White River Valley were "hardy, brave, independent people, . . . frank and generous," and the men "would form the most efficient military corps in frontier warfare which can possibly exist."[9]

Nevertheless, the young New Yorker's ultimate verdict on the inhabitants of the Ozarks was firmly in the negative. He reserved his harshest criticism for the men he encountered, the semi-savage hunters who ruled, as much as anyone could rule, this wilderness and whose survival skills—and

Henry Rowe Schoolcraft. Courtesy of Library of Congress Prints and Photographs Division.

open disdain for the greenhorn's lack of same—undoubtedly challenged and intimidated Schoolcraft. "The hunter, although habitually lazy, and holding in contempt the pursuits of agriculture, so far, at least, as is not necessary to his own subsistence is nevertheless a slave to his dog, the only object around him to which he appears really devoted. . . . To him all days are equally unhallowed, and the first and the last day of the week find him alike sunk in unconcerned sloth, and stupid ignorance."[10] Laziness was far from the only characteristic of the hunter, and of the Arkansaw image. Schoolcraft found these early Ozark settlers to be superstitious and prone to drunkenness as well. One Mr. Fisher, a new arrival on Beaver Creek in present-day Taney County, Missouri, was convinced that a neighbor had bewitched his rifle, which suddenly refused to hit the mark. At present-day Norfork, the fastidious Schoolcraft endured a night of drunken revelry by a party of hunters—a "grand exhibition of human noises, beastly intoxication, and mental and physical nastiness."[11]

Perhaps most troubling to Schoolcraft was the casually violent ways of those he encountered in Arkansas, a characteristic at the heart of the nineteenth-century Arkansaw image. Particularly foreboding, according to our observer, was the next generation's absorption of their fathers' violence. "Without moral restraint, brought up in the uncontrolled indulgence of every passion and without regard of religion, the state of society among the rising generation in this region is truly deplorable. In their childish disputes, boys frequently stab each other with knives, two instances of which have occurred since our residence here. No correction was administered in either case, the act being rather looked upon as a promising trait of character."[12]

All of the essential elements of the Arkansaw image are present in Schoolcraft's journal. Emerging from the Ozarks and from Arkansas is a backward, semi-savage society of whites, lazy, drunken, violent, slovenly, mostly illiterate. A bleaker picture of humanity one could hardly concoct. Women reside largely in the shadows, "inured to servile employments"; the harshness of a life of childbearing and -rearing and incessant labor leaves them physically "by no means calculated to inspire admiration, but on the contrary disgust."[13] Children, wrenched from the civilizing influences of religion and schooling and at liberty to pursue the basest and most animalistic passions, will unfortunately perpetuate their parents' barbarism, wholly ignorant of the civilization that should have been their birthright.

What is rarely evident in Schoolcraft's account is the flipside of the Arkansaw image coin, the alternative rendering of the sensory data, the paradigm of the romantic. But it will emerge soon enough. It will reveal to us the Arkansas of sturdy pioneers—of courageous bear hunters and self-sufficient, resourceful dwellers of the hills and swamps, of independent-minded forest clearers and frontier tamers. But rarely were the chroniclers of early Arkansas so firmly of one mind or the other. And some even turned the coin over and over or recognized the complexity of the Arkansaw gestalt.

Every state in the union has its shelf of early traveler accounts. We often use these observations on the early days as windows into the murkiest rooms of our past and as instruments by which to gauge our progress. In Arkansas, though, we may be troubled by the familiarity of these accounts —or at least by the recognizable condescension in the voices of the writers. We may also be struck by the persistence of an image of frontier life that, for most states, remains just that—a quaint portrait of rough-and-tumble pioneers—but that has managed to endure in Arkansas and to color every discourse concerning the state, past and present.

Arkansas's unique historical and geographical location—blocked on the east by an often impenetrable maze of swamps and thickets and on the west by an equally formidable, if man-made, barrier, Indian Territory—rendered it something of a backwater. This contributed to the development of the Arkansaw image, and in varying degrees to a very real society tailor-made to spawn such an image, but this inaccessibility also meant that comparatively few people just passed through Arkansas, with the exception of those leaving the Midwest and mid-South for Texas. Consequently, Arkansas's travel account shelf may be somewhat thinner than that of other states. The chroniclers and letter-writing observers we did have, though, offered accounts of life and people in a variety of Arkansas locations in the two generations between Schoolcraft's journey and the outbreak of civil war.

Most accounts second the disparaging statements of Schoolcraft, focusing on any number of elements in the Arkansaw image. Thomas Nuttall, an English-born naturalist who arrived in Arkansas before Schoolcraft had finished his brief sojourn in the Ozarks, shared Schoolcraft's disapproval of most of the white settlers he met. "It is to be regretted that the widely scattered state of the population in this territory, is but too favourable to the spread of ignorance and barbarism. The means of education are, at present, nearly proscribed, and the rising generation are growing up in mental darkness . . . and . . . have almost forgot that they appertain to the civilized world."[14]

Like most visitors to the territory and later the state, Joseph Meetch, traveling down the Southwest Trail, or Military Road, in the mid-1820s, noted the "poor looking cabins of northeastern Arkansas."[15] The slovenliness of living conditions—a popular lament of America's better class going back at least as far as colonial Virginia planter William Byrd II—was a staple of testimonials by Arkansas travelers and visitors. English-born geologist George W. Featherstonhaugh, traversing Arkansas in 1834, expressed "great mortification" upon finding a local judge in northeastern Arkansas "living in one of the most dirty and unprovided holes we had yet got into." Farther down the White River he found a couple and their three slaves "living in a wretched, filthy cabin." On the Saline River southwest of Little Rock, Featherstonhaugh reluctantly passed the night in a "den of rags and nastiness" maintained by a black woman. A rare example of an African American contribution to the burgeoning Arkansaw image, the cabin featured a broken window, a broken table, and a door that would not shut. Near present-day Caddo Valley, Featherstonhaugh encountered an abode that would have done any twentieth-century hillbilly postcard proud. The cabin of the Barkman family "was a sort of permanent camping out of doors; the logs of it were at least six inches apart, the interstices, without any filling in, staring wide open; one of the gable ends was entirely wanting, the roof was only closed at one end, and . . . his family, consisting of a wife and several young children, were warming themselves at a fire—*not in the house,* but out of doors."[16]

New York native Henry Merrell, upon moving to southwestern Arkansas a generation after Featherstonhaugh's excursion, found his Pike County neighbors a sickly and "miserable population," living in "houses of logs, & very rude lots at that, scarcely higher than a man could stand up in, with stick & mud chimneys not a great deal taller than the man himself." The women, wrote Merrell, "slept . . . in their frocks and bonnets, the same they wore by day," and all "ate with a one-tined fork or no fork at all."[17]

If the palettes and gastronomical reactions of these early Arkansas chroniclers are to be believed, then a one-tined fork might have been fitting flatware for the frightening fare of the backwoods table. Featherstonhaugh, especially, was critical of the slop—albeit usually free slop—served up on his travels in Arkansas. "Every repast, whether it be breakfast, dinner, or supper . . . consists of the worst possible coffee, indifferent dirty frothy-looking butter, black sugar or honey, as the case may be, a little bacon, or some sort of dried meat cooked, I do not know how, and as tough as leather, and miserably made Indian corn bread." Of the vittles at a Hot Springs tavern, the persnickety Brit griped: "Nothing could be less tempting and more rude than the fare we got; and if it had not been for the supply of tea and sugar we had laid in at Little Rock our stomachs would have gone to bed very discontentedly." The situation did not improve at the Mitchell home on the Military Road near the Ouachita River. "The supper consisted of some pieces of dirty looking fried pork, corn-bread eight days old, mixed up with lumps of dirt, and coffee made of burnt acorns and maize; they had neither milk, sugar, nor butter." Featherstonhaugh was joined at this final meal by James Conway, a southwestern Arkansas planter and surveyor who would be elected Arkansas's first state governor in less than two years' time. The dignified "Col. Conway" seemed immune to Arkansas's backcountry poisons as he instructed the incredulous visitor in the fine art of holding one's nose while swallowing the frontier coffee substitute.[18]

Like Schoolcraft before them, later Arkansas travelers found the colorful, backwoods hunter in abundance. The descriptions of these Arkansas hunters evoke the insularity, irresponsibility, and independence that contributed to the Arkansaw image. Featherstonhaugh offered a portrait of a bear hunter he encountered in Hot Springs in late 1834. "This man was a very singular fellow, who shunned society, was dressed altogether in the skins of animals he had killed, and seemed never to have been washed . . . He lived in the woods many miles from the Springs, and only visited them when he had bear and deer skins to sell." A few days later he met yet another of the species near the Caddo River: "a genuine hunter, dressed in leather prepared by himself from the skins of animals he had killed . . . was going with his rifle on his shoulder, and his dogs, some twenty miles off to hunt bears. This man, although between thirty and forty years old, had never been out of this neighborhood, and had no idea of the world beyond his own pursuits."[19] A generation later Henry Merrell hired to work in his Pike County mill one Charley Ray, "a genuine Arkansawyer . . . the type of a class to be found no where else in such perfection as in Arkansas." A big and powerful man, Ray "could pack home on his back a large deer that he had killed five miles away in the wood, but he could not work half a day without sleeping more or less on a log."[20]

Merrell's judgment of Ray as a lazy worker but an energetic sportsman is a common refrain in the memoirs and travelogues of visitors to the American frontier, especially the Old Southwest. Hunters in territorial Arkansas expended much energy and traveled for days and miles to pursue bears and deer for their hides, a principal source of currency, and for their meat, a staple of the frontier diet. Yet, their failure to conform to the standards of eastern society and their obvious unfamiliarity with the Protestant work ethic convinced visitors that laziness was endemic to the Arkansas backwoods, or at least to the menfolk of the backwoods. Henry Merrell criticized "the general good-for-nothing & lazy disposition of the mountain people."[21] Near the Black River in northeastern Arkansas, Featherstonhaugh encountered a squatter and hunter who "had no property of his own but his rifle, and never has possessed any save that which he acquired by his wandering and desultory pursuits. He had a prejudice against all men who were not, like himself, freed from every kind of restraint, and did not go willingly amongst them." On the road to Hot Springs, Featherstonhaugh found that travelers by wagon and horseback simply went around fallen trees instead of clearing them from the road—an "unjustifiable indolence

THE FATAL BEAR HUNT.

Illustration of an Arkansas bear hunt, from Friedrich Gerstäcker's *Wild Sports in the Far West* (Philadelphia: J. B. Lippincott & Co., 1876). Special Collections, University of Arkansas Libraries, Fayetteville.

on the part of the settler."[22] Friedrich Gerstäcker, an adventurous young German who spent a few years in Arkansas in the late 1830s and early 1840s, discovered that "the western settlers, and particularly those in the south-western states, are not very fond of hard work; in those wild regions they prefer rearing cattle and shooting to agriculture, and are loth [sic] to undertake the hard work of felling trees and clearing land."[23]

Arkansas's backwoodsmen may have been unwilling to give it the old Yankee effort in the fields and shops, but this laziness apparently dissipated in the face of a good scrape. No characteristic of the Arkansas frontier was more commented upon, or more crucial to the creation of the Arkansaw image, than violence and criminality. The territorial and early statehood days of Arkansas were so synonymous with the violent culture of the West that the state gave birth to a famous symbol of American frontier violence, the Bowie knife, and lent its name to yet another, the Arkansas toothpick. Even by the time Joseph Meetch entered Arkansas in 1826, the territory's reputation for violence preceded it. Meetch expressed concern over "the many murders, robberies, and theft[s]" of which he had been told and worried that "every man has his rifle, tomahawk, butcher knife and very often a dirk and brace of pistols." Writer Washington Irving, scribbling observations on his trip down the Arkansas River in 1832, found the territory's scenery peaceful and serene but its inhabitants anything but, referring to Arkansas as the "land of the *bloody hand*" at one point. "Justice runs wild in this part of the country," Irving noted in his journal, "She uses the sword more than the scales." Some believed that Arkansas served as a sort of magnet for unsavory characters from east of the Mississippi. Writing in the 1830s, British traveler Charles Joseph Latrobe repeated the common opinion that the territory had provided "the sinks into which the offscourings of the more settled parts of the country precipitated themselves." Even into the 1840s, according to British novelist Frederick Marryat, foreign visitors were "frightened away by the numerous stories of Arkansas murders, with which a tourist is always certain to be entertained on board one of the Mississippi steamboats." Although Marryat admitted that the stories of Arkansas violence had been "much exaggerated," he nevertheless claimed "that the assizes of Arkansas contain more cases of stabbing and shooting than ten of the other States put together."[24]

But in spite of the fears of British travelers and Schoolcraft's reports of juvenile knife fights and in spite of the preponderance of weapons of all kinds in the back country, the violence observed first- or second-hand by travelers in Arkansas tended to occur in towns or along the routes of commerce and travel, and the perpetrators were not so much *of* Arkansas as *in* it. Traveling down the Mississippi in the early 1830s, Scotsman Thomas Hamilton learned from fellow steamboat passengers that the squatters who

lived along the banks were outcasts and criminals, "men of broken characters, hopes and fortunes who fly not from justice, but contempt."[25]

"Quarrelling seemed to be their principal occupation," Featherstonhaugh
wrote of residents of the territorial capital. They "were continually resort-
ing to what they called the 'Laws of Honour,' a part of the code of which,
in Little Rock, is to administer justice with your own hand the first convenient opportunity. A common practice with these fellows was to fire at
each other with rifle across the street, and then dodge behind a door; every
day groups were to be seen gathered round these wordy bullies, who were
holding knives, in their hands, and daring each other to strike, but cherishing the secret hope that the spectators would interfere." Little Rock, in
Featherstonhaugh's estimation, was little more than a town of "criminals,
gamblers, speculators, and men of broken fortunes, with no law to restrain
them, no obligation to conceal their vices, no motive to induce them to
appear devout or to act with sobriety." And Little Rock was simply one stop
on a riverboat trail of vice and danger. Leaving the territory aboard an
Arkansas River steamboat, Featherstonhaugh found himself amid a "collection of unblushing, low, degraded scoundrels" who gambled away their
time waiting for an unsuspecting visitor to swindle or rob.[26]

In the nineteenth century no Arkansas town was more notorious than
Napoleon, a Mississippi River town that Henry Merrell described as "a bad
place, not for rows with the fists and shalaley, . . . but for street fights and
nightly assassinations with pistol & bowie-knife. Any day there was some-
body killed or wounded." Noting that Napoleon's sinister influence even
extended into the state's delta interior, Merrell retold the stories of a wealthy
planter who had been wounded nine times before finally dying and a
woman who boasted of losing six of seven sons to the knife or pistol.[27]
Friedrich Gerstäcker informed his German readers that "Arkansas was over-
run at this time [late 1830s] with a number of bad characters, gamblers,
drunkards, thieves, murderers, who all thought that the simple-minded
backwoodsmen were easier to be cheated than the wary settlers in the
older states. This circumstance had given so bad a name to Arkansas, that
many thought all its inhabitants went about armed to the teeth with pistols and bowie-knives."[28]

But young Gerstäcker followed this recitation of popular perception
with a more reassuring note: "I have traversed the State in all directions,
and met with as honest and upright people as are to be found in any part
of the Union."[29] This attempt at reputation rejuvenation was not unusual
for, unlike the accounts of Schoolcraft, Featherstonhaugh, and Merrell,
Gerstäcker's estimation of Arkansas was for the most part a positive one. In
the one-man's-trash-is-another-man's-treasure category, the romantically
inclined Gerstäcker found in Arkansas what he had gone looking for when

he abandoned his middle-class German existence. In the swamps of eastern Arkansas and in the Boston Mountains of rugged northwestern Arkansas,
he had discovered Rousseau's natural man, real-life Natty Bumppos who
exuded the primitive impulse that inspired Caspar David Friedrich and
Wordsworth. Gerstäcker had escaped civilization, and he loved it. The
young German found Little Rock, Arkansas's nearest approximation to
modernity, a "vile, detestable place." But in the back country he found
ingenious and independent settlers with a range of skills "for all which
operations Europeans require so many different workmen." He grew especially fond of his Ozark hosts, the Conwells, and wrote of the patriarch of
that clan: "If ever uprightness was stamped upon any countenance, it was
upon his." Upon leaving his adopted state in 1842, Gerstäcker lamented:
"Of all I had seen in America [Arkansas] was the one which pleased me
most; I may perhaps never see it again, but I shall never forget the happy
days I passed there, where many a true heart beats under a coarse frock or
leather hunting-shirt."[30]

Perhaps well beyond the clutches of youthful romanticism, middle-
aged Washington Irving nevertheless felt pangs of primitivism when he
visited the descendants of the French settlers along the lower Arkansas
River. Like Gerstäcker among the pioneers of the swamps and hills, Irving
delighted in the creoles because they were everything sophisticated east-
erners were not: honest, kind, neighborly, simple, even unambitious. They
seemed gloriously uninfected by the Puritan's work ethic and stodginess.
"The inhabitants . . . have none of that eagerness for gain, and rage for
improvement, which keep our people continually on the move." Residing
in a "state of contented poverty," these territorial Arkansawyers "work[ed]
but little, they dance[ed] a great deal; and a fiddle [was] the joy of their
heart." Like the romantics who would come after him, though, Irving
hoped against hope that these Frenchmen would somehow remain
immune to Anglo-American acquisitiveness. "As we swept away from the
shore, I cast back a wistful eye upon the moss-grown roofs and ancient
elms of the village, and prayed that the inhabitants might long retain their
happy ignorance, their absence of all enterprise and improvement, their
respect for the fiddle, and their contempt for the almighty dollar."[31]

Gerstäcker, Schoolcraft, Irving, and their fellow chroniclers of early life
and society in Arkansas were not the only ones molding this image of
Arkansaw. Three distinct but overlapping streams fed the image in the
years before the Civil War. In addition to the travel accounts by Schoolcraft
and other visitors before and after, the Arkansaw image grew from the
imagination of a coterie of uniquely American storytellers known as the
southwestern humorists and from an early-day multimedia phenomenon
based on a new twist to an old folk humor motif.

Friedrich Gerstäcker, from an illustration in an 1876 reprint of his Wild Sports in the Far West (Philadelphia: J. B. Lippincott & Co.). Special Collections, University of Arkansas Libraries, Fayetteville.

Southwestern Humorists

It is difficult to gauge the impact of travel accounts and personal memoirs on the developing Arkansaw image. Just how many people read the published journals of Schoolcraft, Nuttall, Featherstonhaugh, and Gerstäcker will never be known. Gerstäcker's later fictionalizing of many of his Arkansas experiences exposed them to a larger audience, but an audience made up primarily of Germans. In terms of crafting the Arkansaw image, the Schoolcraft and Nuttall accounts undoubtedly played a more crucial role, if only because of their earlier publication. By the time Featherstonhaugh's depiction of Arkansas came to print in 1844, the southwestern humorists were busy putting their own, usually comic, stamp on the Arkansaw image, and by the time Gerstäcker's account of his wanderings appeared in an English translation in 1854, the very word "Arkansas" had become American shorthand for backwoods naivety on the one hand and unbridled violence on the other. No less a writer than Herman Melville, in fact, compared Captain Ahab's mad attack of the whale to that of "an Arkansas duellist at his foe."[32]

If the travelers were responsible for putting an early version of the Arkansaw image before the public, then the southwestern humorists were responsible for popularizing the image in the quarter century preceding the Civil War. Southwestern humorist is a term that modern scholars use to categorize a group of writers who fused the romantic sensibilities of the day with frontier "realism" to create comic portraits of life in the Old Southwest, a region stretching from Tennessee and Georgia to Louisiana and upriver as far as Missouri. The primary vehicle of the southwestern humorist was the short story, hundreds of which appeared in the era's new sporting magazines, most notably William T. Porter's New York weekly, *Spirit of the Times*. Augustus Baldwin Longstreet's sketches of rural Georgia society jumpstarted the genre in the early 1830s, but it wasn't long before Arkansas became arguably the most popular setting for this rough American brand of humor.[33]

Among the earliest Arkansaw stories to appear in the pages of the *Spirit of the Times* were those contributed by Batesville resident Charles Fenton Mercer Noland, most published in the late 1830s and early 1840s and attributed simply to "N. Of Arkansas." Noland's stories covered the typical range of topics: fighting, bear hunting, horse racing, politics, country dances. And most were recounted through the perspective and in the dialect of fictional Pete Whetstone, perhaps the single best depiction of the Arkansaw type found anywhere in the genre. Never one to avoid a good fight or bear hunt, Pete is perfectly representative of his Devil's Fork community in the Ozarks but transcends the ordinary backwoods character for excellent comic effect when he finds himself in Little Rock or even Washington, D.C., oddly enough at the same times that Noland happened to be in these places. In a story published in the *Spirit of the Times* in December 1838, Pete Whetstone related the age-old fish-out-of-water / country-boy-goes-to-the-city story of a visit to a Little Rock "the-a-ter," where patrons "were piled up as thick as pigs in cold weather."[34] Later, he attends a formal supper in town, with predictably humorous results.

> I sat next to a young lady, and I heard them saying, "Miss, with your permission, I'll take a piece of the turkey," and so on. I sees a plate of nice little pickles.—"Miss, with your permission, I'll take a pickle," and she said I might do so. I reached over and dipped up one on my fork—it was small, and I put the whole of it in my mouth. Oh, lordy! But it burnt;—well, the more I chawed the worse it was. Thinks I, if I swallow, I am a burnt koon. Well, it got too hot for human nater to stand; so says I, "Miss, with your permission, I'll lay this pickle back," and I spit it out. Oh, lordy! What laughing. "Excuse me, ladies, if I have done wrong," says I, "but that pickle is too hot for the Devil's fork."[35]

Noland may have contributed a greater number of Arkansas-based stories, but a story by a New Yorker living in Louisiana would become the most famous example of southwestern humor, and a prime contribution to the Arkansaw image. The *Spirit of the Times* of 27 March 1841 carried a short story titled "The Big Bear of Arkansas," penned by a young visual artist and budding writer named Thomas Bangs Thorpe. "The Big Bear of Arkansas" would become synonymous with southwestern humor, so synonymous, in fact, that twentieth-century literary scholar Bernard DeVoto would label the genre the "Big Bear School of Southern Humorists."[36]

"Big Bear" is a story within a story. On board a Mississippi River steamer, the narrator listens enraptured to the tale of bombastic bear hunter Jim Doggett as he leads listeners on the chase of a giant bear in the wilds of Arkansas. Doggett, who proclaims himself the "Big Bar of Arkansas" and brags on his favorite dog, Bowie-knife, relates his Ahab-like obsession with killing the animal—though it should be noted that Thorpe's bear hunter beat Melville's whaler into print by a decade. Much of the appeal of Doggett —and Whetstone—emerges from the contrast between his own coarse and direct language and the more refined but abstract conversation of his more polished listeners. According to Thorpe's biographer, Doggett "is boastful when polite society is modest. He is self-reliant—an individualist—at ease with himself even though he is quite aware that he deviates from the accepted pattern of proprieties and timidities." As such he embodies the romantic's vision of man in his natural state and becomes the heroic heart of the story, which, in the words of literary scholar J. A. Leo Lemay, "is basically an elegiac tribute to a fast-disappearing type, the gamecock of the wilderness."[37]

Here we find the ever-present Janus-faced nature of the Arkansaw image. Although at first glance the Arkansawyer of southwestern humor emerges as vulgar, uncouth, and naive, a more nuanced approach to the literature reveals the writers' admiration, even romantic envy, of the backwoods denizen and his life of simplicity. It is nothing more than modern man's simultaneous rejection and embrace of the primitive, the natural. Whether called romanticism, primitivism, the simple life, counterculture, it boils down to that universal struggle and to the projection of one's desires and edenic visions onto those individuals or peoples whose seemingly uncluttered and angst-free existence we covet but cannot truly experience.

Arkansans have generally decried the influence of Thorpe's "The Big Bear of Arkansas" on the development of the Bear State reputation in the nineteenth century and on the Arkansaw image in general. But this has been misplaced condemnation. We could have done worse for a symbol than Jim Doggett.

Thomas Bangs Thorpe's illustration from his short story, "The Big Bear of Arkansas." From *The Hive of 'The Bee Hunter,' A Repository of Sketches, Including Peculiar American Character, Scenery, and Rural Sports* (New York: D. Appleton and Company, 1854). Special Collections, University of Arkansas Libraries, Fayetteville.

The Big Bear of Arkansas.

Later humorists continued to capitalize on the well-established Arkansaw image with less balanced depictions of antebellum Arkansawyers. One such writer was former minister and politician Alfred W. Arrington, whose 1847 novel *The Desperadoes of the South-West* focused on the violent characters whom the writer had met or heard about during his sojourn in northwestern Arkansas. Another writer, in an 1854 *Spirit of the Times* story titled "Storming an Arkansas Courthouse," alluded to the fact that "the never ending Arkansaw stories of the 'ancient regime' become the more vivid, thrilling or ludicrous, contrasted with the present order of things in that part of Uncle Sam's farm," but then proceeded to spin a tale of Judge Buzzard of Wild Cat County that would make Al Capp proud. The anonymous author of "An Arkansas 'Sell'" two years later echoed the common disdain for and grudging leeriness toward the backwoodsman: "With all the laziness and degradation of the race, they are by no means deficient in shrewdness and cunning, and the stranger who thinks to get the advantage of them in any way will find to his chagrin that he is very much in the position of the trusting individual who went out for fleece and came home shorn."[38]

Yet the southwestern humorists never completely extinguished the romantic appreciation for the backwoods Arkansawyer. A combination of good-natured jibing and romantic admiration is evident in *The Life and Adventures of an Arkansaw Doctor,* which folklorist W. K. McNeil described as "the first volume solely devoted to Arkansas humor." Written by real-life doctor and Tennessee-native Marcus Lafayette Byrn, using the pen name David Rattlehead, this 1851 book relates a series of humorous anecdotes and harrowing wildlife encounters of Dr. Rattlehead's brief service in swampy eastern Arkansas. Byrn first introduces us to the state through the letter of a barely literate Arkansawyer whose community, Raccoon Bayou, was in dire need of medical expertise.

> Sallye gott hur legg broak thee uther daa an eye sent fur doktur Cadely. Thee legg wass soe badd wheen hee goot tu hur he sayed itt mus bee saud off. He commenced wythe hiss insurments an bi jolley the fus thing eye nowed hee hadd oft thee legg an thee rong *one* att that. Wheen hee had it drest eye lucked at itt an eye were so madd eye coomenced on hymn and beat himn intu flynders. Thee legg which were broked gott wel without anny trubble.

In addition to the spelling-challenged farmer, we find in *The Life and Adventures of an Arkansaw Doctor* stereotypically naive and duplicitous slaves and drunken Indians. Byrn also treats us to a brief version of the Arkansas Traveler legend—the first to appear in print—though the squatter is replaced by a taciturn and fiddle-less lad who eventually succeeds in turning the unwanted guest away. But, like Gerstäcker before him, Byrn reveals a fascination with this untamed frontier and its swamps full of dangerous panthers, snakes, and bears. Ultimately Rattlehead recognizes the humanity of his rough-hewn neighbors. In the end he mourns the tragic death of the letter writer who had invited him to Raccoon Bayou, calling him "one of the best friends that I have ever met with in life" and noting that "kinder hearts never beat in human breast than" those of his "devoted and affectionate" family.[39]

But no southwestern humorist should ever end his tale on such a somber note as the last description of a panther-mauled dead man. So we won't end our discussion that way either. Our old friend C. F. M. Noland knew better. Though in increasingly poor health, he reemerged in the 1850s to pen a few more letters from his fictional alter ego, Pete Whetstone. His last missive found that the passage of two decades had not sapped the Devil's Fork's Dan Looney of his strength or his appreciation for a good scrape, as Pete relates Looney's fight with a sassy-talking Yankee on his trip down the Ohio River. As one would expect, the Arkansawyer got the best of his adversary. "I had out-winded him—too much whiskey, I reckon—and this time I flung him an old fashioned Sam Hinton fall, and he did not rise; but I played my thumbs into his eyes, and he sung out; but before they got me off, I reckon my right thumb got mighty near to the fust jint."[40] The Arkansawyer remained as ornery and untamable as ever.

Arkansas Traveler

By the time the southwestern humorists began to close up shop in the 1850s, a new phenomenon had emerged to play chief propagator of the Arkansaw image. No symbol of Arkansas's lowly origins and national humiliation has been more enduring than the "Arkansas Traveler." The legend of the Arkansas Traveler spawned a humorous dialogue in countless variations, a popular fiddle tune, a play, and the two most recognizable artistic images of Arkansas in the nineteenth century. Generations of defensive Arkansans have resented the legend as "'a misrepresentation and a slur'" that has "'done incalculable injury to the State.'" As journalist and novelist Clyde Brion Davis observed, "Native Arkansas historians don't like this story very well" and "feel obliged to tell some version of the legend, together with apologies, asserting the story never was typical of Arkansas, not even of the backwoods squatter."[41] In spite of this defensiveness in certain quarters, the Traveler name has been co-opted over the years by citizens of Arkansas. The state has been granting "Arkansas Traveler Certificates" to visiting dignitaries since 1941, Little Rock's professional baseball team has been the Arkansas Travelers since 1895, and the student paper at the University of Arkansas in Fayetteville is still known as the *Arkansas Traveler.*[42]

But before we get too caught up in analysis, let's take a look at one version of the dialogue:

Traveler: Hello, stranger.

Native: Hello yourself. (fiddles)

Traveler: Can I get to stay all night with you?

Native: You kin git to go to the Devil. (fiddles)

Traveler: Well, have you got any spirits here?

Native: We shore have. Sal seen a big white-un down by the holler gum last night—skeered her damn near to death. (fiddles)

Traveler: You mistake my meaning. Have you any liquor?

Native: Naw, we ain't. The old hound got in the shanty, an' lapped it all up out'n the pot. (fiddles)

Traveler: I don't mean pot-liquor, I mean corn liquor. Have you got any whiskey?

Native: Naw. I drinked the last of it this mornin'. (fiddles)

Traveler: I'm hungry—haven't had a bite since breakfast. Can't you give me something to eat?

Native: Haint got a dawg-gone thing. Nary mouthful o' meat or a dustin' o' meal in the shanty. (fiddles)

Traveler: Well, can't you feed my horse?

Native: Naw. Ain't got nothin' to feed him on. (fiddles)

Traveler: How far is it to the next house?

Native: I ain't got no idee stranger. Ain't never been thar. (fiddles)

Traveler: Well—what might your name be?

Native: It mought be Dick, an' then ag'in it mought be Tom. But it ain't. (fiddles)

Traveler: Well, sir! Will you tell me where this road goes to?

Native: It ain't never went nowhere, not since I been a livin' here. (fiddles)

Traveler: What do you do here anyhow?

Native: Purty well, thank ye. (fiddles)

Traveler: I mean, what do you do for a living?

Native: Keep tavern. (fiddles)

Traveler: Keep tavern! Good God, man, I *told* you I wanted to stop here. . . . Say, why don't you play the balance of that tune?

Native: It ain't got no balance. (fiddles)

Traveler: I mean, why don't you play the whole of it?

Native: Stranger, do you play the fiddle?

Traveler: Yes, a little.

Native: Wal, you shore don't look like a fiddler. But if you think you
    kin play any more onto that 'ar tune, git down an' try it!

The traveler proceeds to "turn the tune," after which he is feted to a veritable banquet and proffered the honor of sleeping in the leaky cabin's lone dry spot. This version, one of hundreds, folklorist Vance Randolph collected from Isabel Spradley in Van Buren, Arkansas, in 1933.[43]

In spite of its lack of subtlety, the origins of the Arkansas Traveler legend and dialogue are somewhat mysterious. The dialogue has most often been attributed to Colonel Sanford C. Faulkner, who had reportedly, like the traveler in the story, happened upon a squatter's cabin in the Boston Mountains while campaigning with four other politicians in 1840. Faulkner's telling of the encounter in a Little Rock tavern created quite a stir, so much of one that he was pressed to recount his backwoods experience a year later at a banquet in New Orleans. Faulkner's tale, according to this version, then took on a life of its own, morphing into dozens of variations and becoming a true phenomenon of folk culture. At least one nineteenth-century chronicler of the legend argued that it was a journey by Faulkner and Albert Pike in Yell County that provided the inspiration for the Arkansas Traveler, and George E. Dodge of Little Rock, in whose home the first of the two Traveler paintings was created, believed that Faulkner had concocted the entire scenario from imagination.[44] It is likely that Pike had something to do with it. In an extended letter published in *American Monthly Magazine* in 1836, Pike, a New Englander who made his way to Arkansas territory as a young man, related some details of a trip he had made down the Arkansas River in the summer of 1833. In Pope County he left the river to trudge nine miles into the southern reach of the Ozarks, where he encountered a cabin dweller on Little Piney Creek who sounds like a reasonable model for Faulkner's squatter. "The owner of the clearing was sitting in front, dressed throughout in leather, and playing lustily on the fiddle. Hearing that sound, I judged there would be no churlishness in his disposition, and I marched boldly up. He greeted me heartily, and without any attempt at politeness, and in two minutes we were on the best terms in the world."[45] If only we were privy to the details of that two minutes. Could this undefined space have featured some tête-à-tête between young Pike and the Ozark settler? We'll probably never know for certain, but it is possible that the Arkansas Traveler dialogue and legend sprang from this encounter. If so, it is ironic that the popular story was not infused with Pike's youthful and romantic admiration for the "bold and stalwart backwoodsmen."[46]

Albert Pike. Courtesy of Ancient & Accepted Scottish Rite,
Valley of Little Rock.

Regardless of the legend's provenance, within a couple of decades the Arkansas Traveler was honored in multiple media: as a painting, and eventually two, by Edward Payson Washburn; as a fiddle tune whose origin has undergone as much scrutiny as the legend itself; and by a comic play set in the backwoods of Arkansas—perhaps the first but certainly not the last stage portrayal of the Arkansas rube. The popularity of all things Arkansas Traveler spoke to perceptions of the "real" Arkansas as it took its place alongside the Big Bear image, and eventually overtook it. It must not be forgotten that both the squatter and the traveler—be it Faulkner, Pike, or whomever—were residents of Arkansas, at least in the dialogue's original form. Yet, the squatter quite obviously comes to represent Arkansaw—the fundamental yokelness of her character—in the reading, hearing, or viewing of the story. To the eternal chagrin, or relief, of Arkansas sophisticates, the Arkansas Traveler lets us know that the urbane and cosmopolitan among us may be *in* Arkansas but they will never be *of* Arkansas. The genuine article is the Arkie, the squatter, the Arkansawyer of rude pursuits and base instincts. J. W. Fulbright could never shed the factory-made frock of the bemused traveler, could never be an Arkansawyer. Orval Faubus, adorned in coonskin cap and one-gallused overalls, could never be anything but.

The Arkansas Traveler dialogue in actuality contained little that was original. The convention of the comic conversation between two characters from different classes or circumstances is probably as old as comedy itself. Most of the lines of the dialogue appear in earlier American and European folk humor, some, according to the late folklorist W. K. McNeil, dating as far back as the sixteenth century, and the back-and-forth style would become a staple of vaudeville and radio comedy.[47] More significant for our purpose is the fact that this multimedia comedy phenomenon became not the Mississippi Traveler or the Vermont Traveler or the Missouri Traveler, but the Arkansas Traveler. Let us return to that thought from time to time.

But before we do, let's consider for a moment the positive attributes of the legend. Just as the backwoods hunters and fighters of the southwestern humorists often assumed a sort of romantic, protagonistic stance, in the language of the right teller the squatter could also achieve a Jim Doggett or Jed Clampett-like level of naturalness, if not downright country cunning. The version of the dialogue reproduced by H. C. Mercer in his 1896 study of the Arkansas Traveler is informed by the traveler's bemusement and the squatter's ignorance (a popular version of the middle and latter parts of the nineteenth century made the traveler an easterner instead of a town-dwelling Arkansan) but many versions—and perhaps most versions once found in the folk tradition—give an equal shake, if not the upper hand, to the squatter.[48] And it was this version of the squatter—the winking cornpone jester who delights in exasperating his citified visitor—that Leo Rainey's Arkansaw Traveller Theatre at Hardy peddled to a largely Yankee audience for more than two decades.[49] This is the squatter or settler that the romantic, twenty-three-year-old Albert Pike found on Little Piney Creek. Like Friedrich Gerstäcker an imbiber of the rapturous Rousseauian spirit, Pike gushed over the pioneers he found in remote Arkansas. "I incline to believe that the best and most gallant knights of olden time were much such men . . . The same bold, brave, and careless demeanor—the same contempt of danger and recklessness of the finer courtesies and sympathies of life—the same fighting, reveling, carousing, and heedless disposition—the same blunt and unpolished manners exist in the latter which are recorded to have belonged to the former."[50] Once again, one man's trash is another's treasure.

One other facet of the Arkansas Traveler legend deserves mentioning. The squatter represented the future of the Arkansaw image, a subtle but important reshaping of the Big Bear image. The squatter may be an

Edward Payson Washburn's "The Arkansas Traveler," from an 1870 Currier and Ives lithograph. Courtesy of Library of Congress Prints and Photographs Division.

unsavory character to the more refined, but he isn't dangerous. The hides that Washburn stretched tight on the cabin walls and the remoteness of the setting indicate a certain handiness with a rifle, but the squatter's apparent domestication and carefree sawing on the fiddle reveal his benign nature. We recognize him—more than we do Jim Doggett—in the countless hillbilly caricatures of the twentieth century. Not burdened with relating his own existence—as are Pete Whetstone and Doggett—the squatter becomes a more malleable character, one whose cooptation by the romantic on one hand and the "progressive" on the other has contributed to his endurance as an Arkansas, and American, icon.

And Now a Word from Our Invaders

It should come as no surprise that even more than four decades after the trek of Schoolcraft visitors to northern Arkansas would find little worth writing home about. Actually, they would find plenty to write home about, but rarely in a positive light. "They have barely enough to keep body and soul together which I suppose they make by hunting and I do not think they are fit for anything else." "Not one house in ten has any window. Their school houses and churches (and they are very scarce) have a log sawed out to admit light." Northern Arkansas "was very thinly settled by a wild semi-civilized race of backwoodsmen."[51] These observations reflect the spirit of progressive condemnation found in the accounts of Schoolcraft and Featherstonhaugh, but they come from a different source in a different era—the letters of Union soldiers who found themselves in Arkansas in 1862. These letters, some published in local newspapers and others read by a few family members before being bundled away, can tell us a few things about the Arkansaw image at this crossroads moment in American history.

First of all, their tone suggests the efficacy of rural zoning as a kind of reputation patina; in the event of another invasion from the North, we should at least be prepared to make a better impression. Perhaps as important, the critiques of midwestern soldiers "visiting" Arkansas for the first time reflected the influence of antebellum Arkansaw imagery and helped ensure the perpetuation of that imagery into the postwar era. Certainly, the scene confronting soldiers in northern Arkansas in 1862 would have hinted at the devastation to come and at the generally unprogressive nature of society that antebellum visitors had vilified or romanticized. "There is a general appearance of slovenliness, as if they had all come to the conclusion that there was no use trying to be decent." "The people are ignorant . . . ; schoolhouses are almost or quite unknown." "The few who live here and there look as if they were banished from civilized society for their evil deeds." For one Iowa soldier, Arkansas was "decidedly a land of corndodgers and poor fiddlers."[52] It is unclear if the Iowan was making reference to the fiddlers' economic condition or to their lack of skill. We can only hope for the sake of all that is holy that it was the former. But like so many of the soldiers' observations this one, too, was colored with a regional-cultural prejudice that filtered every sight and sound through the prism of domesticated midwesternness.

Soldiers and war correspondents who judged Arkansawyers in comparison with folks in more settled and agriculturally developed regions, like Schoolcraft and Featherstonhaugh before them, found them—and their rocky, desolate homeland—sorely wanting. A correspondent for a St. Louis newspaper wrote: "We are marching through a region where the sound of the church bell is never heard, where a large portion of the country is a wilderness, and the inhabitants of the small and narrow valleys . . . following a rude and primitive method of agriculture, . . . give but little attention to religion or education. . . . such houses, and orchards, and lawns as you find in the New England, Middle and Western States, are nowhere to be found here."[53]

We should also keep in mind that these soldiers were no strangers to the Arkansaw image, and many of the letters reveal the midwesterners' gleeful reports that people and places in the land of the Arkansas Traveler were just as advertised, or even better. One correspondent for a Cincinnati newspaper, traveling with the Union army, noted: "The semi-barbarous condition of Arkansas has become proverbial in this country; and yet no one who has not traveled in the State can have any idea of the ignorance and immorality that prevail there."[54] "You have often read and heard tell of the curious ways that the people have in this state, but the stories was never bad enough to be true," a cavalryman wrote home to Indiana. Even a soldier from Kansas, an infant state that a few years earlier had been the site of enough violence to be dubbed "Bloody Kansas," felt at liberty to take a swipe at Arkansas. "We told them a few things about America which quite astonished them. They in turn quite satisfied us. If I had time I would tell you some things that would best the 'Arkansas Traveler.'"[55]

All of this is not to suggest that Arkansas was somehow unique among the southern states in being condemned and ridiculed by Union soldiers. The boys in blue could have found, and did find, subjects to criticize in any of the rebellious states they entered. But the letters by soldiers and newspaper correspondents do confirm the power of the prewar Arkansaw image and the unlikelihood that it would go away anytime soon. It was enough to leave citizens of the Bear State wondering, "Why Arkansas?"

Why Arkansas?

The basic assumption that informs this little survey is that Arkansas has been, fairly or unfairly, peculiarly singled out among the fifty states for derision and caricaturing, that the very phrase "Arkansaw image" conjures up widely shared visions in a way that "South Dakota image" or "Ohio image" or "Florida image" or even "Tennessee image" does not. Our premise also assumes that the visions conjured involve some combination of moonshine crockery, toothlessness, flop-eared hounds, barefootedness, shiftlessness, and yokelicity. This assumption may be a product of our own myopia; perhaps someone this very minute sits in Vermont wondering why the rest of the country picks on the Green Mountain State so. Maybe it's a product of Arkansas's hypersensitivity; perhaps as a state we've never progressed beyond the adolescent girl stage and thus suspect that all those muffled whispers wafting inland from the coasts are jokes and snide comments about our acne and bad hair. Maybe there really is no Arkansaw image and what follows is an exercise in futility.

But assuming, at least for the amount of time it takes to read this book, that Arkansas has historically occupied the outhouse on this farmstead we call the United States—that folklorist James R. Masterson was correct when he opined of Arkansas: "Her ill fame has marked her, more than any other State in the Union, as a target for reproach and ridicule"—why is this so?[1] What about this state has so distinguished her from her neighbors? Why Arkansas? Not surprisingly, there would appear to be no simple answer. This lack of clarity on the issue is not for lack of effort. Arkansas's image problem has been a favorite topic for many years, to the point that considering Arkansaw's origins and nuances has become a sort of rite of passage among historians of the state.

The sheer volume of historians' energies devoted to unraveling the intricacies of the Arkansaw image suggests the enduring power of legend, myth, and stereotype, as well as what Bob Lancaster has termed our state's "preoccupation with self-justification."[2] In the spirit of avoiding our penchant for blind defensiveness, perhaps we should begin with a bit of self-flagellation. It is no stretch to say that the Arkansaw image has at times and in places been a representation of reality only slightly tinged with exaggeration. If you've lived in Arkansas for any length of time, you probably have some appreciation for our "Thank God for Mississippi" statistical record.

(Dear Mississippians: It is not my purpose here to use the tried-and-true defense of "Yeah, we may be bad, but look at so-and-so." I realize that you have your own image problems and suspect that you have uttered the phrase "Thank God for Arkansas" more often than did George H. W. Bush's speechwriters in 1992.)

As historian Foy Lisenby has observed: "Unfortunately, statistics over the years reveal the 'backward state' image has been pretty well rooted in actuality." But we now know that poverty and backwardness long predated the statistical proofs of their presence. In his study of colonial Arkansas, Morris S. Arnold finds that "Arkansas was undeveloped compared to its neighbors in the rest of Louisiana." A combination of physical limitations and colonial governmental blunders rendered Arkansas Post insignificant and impoverished in comparison with such younger settlements as St. Louis and New Orleans. Thus, argues Arnold, "many of the recurrent themes of Arkansas history, especially its persistent poverty and relative cultural backwardness, have their roots deep in the eighteenth century." Similarly, historian S. Charles Bolton has uncovered a factual basis for the developing image in the early nineteenth century. "The Bear State concept was real," writes Bolton, "in the sense that crudeness, violence, and a penchant for hunting were very much a part of life in Arkansas, real also in that it reflected the settlement of Arkansas by southern people, many of whom lived in a manner that was looked down upon by northern visitors."[3]

Historians and writers have compiled a litany of reasons for Arkansas's negative reputation. Lisenby cites as culprits fundamentalism, provincialism, indifference to social justice, racial prejudice, a barbaric prison system, and poor schools. Of course, as Lisenby himself observes, Arkansas has never cornered the market on any of these characteristics, and all of them at one time or another have been highlighted in condemnations of the South in general. Bolton has focused on racism as a "distinguishing quality" of Arkansas. Again, there is plenty to talk about: slavery, the Ku Klux Klan, Jim Crow, the Elaine massacre, race-baiting governors from Jeff Davis to Ben T. Laney to Orval Faubus, and the unforgettable Little Rock integration affair. Nevertheless, we share our heritage of racism and race-fueled oppression and violence with the rest of the South—even the rest of the nation—and, in spite of the international spotlight shone on Little Rock in 1957, Arkansas carries fewer race-related image scars today than do states such as Alabama and Mississippi.[4]

This is not to suggest that race played no role in the advent and development of the Arkansaw image. Slavery, and its effects on society, helped set Arkansas apart from peer frontier territories and states like Michigan and Iowa, though both likely laid claim to a number of colorful backwoods denizens at the time. And historian Michael B. Dougan has demonstrated the prominent place of the bigot in Arkansas fiction, especially in the twentieth century. As we shall see later, race and the Arkansaw image have been inextricably linked, but the bigot has impacted the image only in a peripheral manner. In spite of Arkansas's myriad problems, observes Lisenby, "it is probably the stereotype of the ignorant, backwoodsy hillbilly—combined with the low rank of Arkansas in economic and educational statistics—that has become most firmly fixed in the popular perception of the state." It was this "quaint and archaic rural type" that, according to historian Lee A. Dew, "Arkansas, in the public mind at least, seemed particularly to be inhabited by . . ." Once again it would appear that Arkansas had no monopoly on hayseeds and bumpkins. So why did Arkansas seem to be "particularly inhabited by such characters?"[5]

Writing more than half a century ago, the late historian E. E. Dale attributed Arkansas's backwardness—and thus enduring reputation for backwardness—primarily but not solely to the nineteenth-century "millpond effect" caused by the Indian Territory.[6] With the Indian Territory blocking what could have been a natural flow of westward-moving traffic through the state, so goes the argument, Arkansas society grew stagnant, became more isolated, and lost touch with the rush of American life happening outside her borders. In the most thorough analysis of the making of Arkansas's nineteenth-century Bear State image, historian C. Fred Williams argues that the millpond effect was but one of several factors that accounted for "the persistent association of this image with Arkansas." Among these factors were a reputation for violence—a murder on the statehouse floor, committed by the speaker of the house no less, tends to solidify such a reputation—and the state's highly publicized debt problems. Again, the fact that Arkansas's two antebellum banks failed so miserably that the good people of the state thought it preferable to not even have banks anymore was bound to raise an eyebrow or two. Travel accounts, too, as we have seen, spread the news of Arkansas's violent and backward ways and presented a generally negative view of the place. But Arkansas was by no means the only territory or state plagued by killings, cooked ledgers, and bad press.[7]

Therefore, it seems likely that two other factors identified by Williams played more crucial roles in image development and perpetuation: geography and chronology. Arkansas's geographical challenge was truly unique. Primeval swampland covered much of the eastern part of the state, providing a barrier to Americans' typical east-west migration. Those who did make it past the swampy gates found their way westward blocked by the Indian Territory, a geopolitical obstacle that created the millpond effect. Furthermore, the combination of impenetrable swampland and rugged plateau and mountain terrain posed a serious challenge to transportation and commerce. Thus, Arkansas's geography contributed to its arrested development and to its lingering frontier lifestyle.[8]

The timing of Arkansas's statehood was also significant. Hurried into the Union as part of a slave state / free state Senate balancing act, Arkansas was plagued from the beginning by an inadequate infrastructure and weak system of law and order. Arkansas also found herself competing for immigrants, usually unsuccessfully, with more popular destinations such as Texas and Oregon.[9] And one could argue that timing factored into the equation in another way. Although the genre of literature known as southwestern humor did not originate with tales of Arkansas, its emergence in the 1830s coincided with the late territorial / early statehood era of Arkansas's development, a stage of development during which Arkansas was ideally suited for supplying colorful tales of the backwoodsmen and for the creation of the Bear State image. Arkansas eventually progressed beyond this free-wheeling frontier stage of existence, but the Bear State / Arkansas Traveler / Arkansas Toothpick image persisted in the nation's consciousness. Image frequently trumps reality, especially when money and careers may depend upon the perpetuation of an image.

The fact that Arkansas was off the beaten path—it has never been a prime destination or even on the way to any prime destination—likely contributed to its role as national pariah. Very few people ever visited Arkansas, rendering it the perfect blank slate on which to sketch a variety of fanciful tales and caricatures. As Cephas Washburn described it, "Arkansas was a perfect *terra incognita*. The way to get there was unknown; and what it was, or was like, if you did get there was still more an unrevealed mystery."[10] Arkansas's lack of a destination area underscores another geo-cultural characteristic that set the state apart. Though the southwestern humorists were as likely to locate their characters in Mississippi and a few other Old Southwest states as in Arkansas, the Bear State seemed to lag behind these other places in an important way. Literary historian Elmo Howell found that "the neighboring states were not very different [from Arkansas], except that they were older and could boast of a few areas of settled culture."[11] Louisiana had New Orleans; Missouri had St. Louis and the lower Missouri River Valley; Tennessee had joined the Union when Arkansas was yet sparsely settled, Spanish-empire wilderness; and even Mississippi had its vaunted Natchez district, home to some of the South's most affluent planters. By contrast, most of Arkansas's fertile land lay beneath fetid swamp water; Little Rock, her only significant town to speak of, received poor reviews by travelers; and Napoleon, the most significant antebellum Mississippi River town on the Arkansas side, was such a den of lawlessness that its death at the hands of the shifting waters seemed to confirm God's displeasure. Given another decade or two, Arkansas might have developed a plantation belt to rival those of her sister states in the Southeast, along with the conscious cultural cultivation that accompanied the planter's triumph. But the drums of war found Arkansas and its small population in the early stages of transition from frontier to civilization.

When it comes down to nut-cutting time, there would seem to be two main camps: those who attribute the Arkansaw image to the state's quite real shortcomings and eccentricities and those who, finding nothing exceptional or unique about Arkansas, blame the serendipitous confluence of the territory/state's awkward frontier stage with the nation's Jacksonian era humor-mining. Regardless of which camp you've pitched your tent in, it should be pointed out that today we're probably no closer to uncovering the secret of the genesis of the Arkansaw image than the good folks of Arkansas were in the twentieth century or the nineteenth. "Just why they picked on Arkansas is still a mystery," a WPA writer intoned on the eve of World War II.[12] Almost seventy years later the answer to the question "Why Arkansas?" retains an element of mystery. What we can say for certain is that this image had legs, legs that carried the Bear State reputation into the Gilded Age and beyond, legs that only grew stronger in the twentieth century and show no signs of giving out anytime soon. And it's a sure bet that the Arkansas obsession with the Arkansaw image is around for the long haul as well.

✧ CHAPTER TWO ✧

Aboard the Arkansaw Train

The names Opie Read and Thomas W. Jackson are rarely recognized in the twenty-first century, a shocking circumstance considering the amount of fretting these two gentlemen once caused in Arkansas. Both natives of middle Tennessee and from humble backgrounds, the comparisons would stop there if not for their most significant connection—their contributions to and perpetuation of the Arkansaw image. A tall, raw-boned twenty-something when he first arrived in Arkansas in 1876, Read, after brief newspaper jobs in Carlisle and Conway, spent three years working for three different Little Rock papers before his penchant for embellishing his stories got him fired from the *Arkansas Gazette* in 1881. The following year he and his brother-in-law, Philo D. Benham, founded in Little Rock the *Arkansas Traveler,* the humorous weekly that would forever tie Read's name and reputation to the state. And a fitting title it was, for the paper was in a very real sense the spirit of the Arkansas Traveler legend in periodical form. Read claimed that he gathered many of his stories—populated with country bumpkins, worldly travelers, and naive blacks—on his railroad trips into rural and small-town Arkansas, and railroad passengers and other readers couldn't get enough. Within three years the *Arkansas Traveler* boasted a nationwide weekly circulation of eighty-five thousand. By 1887, the combination of the paper's massive circulation and increasing acrimony over its demeaning portrayal of Arkansas led Read to move his operation to Chicago, where he would spend the remainder of his long life.[1]

Thomas W. Jackson, too, would eventually end up in Chicago and on the hit list of the defenders of Arkansas's honor, but through a different and perhaps more unlikely journey. Born in Manchester, Tennessee, in 1867, he grew up in northeastern Texas and as a young man there went to work on the railroad. His job as a brakeman eventually took him to Arkansas and southern Missouri, where he found a wife, and finally to the Pacific Northwest. It was there that the barely literate Jackson began dictating to his wife the jokes and anecdotes he had absorbed from two decades on the rails. His little paperback joke book, *On a Slow Train Through*

Arkansaw, was published in Spokane, Washington, in 1903; peddled by railroad news butchers for a quarter a copy, it sold by the thousands, prompting the author to quit his brakeman job, move to the Windy City, and found the Thomas W. Jackson Publishing Company, which would churn out hundreds of thousands of copies of *Slow Train* and Jackson's twelve joke books that followed.[2]

Read and Jackson were by no means originals. Both seized on an Arkansaw image already alive and well in their day. Although both were intimately connected to Arkansas, or at least the Arkansaw image, their true relationship with the state was little more than cosmetic. Most of what the prolific Read wrote had nothing to do with Arkansas, and as we shall see Jackson's association with the state went little deeper than the title of his first book. Still, the two men and their works represent well the era covered in this chapter—the half-century-plus between the end of the Civil War and the end of World War I—for during this period the Arkansaw image drifted farther away from any mooring in reality that it arguably possessed in the era of the travel writers and southwestern humorists. The image, due in no small part to the efforts of Read and Jackson and many more like them, increasingly achieved one-note status as the backwoods buffoonery of Arkansaw shoved other elements and characteristics to the periphery. The defenders of Arkansas would blame Read and Jackson for perpetuating this image—which they certainly did. But the Arkansaw image was already strutting its stuff across the national stage long before Read and Jackson caught on; they were just shrewd promoters who capitalized on it.

Considering the momentous changes of the period between the Civil War and World War I, one might reasonably have expected the Arkansaw image to simply fade away. But it didn't. In spite of—or, it can be argued, because of—developments such as massive immigration and demographic alteration, industrialization and the rise of the corporation, rapid settlement of the West, and the tremendous expansion of cities, Arkansas's reputation remained unfazed—altered somewhat but fundamentally similar to the Big Bear / Arkansas Traveler image. One major reason for this perseverance was that Arkansas herself, in a most fundamental way, remained unchanged. The monumental developments that so transformed America in this era ultimately exercised only an indirect effect on the overwhelmingly rural and agricultural state. By the end of the nineteenth century, Arkansawyers had largely killed off the bear, but not the Bear State. The squatter in the coonskin cap was a figure, romantic or unfortunate, of the state's frontier past—of practically every state's frontier past. But myth and memory are powerful shapers of perception. Besides, compared with most of the places Americans lived, Arkansas did remain rural and undeveloped.

Arkansas also retained a measure of its violent and dangerous spirit into the postbellum era. Animosities stirred by Civil War divisions and Reconstruction politics plagued communities long after hostilities officially ceased. The so-called Brooks-Baxter War—in which Arkansawyers divided into warring factions a full nine years after Lee's surrender—seemed a fitting sequel to the guerrilla warfare and clannish violence that had rendered the Arkansas countryside a lawless no man's land during the war. Visitors to the state continued to recoil from a society that "will never improve much in the face of ignorance, whisky and weapons." Describing this state of affairs in western Arkansas in 1874, a *Scribner's Monthly* reporter observed "deadly broils . . . between drunken ruffians, whose only sentiment is revenge by pistol shot, and whose chief amusement is coarse and bestial intoxication. . . . Murder is considered altogether too trivial an offense in Arkansas."[3] And even after the self-proclaimed Redeemers had imposed their brand of law and order on the state, Arkansas maintained its link with a heritage of frontier savagery, at least in the eyes of the American public, through the highly publicized and frequently exaggerated exploits of Isaac "The Hanging Judge" Parker and his western district federal court.

For the few northern visitors who came to judge the state of affairs in Arkansas, the sparsely populated state seemed as benighted as ever. The Reverend D. A. Quinn, a Roman Catholic missionary assigned to tend to a bevy of small and scattered flocks in eastern Arkansas in the 1870s, found himself in the midst of a mass of "unsavory expectorant country 'folk.'" Calling this "low type of Caucasian humanity" Hoosiers, Quinn "began to speculate which of the twelve tribes of Israel emigrated to Arkansas." As for the Arkansawyer's appearance, the Catholic missionary found "the Arkansian Hoosier's body . . . a pitiful wreck of humanity. It is the color of the clay on which he stands. I have seen them *dipping* snuff and eating *clay*."[4]

"The masses of the whites are ambitionless, and even the most enthusiastic that I met seemed dubious about the State's prospects," proclaimed *Scribner's Monthly* in 1874. Churches and schoolhouses were still too few and far between to suit an easterner's preference. "The grade of intelligence in the interior districts . . . is much the same as in Eastern Tennessee," which, we infer from the author, must have been somewhere between a touch slow and downright moronic. But the situation wasn't completely hopeless, for "the cultured people living in the larger towns are making special efforts to redeem the commonwealth from the bad name it has received."[5]

The cultured people put up a valiant fight, which will be chronicled in detail later, but their efforts ultimately did little to reform the state's bad name. The Arkansaw image cultivated by Read and Jackson maintained its powerful hold on the American imagination, and Arkansas people, for good or ill, continued to be defined and labeled by it. That image—still essentially the semi-savage, Anglo-American backwoodsman—faced some stiff competition in the ethno-cultural caricature contests of the era: red-skinned savages on the Great Plains and the cowboys and sodbusters who took their lands, drunken Irishmen, money-grubbing Jews, and any number of other melting pot undesirables. In the process of surviving and thriving, the image produced a little something for everyone: novels, short stories, jokes, yellow journalism cartoons, and songs. What follows in this chapter is a survey of the era's backwoods banality, cornpone comedy, and mountain melodrama.

Twain's Thing for Arkansaw and the Bearless Bear State

Although the old southwestern humorists went the way of the Confederacy, the regionalist spirit in literature survived into the late nineteenth century, as did Arkansas's utility as a land tailor-made for comedy. The century's most famous regionalist, reared on the southwestern humorists and familiar with the tales of Arkansas that chugged up and down the Mississippi with every shining steamer, found good use for old Arkansaw. In *Roughing It,* Mark Twain's own travel account from his days out west in the 1860s, he described a rough character who seemed to fit the old Bear State image so well that he went by the name "Arkansas." A "stalwart ruffian . . . who carried two revolvers in his belt and a bowie knife projecting from his boot, and who was always drunk and always suffering for a fight," Arkansas "was so feared, that nobody would accommodate him."[6]

A dozen years later the Arkansaw image enjoyed a brief but colorful appearance in Twain's most celebrated novel, *The Adventures of Huckleberry Finn.* On their journey down the Mississippi, Huck and runaway slave Jim, along with their newly acquired companions the Duke and the King, ventured into an "Arkansaw" river town in which "all the streets and lanes was just mud; they warn't nothing else *but* mud . . . The hogs loafed and grunted around everywhere." Many an antebellum traveler, and reader, would have recognized the scene. "There was empty dry-goods boxes under the awnings, and loafers roosting on them all day long, whittling with their Barlow knives; and chawing tobacco, and gaping and yawning and stretching—a mighty ornery lot." Huck Finn listened to enough banal conversation over "tobacker" to repulse any street urchin and witnessed "considerable whisky-drinking going on," as well as three fights, a shooting, and a near lynching.[7] Even Huck, himself no paragon of respectability, found this hive of sadistic poor whites unpleasant beyond belief.[8]

But, as with his southwestern humorist predecessors, Twain's treatment of Arkansas was more complex than it might at first appear. It should not surprise anyone that a writer of his generation—and a Missourian no less—would portray Arkansas as an uncouth and violent backwater. Still, Twain's overall body of work evinced a familiar romantic, even nostalgic, appreciation for the sometimes unsavory people of the Mississippi Valley. His was no romantic fascination with a strange and colorful population, such as that of Gerstäcker, for we are incapable of finding the commonplace truly fascinating. As literary historian Elmo Howell wrote of Twain's ambivalent relationship with Arkansawyers: "If some of them are 'lunkheads,' they still amuse him for they are the sort of people he grew up with."[9] Twain's best-known works grew in large part out of his nostalgia for a Mississippi River world that, he thought, had disappeared, a nostalgia intensified by his Victorian Connecticut surroundings. According to Howell, he shared with a later literary giant of the Mississippi Valley, William Faulkner, a simultaneous love for and hatred of his native region and its people. "Although he falls into the easy manner of his time of using Arkansas to suggest frontier raucousness, his generalizations belie his treatment of Arkansas people, which is uniformly kind."[10]

With the exception of a notable Twain scene or two, in terms of American fiction Arkansas kept a lower profile in the latter part of the nineteenth century than it had in the antebellum era. As the frontier moved on to the Rockies and beyond, the Wild West supplanted the Old Southwest in the hearts and minds of readers. Though the South continued as a source of fascination for the reading public, Arkansas's position on the periphery of the Deep South made it an unlikely setting for Old South novels. Furthermore, even though John Fox Jr. and Charles Egbert Craddock (née Mary Noailles Murfree) were busy introducing the nation to the quaint ways of Appalachia, the Ozarks and Ouachitas received little literary treatment, fictional or otherwise, before the twentieth century.[11]

Among the most notable fiction writers to use Arkansas as a setting in this era were Octave Thanet (né Alice French) and Opie Read. Primarily a writer of short stories, Thanet, a New Englander by birth and disposition and Iowan by raising, spent her winters in the little Lawrence County, Black River community of Clover Bend and mined the local scenery, dialect, and culture in an attempt to bring verisimilitude to her stories. A local colorist, yes, but Thanet was no romantic in the sense of identifying with the backwoods characters she discovered and wrote about. Her stories remained firmly rooted in her Victorian, middle-class morals and sensibilities, and this lens more often than not rendered the lower classes "shiftless, sickly, and lacking foresight or ambition." In Thanet's Arkansas only the planters gain approval as responsible and trustworthy, while the narrator remains ever the "superior outsider, reporting the shocking, amusing, or irritating ways of people who are clearly her—and her readers'—inferiors."[12]

Opie Read. Courtesy of
Butler Center for
Arkansas Studies,
Central Arkansas
Library System, Little
Rock.

Read's work, though as obscure today as Thanet's, was widely read in the late nineteenth and early twentieth centuries. Despite his deep association with Arkansas, only a handful of his almost three dozen novels were set in the state. *Len Gansett* (1889) and *Emmet Bonlore* (1891) both revolved around the experiences of small-town, Arkansas newspaper publishers, a subject on which Read could speak with some authority. *An Arkansas Planter* (1896) was typical of lots of stories of the postwar South, set as it was in Arkansas's plantation district. As a matter of fact, there was nothing in any of Read's Arkansas novels that would suggest an Arkansas exceptionalism. Most of Read's novels were set in the states of the upper South and, typical of the era, were burdened with thick dialect and filled with eccentric characters and romantic, backwoods settings.[13]

The Persistence of the Arkansas Traveler

Readers in the twenty-first century are more likely to encounter Twain's vision of Arkansaw, but it was Read whose name was synonymous with Bear State humor in the late nineteenth century. His urge to spin yarns had begun to overwhelm his reportage early in his newspaper career. According to his biographer, Read ruffled feathers with his colorful Conway commentary even before leaving for Little Rock. *The Arkansas Traveler,* launched in June 1882, freed Read from the constraints of traditional reporting. Though many of his Arkansas readers may have been unaware, *The Arkansas Traveler* was not unique in the late nineteenth century. *Texas Siftings, California Maverick,* and other weeklies mined the same vein of humor with a hodgepodge of editorials, feature stories, literary and theatrical criticism, and fiction.[14]

Given the cultural resonance of the Arkansas Traveler image, it should come as no surprise that Read's paper may have had more fun at its state's expense than did the others in the genre. Read himself claimed that *The Arkansas Traveler* became such an anathema that one of the paper's subscription collectors was harassed in the hill country and that a country politician was elected to office largely on the promise to hang Opie Read. But, given the generally positive responses from readers and other papers around the state upon the *Traveler's* debut, these claims likely emanated from Read's attempts to generate publicity through controversy. And, considering Arkansawyers' later appreciation for Bob Burns and the Clampetts, it should also come as no surprise that some of the paper's most loyal readers

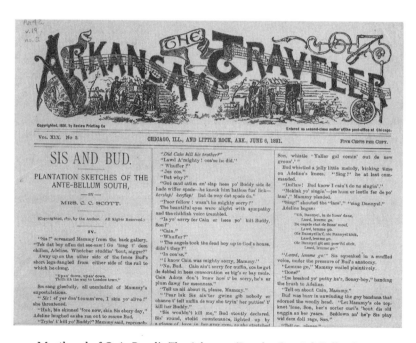

Masthead of Opie Read's *The Arkansas Traveler.* Special Collections, University of Arkansas Libraries, Fayetteville.

were the very small-town and country folk who were supposedly the comic foils of the enterprise. One reason for this may have been Read's willingness to spread the comedy around, geographically, racially, and socioeconomically. *The Arkansas Traveler*, like the twentieth-century joke books that it in part inspired, was an equal opportunity ridiculer. The publication's stories of poor mountaineers were just as likely to be set in Tennessee or Kentucky as they were in Arkansas, especially after the move to Chicago in 1887, and readers consumed generous doses of standard slow railroad humor and dialect-laden, silly Negro stories. Although Read's outlook tended to follow the middle of the road, he wasn't above using his stories to criticize Victorian self-righteousness and hypocrisy. Like most local colorists, Read had a romantic streak, one that influenced a preference "to indentify himself with the swamplands and the Ozarks." In fact, one suspects that Read gained a certain degree of satisfaction from raising the hackles of Little Rock's better sort, a group more likely to voice its displeasure than was the common run of clodhoppers and hayseeds.[15]

More than the title of his weekly kept the spirit of the Arkansas Traveler legend alive. According to Read's biographer, the "Arkansas Traveler dialogue was probably the basic structure of all of Read's fiction."[16] And the legend—with its celebration/condemnation ambivalence—provided the basic structure for the presentation of Arkansas in American popular culture in the late nineteenth and early twentieth centuries.

The Arkansas Traveler title and tune, if not the spirit of the legend, flourished in the late nineteenth century in song, in the form of a popular stage production, and perhaps most bizarrely as the centerpiece of one of the earliest tourist traps to capitalize on the state's backwoods image. This tourist trap was McLeod's Amusement Park, commonly called Happy Hollow, in Hot Springs. Established as a photography studio in 1888 by Georgia native Norman McLeod, Happy Hollow eventually boasted a zoo, a shooting gallery, and a souvenir shop. By the end of the nineteenth century it had gained a reputation for its comic photographs, courtesy of its Coney Island–style gag backgrounds and props, many of which played on Americans' images of Arkansaw. Visitors could have their photographs taken astraddle a donkey, lounging in an old bathtub, or peering out of headless plywood backdrops depicting a number of humorous scenes. The nexus of this amusement park was a dilapidated log cabin on whose slatternly roof perched a hand-scrawled sign that read "Arkansaw Traveller."[17]

The Arkansas Traveler legend remained a central motif in other endeavors meant to entice the general public. One of these was the stage production *Kit the Arkansas Traveler*, which, according to the late folklorist James R. Masterson, played coast to coast for thirty years. Written by Edward Spencer and significantly revised by Thomas B. de Walden, *Kit,*

McLeod's Amusement Park, "Happy Hollow," in Hot Springs, Arkansas.
Courtesy of Butler Center for Arkansas Studies,
Central Arkansas Library System, Little Rock.

which debuted in Buffalo, New York, in 1869, made use of the legend's setting—backwoods cabin, meeting between squatter and stranger, and turn
of the fiddle tune—in the first act, but the remainder of the play took to
the Mississippi River and drew more heavily from the antebellum stories
of desperadoes and ruffians in the wide-open Southwest. In a violent and
melodramatic twist to the legend, the stranger in *Kit* abducts the squatter's
wife and small child; the wife dies in the villain's harrowing escape, and
only years later in St. Louis and then again aboard a Mississippi steamboat
does the now wealthy but drunken squatter, Kit, encounter his grown
daughter and her captor. What follows is a thrilling if formulaic dash from
gambling to explosions to familial reunion, culminating in the villain's
murder courtesy of Kit's Bowie knife.[18]

As Masterson observed, *Kit*'s "plot and the characters . . . have no
essential relation to Arkansas."[19] There is no evidence that the original version of the play was even set in the state. But the revisionist's decision to
utilize the Arkansas name and the familiar Arkansas Traveler setting speaks
to the power of the Arkansaw image in American popular culture. And

nowhere was that image better conveyed than in popular song. According to the late folklorist W. K. McNeil, "Pop and folk songs . . . have probably reached a greater audience than any other type of cultural material . . . [and they] offer a more candid body of opinion than can be found in more formal sources."[20] That candid opinion frequently found Arkansas "the hands-down favorite candidate for criticism." When combined with printed caricatures of Arkansaw, according to folklorist Erika Brady, popular songs "have created a myth of a land at the back of the beyond, peopled by a wild, shiftless, shrewd cast of characters indifferent to or at odds with the mainstream of American life."[21] The two most popular nineteenth-century musical representations of the state were "The Arkansas Traveller and Rackinsac Waltz" and "The State of Arkansaw." The fiddle tune known as "The Arkansas Traveler (or Traveller)" dates at least as far back as the mid-1840s, and an obscure musician by the name of William Cumming first published an arrangement of the tune, "The Arkansas Traveller and Rackinsac Waltz," in Louisville and Cincinnati in 1847. There is some evidence that the tune may have been the composition of a Cincinnati-based, Spanish-American violinist named José Tasso. Regardless

"The Turn of the Tune: Traveller Playing the 'Arkansas Traveller," 1870 Currier & Ives lithograph by John Cameron, based on the uncompleted painting by Edward Payson Washburn. Courtesy of Library of Congress Prints and Photographs Division.

of the tune's origin, what concerns our little foray is the dialogue, and it is likely that the most popular postbellum version of the Arkansas Traveler dialogue was the one published and performed by an albino African American during the Civil War. A guitarist and performer of some renown, Mose Case turned the traveler into an urbane easterner and the squatter into a ruder and more witless customer than the one who slyly held his own with, or got the best of, the traveler in the versions more likely to turn up in Arkansas.[22]

Known by a multiplicity of names—"Bill Stafford," "Sanford Barnes," "When I Left Arkansas," as well as "The Arkansas Traveller"—"The State of Arkansaw" offered a similarly bleak picture of the state. A true song of the people, "The State of Arkansaw" is of unknown authorship and appeared in print for the first time in 1891. Though dozens of different versions of the song have been collected over the years, the crux of the story remains pretty consistent. A wanderer, usually named Bill Stafford or Sanford Barnes, travels by rail to Arkansas, where he takes up residence at a hotel run by a tall, skinny man with long hair. Overcharged for his sorry room and sorrier board, the wanderer soon finds himself in the employ of his hotelier, who almost works the wanderer to death draining land. Ultimately, the wanderer escapes Arkansas and vows never to come back.[23] Here is a version of the song collected by folklorist John Quincy Wolf Jr. in Batesville in 1952.

My name is Sanford Barnes; I came from Buffalo town.
I've traveled this wide world over; I've roamed it 'round and 'round.
I've had my ups and downs through life, and better days I've saw,
But I never knew what misery was 'til I struck old Arkansas.

It was in the year of '82, in the merry month of June.
I landed in Hot Springs one sultry afternoon.
Up came a walking skeleton and handed me his paw,
Inviting me to his hotel, the best in Arkansas.

I followed my conductor unto his dwelling place.
There was misery depicted in his melancholy face.
He fed me on corn dodgers and beef I couldn't chaw;
He charged me fifty cents a day in the state of Arkansas.

I got up early next morning to catch the early train.
He said I'd better work for him; he had some land to drain.
He'd give me fifty cents a day, my wash and board and all.
He thought I'd be a different man when I left old Arkansas.

I worked six weeks for this galoot, Jess Harrell was his name.
Six foot seven inches in his stocking feet, and as slim as any crane.
His hair hung down like rattails over his long lantern jaw;
He's a photograph of all the gents that was raised in Arkansas.

He fed me on corn dodgers as hard as any rock
'Til my teeth began to loosen and my knees began to knock.
I got so thin on sassafras tea, I could hide behind a straw.
You bet I was a different man when I left old Arkansas.

Farewell to the old swamp angels, the canebrakes and the chills.
Farewell to sage and sassafras tea and popcorn dodger pills.
If ever I see that place again—I'll give to you my paw—
It'll be through a telescope from H[ell] to Arkansas.[24]

Other songs from this era found mirth at the expense of Arkansas's dignity. "The Arkansas Sheik," a song of murky origins that was often recorded in the 1920s and 1930s, warns "Missouri gals" against marrying an Arkansas boy, who dresses in "an old flop hat with more brim than crown / An old pair of shoes with the heels run down." The Arkansawyers in "The Arkansas Sheik" live in a decrepit old cabin, slobber tobacco juice on their chins, and own little besides "an old blind mule and an old milk cow / A razorback hog and a bull-tongue plow."[25] "In Arkansas" was no more likely than "The Arkansas Sheik" to be named official state song. In a version recorded in 1930 by Jimmie Davis—he of "You Are My Sunshine" and Louisiana gubernatorial fame—Arkansas was no place for the overly refined. "The babies all dip Garrett snuff, Way down in Arkansas / They use possums for yard dogs, Way down in Arkansas / The people sleep in hollow logs, Way down in Arkansas." Among the other habits and achievements of Davis's Arkansawyers: "They climb grapevines and scale the trees . . . And they crack hickory nuts on their knees . . . They eat wildcats at early morn . . . They don't drink coffee, they drink corn . . . They don't wear pants, haven't got 'em for sale . . . They wear long shirts with great long tails."[26]

With Mose Case's "The Arkansas Traveller," "The State of Arkansaw," and other popular songs we find the Arkansaw image drifting away from its traditional ambivalence. Depending on the person doing the telling or the singing, Arkansas might have retained a sliver of its country wit and romance, but the general tone of these numbers was one of ridicule. This shallower, hyperbolic assessment of Arkansas blossomed with the coming of a new century. Thomas W. Jackson's *On a Slow Train Through Arkansaw* was only the most successful of a string of one-note books that recaptured the spirit of condemnation once inhabited by Schoolcraft and Featherstonhaugh. Only this time it was played for comic effect.

You Might Be a Hillbilly If . . . : Slow Trains and Slower Brains

We might refer to this new phase in the development of the Arkansaw image as the dawn of the hillbilly—but only because Patrick Huber's recent study of a certain amorous mountaineer figurine has rendered the phrase "rise of the hillbilly" forever off limits in mixed company.[27] (Besides, I'm plagued by the same red-faced, hypocritical prudery that Vance Randolph discovered in my ridge-running forebears, to the point of cursing the procreative suggestions embedded (pardon) . . . implied in the very term "forebears.") By now we've been bombarded with images that smack of hillbilly—the Arkansas Traveler phenomenon is a veritable Hillbilly 101 thesis—but to this point I've been careful to avoid the term hillbilly, or at least careful with its usage. This is not because of a hyper-political correctness; the descendants of Pete Whetstone, last I checked, have received little protection by the P.C. police. Rather, it is because to the amazement of most of us in the twenty-first century, the term hillbilly achieved common usage little more than a hundred years ago.

Perhaps it is no coincidence that the most caricatured, one-dimensional versions of the Arkansaw image followed close on the heels of the first-known published use of the word "hillbilly," in the New York *Journal* in 1900.[28] One of the first books to use the term in relation to Arkansawyers was the 1902 novel *Down in Arkansas,* by Charles H. Hibler. *Down in Arkansas* follows three Arkansas travelers—an educated Bostonian, a cynical Philadelphia attorney, and a rotund Kansas City land speculator—as they try to make their way through the Ouachitas. Taken captive by a gang of armed and masked moonshiners who mistake these citified interlopers for revenuers, the trio is sprung from their prison cave by an undercover federal agent. But the transparent plot seems nothing more than Hibler's excuse for page after page of fanciful description of the Arkansas backwoods—"the wildest, strangest, and dullest neck of woods in the wide world." For Hibler, "the Hill Billy is a character in many respects unlike any other on the globe, and to do him justice would require the facile pen of a Dickens." The author's own pen, facile or not, described a moonshining hillbilly that any modern American could recognize: an "ill-proportioned figure of a man, whose head was covered with long black hair, and whose microscopic eyes seemed to blaze . . . a full-fledged wonder, grim and threatening, with a trusty double-barreled shotgun in his big rusty hands; a large man, nearly seven feet tall, thin of girth, though broad-shouldered and powerful." Sounds remarkably like Bill Stafford's tormentor. While we're at it, we'll let Hibler finish the postcard. Many Arkansas hillbillies, "suspicious by nature, look upon strangers . . . [as a] menace to their 'liberties.'" Finally, the trio's captors "were a thin-visaged, long-shanked, and cadaverous lot of Hill Billies."[29]

Let's not be so fast to throw *Down in Arkansas* into the furnace, however. In spite of the cool reception by Arkansans, then and now, Hibler's novel reveals the same ambivalence reflected in the stories of many southwestern humorists and in the dialogues of the Arkansas Traveler. Evident in the novel is the romantic impulse to exalt and envy the supposed and unattainable simple life of the hillman. "Among his inherent qualities are integrity and prodigality, and in the matter of contentment and enjoyment, he is a step higher on the ladder of man's worthy, but visionary ambition, than any being of his color on the face of Mother Earth." Hibler's narrator underscores the fin de siècle–inspired anxieties of the modern. "The dweller in the cabin, secluded and secure, is far happier than he who resides in a mansion, mid trials and turmoil, worry, and strife. . . . Therefore, though his fare be frugal, his home humble and his life quiet, he is contented with his environment, happy in his seclusion."[30]

The spate of joke books that followed *Down in Arkansas* in quick succession suffered few pains of ambivalence, however. Within the span of about five years no fewer than four cheap paperback joke books carrying

What You See in the Hills of Arkansaw

Illustration from Thomas W. Jackson's *On a Slow Train Through Arkansaw*, 1903. Special Collections, University of Arkansas Libraries, Fayetteville.

the name "Arkansas(aw)" in the title made their appearance. These harbingers of the twentieth-century Arkansaw image were not the first Arkansaw-themed joke books—a compilation of jokes and sketches from Opie Read's *The Arkansas Traveler* published in the 1880s may have been the first of its kind—but they did ring in the new century with a bang worthy of a good old-fashioned firing of the anvil. Though Thomas W. Jackson's 1903 book is best remembered today and most often condemned for its reputation-poisoning effect, the content of *On a Slow Train Through Arkansaw* was less Arkansas-related than that of the other three.

> It was down in the state of Arkansaw I rode on the slowest train I ever saw. It stopped at every house. When it came to a double house it stopped twice. They made so many stops I said, "Conductor, what have we stopped for now?" He said, "There are some cattle on the track." We ran a little ways further and stopped again. I said, "What is the matter now?" He said, "We have caught up with those cattle again." . . .
>
> The news agent come through. He was an old man with long gray whiskers. I said, "Old man, I thought they always had boys on the train to sell the pop corn, chewing gum and candy." He said he was a boy when he started. They stopped so often one of the passengers tried to commit suicide. He ran ahead for half a mile, laid down on the track, but he starved to death before the train got there."

Beyond a few slow train jokes like these, there is little Arkansas material to be found. Unless you happened to have been an employee of the railroad in the early twentieth century, there seems to have been little reason to take offense. In fact, the book's typically irreverent skewering of blacks, Jews, and other popular targets of the era was more demeaning than any slur against Arkansas. But Jackson's decision to locate his slow train in Arkansas likely suggests the popular perception that a slow people would naturally have slow trains. As folklorist W. K. McNeil remarked in his introduction to a reprinting of the book, "By 1903 Arkansas was well entrenched in burlesque and in the minds of many people as the worst state in the Union."[31] Thus, *On a Slow Train Through Arkansaw* was just as much a product of the Arkansaw image as a purveyor of it. The most significant aspect of Jackson's book is that he chose "Arkansaw" for the title, recognizing the humorous resonance of the very word. No other state name carried such an immediate recognition of comic backwardness.

Unlike Jackson, the author of *Three Years in Arkansaw,* a thin paperback published in Chicago in 1904, aimed all his barbs directly at Arkansas's country folk. A wanderlust-stricken Indiana native and former resident of Polk and Sevier counties in southwestern Arkansas, Marion Hughes recounted the odd ways and backward lifestyles of his former neighbors in such out-of-the-way places as Horatio, where he "existed . . . for nine months. You see, people in Arkansaw don't live; they only exist." Hughes's Arkansaw was populated with snuff-dipping grannies, slow-witted yokels, lazy farmers, moonshiners, and no fewer than ten different kinds of wild hogs. Shoes were practically unheard of. Much of the booklet consisted of jokes and stories that, like *Slow Train*'s contents, were circulated widely in the folk humor of the day. Hughes even included his own obvious rip-off of the Arkansas Traveler legend.

> I stopped in out of the rain one day at a typical Arkansawyer's home. The old man was sitting in the corner sawing away on an old fiddle, his wife was trying to start a fire with some wet wood, while the barefooted, half-naked children were shivering with cold, but the old man didn't appear to pay any attention to me, his wife or the freezing children, but kept sawing away on the old fiddle. Finally he said to me, "I am larning to play a new tune called 'Hell among the yearlings.' I thought it would be more appropriate if he would call it "Hell in Arkansaw."[32]

Hughes's most valuable contribution to the Arkansaw image was the collection of illustrations scattered throughout *Three Years in Arkansaw*. With their haggard old women dressed in tatters, lanky, floppy-hatted men, gaunt hounds, and cabins full of children, chickens, and hogs, the Hughes drawings were among the earliest examples of the Arkansaw image in its twentieth-century, visual hillbilly mode. The intrepid author concluded his dissertation on life in Arkansas with a bit of his own poetry:

I hav lived in 16 States
But of all I ever saw
There is no place like living
Down in old Arkansaw.
They all wear homade clothing
Both the men and females
While the children with dirty faces
All go in their shirt tails.
The men drink moonshine whisky
The women chew and dip
And the big gals go barefooted
With tobacco on their lip.

They cook by the fireplace
With a skilit and a lid
And all liv on black coffee
Sow bossom and cornbread.
All are free-hearted
And respect the moral law
Is the reason I love to liv
Down in old Arkansaw.[33]

Hughes's closing stanza suggests a certain romantic attachment to his simple Arkansas subjects. But lest you grow weary of my jug-half-full interpretation of the Arkansaw image, it should be noted that the sheer volume of mockery and derision blacks out the faint glimmers of romanticism in *Three Years in Arkansaw*.[34]

Likewise, the page-upon-page of indecipherable dialect obscures the fundamentally romantic tone of Herb Lewis's long-forgotten—and largely forgettable—work of fiction, *Eb Peechcrap and Wife at the Fair* (1906). The fair in question is the 1904 Louisiana Purchase Exposition (World's Fair) in St. Louis, and Lewis's story is typical of many country-folks-go-to-the-big-city tales. Told in the words of Elberter Peechcrap from "Possom Ridge, Arkansaw," *Eb Peechcrap* consists of a series of shocks and mishaps the Peechcraps experience on their big outing, such as Eb's recollection of their

Illustration from Marion Hughes's *Three Years in Arkansaw*, 1904.
Courtesy of Arkansas History Commission.

arrival in the city and his first brush with railroad porters: "Wal, by gum! That thar' city o' St. Louis war bigger'n Fount'in City, an' Gait City, an' Persimmon Center, with Squar' Hank Austum's an' Bill Frazher's real estate ter boot . . . An' when we uns lit on the ground more 'an a dozen the dad gumdest iddyots jist cum runnin' an' grabbed my poke an' verleece rite out'n my han' an' tried tu steel 'em rite thar' in daylite." As one might expect of a book whose title page epigram is "Wal,' by gum! I reckon," the hilarity that ensues is more than a little corny and clichéd. Nevertheless, the author's stated aim is to depict "a natural character in the good old time Arkansawyer," a people "possessed of a genuine human sociability, considerable wit, hidden-shrewdness, . . . a little 'quar' in speech, yet more from habit handed down than otherwise, and full of the 'perklivyties' to protect himself and his own reputation and family." In other words, Herb Lewis's Peechcraps were Clampetts for the age of Teddy Roosevelt, and, like their 1960s-era descendants, they maintained a countrified high ground amid the shiftiness and unpredictability of the urban world.[35]

Harold Bell Wright and the Bucolic Ozarks

If On a Slow Train Through Arkansaw and its imitators distilled the shiftless and dim-witted hillbilly into his modern and publicly palatable flavor, a simultaneous development resuscitated the romantic spirit long present in the Arkansaw image and transformed it into an appealing vision of a land and a people divorced from the march of time—in a mostly good way. In the process it helped narrow the twentieth-century parameters of the Arkansaw image, zeroing in on a particular geographic setting and that set-ting's dominant ethnic group—though almost no one at the time would have considered the supposedly pure Anglo-Saxon whites of the Ozarks and Ouachitas an ethnic group.

A century ago the United States was not yet an urban nation, but there were plenty of urbanites suffering a sort of separation anxiety. They feared rapid urbanization and industrialization and the young nation's concomi-tant separation from its rural and agrarian past. They feared the deleteri-ous effects of overcivilization on the mind and body and spirit. This antimodernism was in a sense just the newest incarnation of the romantic and primitivist spirit, with new champions and new catch phrases and new obstacles. But all who embraced the new romantic spirit agreed that the restoration of personal spiritual vigor, if not by extension a broader social salvation, depended on making contact with the natural world, get-ting away from the cities, at least temporarily, going back to the land. Psychologists of the era postulated that depriving children of contact with nature prevented their full and natural development. In the same vein, historians argued that America's frontier and agrarian heritage had been integral to the cultivation of such fundamentally "American" virtues as democracy, independence, and ingenuity; and the closing of the frontier at the end of the nineteenth century left Americans wondering what kinds of virtues, or vices, a highly civilized, urban nation would breed. Middle- and upper-class city folk embraced Liberty Hyde Bailey's Country Life Movement, only the first of several idealistic back-to-the-land models to catch the fancy of affluent, twentieth-century Americans. President Theodore Roosevelt, he of big game hunts and rough riding, championed this plan and urged every American to discover his inner farmer.[36]

Another manifestation of this turn-of-the-century romantic spirit was a pastoral, usually moralistic literature exemplified by a slew of novels peddling "the arcadian myth."[37] Few purveyors of the myth were more successful than Harold Bell Wright, whose novel *The Shepherd of the Hills* sold two million copies in its first ten years on the market. Although *The Shepherd of the Hills* was set not in Arkansas but in southwestern Missouri—and no Branson-area tourism promoter ever plans to let the public forget it—the novel exercised such a tremendous impact on perceptions of the Ozark region in general that it deserves top billing in our survey of the origins of the bucolic, pastoral element of the Arkansaw image.

Harold Bell Wright's
*The Shepherd of the
Hills, 1907.*

Born in upstate New York and raised there and in Ohio, Wright was a thirty-year-old Disciples of Christ minister in Pittsburg, Kansas—home to a boy named Vance Randolph—when he wrote his first novel in 1902. Following a move to Kansas City, poor health forced him to give up the ministry temporarily, and in 1905 Wright and his wife retreated into the White River hills of southwestern Missouri, spending the summer on the farm of John and Anna Ross west of Branson. It was there that he began the first draft of his best-selling novel, which he would continue writing during a preaching sojourn in Lebanon, Missouri. By the time *The Shepherd of the Hills* was published in 1907, the Wrights had moved to southern California. Though most of Wright's later novels were set in the mythical West instead of the arcadian Ozarks, the critically panned author had left his mark on the region that, in his estimation, had rejuvenated him in body and in spirit. Described by historians Lynn Morrow and Linda Myers-Phinney as a "formulaic Arcadian melodrama," *The Shepherd of the Hills* related the story of a successful but weary city pastor "who retreats to the wilderness of the Ozark Mountains in an attempt to recover inner peace and heal his tormented soul." Straight out of the only-in-fiction handbook, the shepherd is taken in by the kindly, salt-of-the-earth parents of the girl whom his own son had years earlier seduced and abandoned. But the shepherd restores his and his family's good name—as well as his faith and mental and physical health—by coming clean to his hosts, by leading the simple life as a country shepherd, and by convincing another young Ozark woman to turn down her citified suitor, and the promises of a life of leisure and material comfort, in favor of the strapping local lad whose only ambitions lie rooted in the rocky soil of the hills. As Morrow and Myers-Phinney point out, "the presumption of the Arcadian myth, that rurality was intrinsically superior to urbanity, was the foundation of Wright's story." For the sickly young preacher—as for the shepherd of his story—"the Ozarks [was] a sanctuary."[38]

Not a great work of literature by the standards of the day, or any other era for that matter, *The Shepherd of the Hills* had an impact all out of proportion to its literary value. The novel's bucolic setting, in the very hills in which Wright had camped and among the real-life people who served as models for his characters, inspired thousands to visit the area known still today as the "Shepherd of the Hills Country." The novel's success inspired imitators. Most—Grover Clay's *Hester of the Hills: A Romance of the Ozark Mountains* (1907), John Homer Case's *Jean Carroll, A Tale of the Ozark Hills* (1912), Caroline Abbott Stanley's *The Keeper of the Vineyard: A Tale of the Ozarks* (1914), William R. Lighton's *Happy Hollow Farm* (1915), William Antony Kennedy's *The Master of Bonne Terre* (1917), and Wright's own follow-up *The Calling of Dan Matthews* (1909)—kept *Shepherd*'s Missouri setting.[39] One writer who found an Ozark Arcadia on the Arkansas side of the line was Missouri-based novelist (and sometime northwestern Arkansas resident) John Breckenridge Ellis, who followed his *Arkinsaw Cousins: A Story of the Ozarks* (1908) with *The Little Fiddler of the Ozarks* (1913). Though located in southwestern Arkansas instead of in the Ozarks, Ruth McEnery Stuart's fictional Simpkinsville was home to the same "simple and kind-hearted folks" who lived in Wright's novels.[40]

It is instructive—and worth mentioning here—that most of the Arcadian novels of the Ozarks were set in Missouri. In general the stereotypes and images associated with the Ozarks have crossed state boundaries, just as the 36°-30' line has created no fundamental sociocultural division within the region. Arkansas's state reputation—the Arkansaw image—and its experiences as a part of the defeated Confederacy and occupied Reconstruction South contributed to real if usually subtle divergences between the imagery of the Arkansas Ozarks and the Missouri Ozarks. Missouri's Union loyalty, however tenuous, and its subsequent transformation into a midwestern—instead of a southern—place dominated by St. Louis and Kansas City businessmen made the Show-Me State a more benign setting for a modern American Arcadia.

As we shall see in chapter 3, though, the Arkansas portion of the Ozarks would receive a share of the Arcadian mythologizing of the years between the two world wars. And no small amount of this romanticizing stemmed from the novels of Harold Bell Wright and others of the early twentieth century. In fact, the long-term effect of *Shepherd*'s Arcadian vision of the Ozarks was even more crucial than the short-term impact, for among the thousands attracted to the region by Wright's bucolic descriptions were Vance Randolph and Otto Ernest Rayburn, two men who would play major roles in the crafting of the Arkansaw/Ozark image in the coming decades.

But before we leap into the interwar period—the great age for everything hillbilly, everything Ozark, everything Arkansaw—I should point out that Wright and his imitators did not have a monopoly on depictions of a pastoral Arkansas or an arcadian Ozarks. By the time the 1920s rolled around, the American popular music repertoire contained dozens of songs trumpeting the good old days back on the farm—the harried urbanite's vision of the agrarian idyll—and a fair number of these were set in Arkansas or in the Ozarks. One of the earliest was Henry DeMoss's "My Happy Little Home in Arkansas," which was debuted at Chicago's World's Columbian Exposition in 1893. Like many a sentimental song to follow, the setting of "My Happy Little Home in Arkansas" was a bucolic paradise—the "Ozarks as Eden," in the words of the late W. K. McNeil. "'Tis a pretty little cottage / Where the grass is ever green / And the streamlet from the Boston Mountains flows," DeMoss wrote of Arkansas, "Where the mockingbird doth sing / 'Til the grove with music rings / At my happy little home in Arkansas." Equally sentimental was James White's 1915 song, "'Way Down in Arkansaw," though White's muse longs for a different geographical region of the state and smacks of the Deep South numbers that emanated from the minstrel tradition. "'Way down south where I was born / Amid the cotton and the golden corn / There's the place I long to be / In that land of hospitality." And no song could top Eva Ware Barnett's "Arkansas" for syrupy sentimentality. One of several songs to be voted an official "state song" by the general assembly, the 1916 number praised above all else the state's bucolic countrysides, "Where the roses are in bloom, And the sweet magnolia too / Where the jasmine is white, And the fields are violet blue."[41] This was certainly a place worth coming home to, or even moving to, unlike the Arkansaw of Charles Hibler's novel or of Mark Twain's violent and backward river town.

The Shepherd of the Hills, "My Happy Little Home in Arkansas," and other products of the nostalgia and romanticism of the era exemplified a new—or at least revived and revised—element in the Arkansaw image, one that would perhaps never become the dominant motif but would contribute to the image's complexity. As we have seen, the romantic influence had been around at least since the days when Albert Pike chronicled his adventures in the Arkansas territory. But Wright's novels of the Ozarks and the nostalgic songs of Arkansas offered a new twist, sentimentality. Romanticism and sentimentality did not always go hand-in-hand, but they would increasingly do so in the twentieth century, especially when the Ozarks was involved.

This Hillbilly State of Mine

Take a minute and think about the images that the word "Arkansaw" evokes. Admittedly, unless for some reason you started reading this book here in the middle, you've been bombarded with caricatures, personalities, and stereotypes from the first one hundred years of the Arkansaw image that are probably jostling for position right about now. If I had started the book with that question, what images would have come to mind? Most likely some of the ones we've already covered, along with several that will crowd the pages of the remainder of the book. In generic terms, I suspect there are a fair number of beanpole-physiqued men in bare feet and raggedy overalls, maybe wearing floppy black hats and slouching with moonshine jugs. Some are haggard old grannies, crouched over a washboard or occupied at a spinning wheel or quilter's loom. There could be fiddles and hoedowns involved, or perhaps just "ballets" about jilted lovers or murderous spouses or train wrecks or Jesse James. Hound dogs and shotguns are probably the most common accessories, shoes and teeth the most uncommon. Maybe your Arkansawyers are more ominous—greasy-headed rednecks in loud, large trucks, drunken, spewing intolerance from tobacco-stained mouths. Maybe not.

If there is definition, specificity to the faces, whose are they? Bob Burns? Lum and Abner? Dizzy Dean? Some anonymous Depression-era family on their way to who knows where in a jalopy that's probably not getting them there. Orval Faubus? Jed Clampett? Lil' Abner, Daisy Mae, Mammy Yokum? Almeda Riddle? Your grandparents? The guide from those float trips on the Buffalo years ago? Chances are the word "Arkansaw" doesn't inspire images of Sam Walton or John Gould Fletcher or Daisy Bates or J. William Fulbright. Chances are the people in just about all those images are common folk (or Hollywood representations thereof), they're white, and they have some sort of connection to the Arkansas upland. In other words, chances are that the dominant motif in your version of the Arkansaw image is that of the hillbilly or the mountaineer.

Like her sister states in the old Confederacy, Arkansas has a less-than-stellar record of racial justice and tolerance. One of the bright spots for Arkansans of African descent, however, may be their historic side-stepping of the Arkansaw image. Sure, African Americans face some of the same image problems—the stigma from low test scores and family income rankings is no respecter of race—but they are largely left out when it comes to hillbilly/ mountaineer imagery, the dominant dual symbol of Arkansawyers in the twentieth century. After all, there have always been blacks in the Ozarks and Appalachia, but everyone knows hillbillies are white.[1] This reprieve for Arkansans of African descent isn't the result of modern political correctness or some miracle of racial good will from an earlier time, though. As we have seen, blacks, slave or free, played only the most peripheral role in the early development of the Arkansaw image, a situation due primarily to the antebellum black's own victimization by racial stereotypes and his near absence from the informal public discourse in the South. After the war, freedmen continued to have little connection to the Arkansaw image. By the twentieth century Jim Crow laws and widespread disfranchisement had rendered African Americans in Arkansas and elsewhere in the South in effect a voiceless minority. Other national (and international) movements combined with their second-class citizenship to force Arkansas's African Americans even off the periphery of the Arkansaw image, though one suspects that few if any protested this particular segregationist slight.

The Arkansaw image's racial specificity emerged as a product of its regionalization. In the twentieth century the Arkansaw image became increasingly indistinguishable from an emerging Ozark image that itself covered the territory between buffoonish simpleton to noble and resourceful spawn of the frontier. In the twentieth century the image obtained a geographical qualification that it did not have throughout most of the nineteenth. For most Americans the residents of the rural Ozarks and Ouachitas became the true Arkansawyers. And if one word achieved synonymity with the Arkansaw image it was "hillbilly." As historian Elliott West recognized, "To the extent that outsiders think of us, they often picture a land of hillbillies, and the Ozarks, of course, are home to that image."[2]

As we have seen, the Bear State/Arkansaw image of the nineteenth century was not tied to a specific geographical region or type of terrain. All Schoolcraft's condemnations were aimed at people living in the sparsely settled Ozarks, but that is because he saw no other region on his brief journey. Featherstonhaugh was an equal opportunity despiser, criticizing with impunity most Arkansawyers he encountered wherever he encountered them: in towns and in backwoods, in the Arkansas and Mississippi River valleys and in the delta, the Ozarks, and the Ouachitas. Pete Whetstone hailed from the Ozarks, but Jim Doggett made his home and his hunts in the swamps and canebrakes. The squatter of Arkansas Traveler legend probably haunted the hills, but the elevation of his homestead was of secondary importance; the legend was, after all, the Arkansas Traveler, not the Ozark or Ouachita Traveler. Friedrich Gerstäcker felt nature's call wherever a good bear hunt could be had, whether in the cypress bottoms of the east or the northwestern Ozark hills canopied in white oak.

If the most obvious question arising from a study of the nineteenth-century Arkansaw image is "Why Arkansas?" then the most pertinent, if not obvious, question facing our twentieth-century image is perhaps best summed up as "Why the Hillbilly/Mountaineer?" We can glean a few clues from a survey of changes within the state. Cotton, which became king in Arkansas only after the Civil War, gradually absorbed the bulk of the cane-brakes and swamplands that the mythical Jim Doggett had hunted. Forests were cleared, swamps drained, land leveled, and cotton planted from state boundary to state boundary in the once-wild lowlands, leaving only nooks and crannies where the medieval forest and its depleted wildlife remained. Cotton also crept into the less rugged sections of the hill country, into river bottoms in western and northern Arkansas, along the fringes of the Ouachitas, and onto the undulating plateau lands of the eastern Ozarks. The railroad lines that snaked into Ozark and Ouachita hollows and coves, mainly after 1900, brought the denuders of forests but not the planters of cash crops. The results were often equally destructive—the disappearance of virgin forests and large game animals and the erosion of hillsides—but the transformations were not so visible to the visitor as were those of the fertile delta. With the exception of a few swampy refuges like northeastern Arkansas's Big Lake area, by the 1920s the Ouachitas and Ozarks contained the state's few truly remote locales, the places so divorced from the fren-zied modernization of twentieth-century America that they were bound to reveal the sought-after "contemporary ancestors" of the day.[3]

But there were larger forces at work—movements emanating far from Arkansas's borders—that defined these contemporary ancestors, found value in their quaint and backward ways, and held them up for apprecia-tion, and often ridicule, from a nervous people. The inhabitants of the Arkansas hills and mountains were belatedly swept into a vortex of Progressive-era nostalgia, xenophobia, racism, and class-consciousness that first focused its fury on Appalachia and that ultimately proved significant to the evolution of the Arkansaw image.

Contemporary Ancestors and Elizabethan Americans

As the Reconstruction era gave way to the Gilded Age, America "discov-ered" the mountaineer. Many northern philanthropists, missionaries, and teachers who had taken it upon themselves to provide education and uplift to the South's freedmen learned of the plight of another southern "ethnic" group through the national press's obsession with backcountry feuds and through the short stories and novels of Charles Egbert Craddock (née Mary

By the middle of the twentieth century the hillbilly and mountaineer had come to dominate the image of Arkansas, as this image illustrates. The genesis for this development, however, lay in the late nineteenth and early twentieth centuries. Automobile decal, c. 1950.

Noailles Murfree) and other local colorists in the final quarter of the nineteenth century. These "mountain whites," as they came to be called, lived in isolation in the coves and hollows of the Appalachians, so isolated, many northerners believed, that visiting their quaint communities and farms was like stepping back in time, like seeing your forebears in the flesh. The archaic ways of these "contemporary ancestors"—their handicrafts, superstitions, outdated agricultural techniques, and British ballads—fascinated middle- and upper-class northerners in much the same way that the lifestyles and beliefs of former slaves had intrigued them in the war era. The mountaineers were an exotic people living in the backyard of the urban Northeast. Their "otherness" struck the chords of romanticism in many northern hearts, prompting young men and, more often, young women from good homes and good families in New York and Boston and Philadelphia to go native in the remote corners of the southern mountains—quite often to save and preserve the mountains and mountaineers from the deleterious effects of industrialization and civilization introduced by other northerners, coal mine and textile mill operators and railroaders.

The otherness of the mountaineer was a special kind of exoticism, however, one that rendered these southerners more provocative and worthy of attention and assistance. "Mountain society differed from black society in only one important respect," writes historian James C. Klotter, "It was white."[4] The mountaineer's whiteness was crucial to northerners' preoccupation with him and to the development of what historian Anthony Harkins has called the "dualistic icon of the hillbilly-mountaineer" at the turn of the twentieth century. The same ambivalent reaction that we have seen in the Arkansaw image awaited the mountaineer. On the one hand, the mountaineer's backwardness and inferiority reinforced the dominant American view that modernization and progress were one in the same and that it was the duty of progressive Americans to modernize the mountaineer. Many northerners were aghast at this land of feuding, moonshining deviants. Ignorance, superstition, and loose sexual mores were thought common among former slaves, but the discovery of such traits in mountain whites seemed to undermine widespread views of racial superiority. On the other, the mountaineer was viewed as the repository of a valuable heritage, the embodiment of a past that northern urbanites and their predecessors had jettisoned over the course of the previous century. And his mountains offered "northern urbanites a welcome sojourn in a mysterious (but ultimately safe) wilderness."[5]

More than that, he was a living symbol of America's Anglo-Saxon, Protestant heritage. The mountaineer's supposed unspoiled Anglo-Saxonism, more than just his whiteness, was the key element. The Northeast's white,

Protestant establishment grew increasingly anxious over the growing numbers of immigrants in the late nineteenth and early twentieth centuries—
especially as higher and higher percentages of them were Roman Catholics
and Jews from southern and eastern Europe. The demographic impact of
such large numbers of newcomers was clear. What wasn't so obvious was
the immigrants' ultimate effect on an American society born of Britain and
Protestant northern Europe. Eugenicists argued that the Anglo-Saxons, however contrived the appellation may have been, were the world's greatest
race. The champions of Anglo-Saxonism—"a kind of patrician nationalism,"
according to historian David E. Whisnant—pointed to the globe-spanning
British empire and to the blossoming United States as proof. But the Anglo-
Saxon race, in the United States at least, was in danger, eyeing with trepidation the hordes storming the gates. For those so anxious, the people of
the southern highlands, while uncultured and wayward, offered the last
best hope.[6]

In the process of studying this "peculiar people," collecting their anti-
quated folkways, attempting to explain their otherness, and holding them
up as a people worth both preserving and civilizing, writers, ministers,
businessmen, and scholars of the late nineteenth and early twentieth centuries introduced the nation to an array of images bookended by the noble
mountaineer and the hillbilly. Arkansas's highland regions played almost
no part in the development and dissemination of the dichotomous moun-
taineer/hillbilly imagery of the late 1800s. The primary reason for this
would appear to be geography. Appalachia is much larger than the Ozarks
and Ouachitas and much closer to the Northeast, whence most of the local
color writers, missionaries, and social workers came.

So, in spite of Arkansas's backwoods reputation in the nineteenth century, it inspired little of the reforming and preserving spirit that exposed
the Appalachian mountaineer to the nation. Only after the turn of the
twentieth century did significant numbers of writers and reporters, as well
as a few missionaries, turn their attentions to Arkansas, and invariably they
found their way to the Ozarks and the Ouachitas, the supposed domains
of Arkansas's pure Anglo-Saxon stock. By the time they arrived, the Appalachian mountaineer/hillbilly model was in place, and all they had to do was
apply it to the Arkansas highlanders. And as our survey thus far has
revealed, it wasn't an uncomfortable fit. The ambivalent Arkansaw image
absorbed the newfangled mountaineer/hillbilly icon and went about its
merry way, thus attaining a geographical narrowness that it had not previously possessed. Arkansaw prepared to burst into the American consciousness once again in the years after World War I. She may not have been a
cast member in the hillbilly pilot, but Arkansaw would quickly make a case
for being star of the show.

✧ CHAPTER THREE ✧

Heyday of the Hillbilly

Fame and adulation are fleeting things. Only a tiny minority of those who achieve celebrity reach a level of transcendence that assures their notoriety among the coming generations. Robin Burn, alas, wasn't among that minority. He was famous all right. Unless you have reached septuagenarian status, you won't have any personal memory of his fame. But there was a time in the not-too-distant past when practically every American could have told you a little something about the "Arkansas Philosopher," the "Sage of the Ozarks," the windy "Arkansas Traveler" whose colorful kin back home never failed to provide enough comic fodder for a weekly feeding, the fellow who sounded like he belonged on any old country store porch and who played a homemade instrument whose moniker is now remembered for the army weapon named after it.

America knew Robin Burn as Bob Burns. Americans knew as well that he was from Arkansas. To many, Bob Burns *was* Arkansas. In the quarter century following World War I, Arkansas produced a number of celebrities, a surprisingly large number that was all out of proportion to the state's population and reputation for backwardness. In the 1930s and 1940s, none was more widely known or more closely associated with the Wonder State than the favorite son of Van Buren, Arkansas. A strapping, drawling man who had spent most of his adult life touring as a musician, a blackface minstrel, and as a vaudevillian rube, Bob Burns made his way to Hollywood near the end of the Roaring Twenties. There he found insignificant roles in a couple of movies before breaking into the radio entertainment business in the early 1930s. He was knocking on the door of middle age by the time he got his big break in 1935, a guest appearance as a Will Rogers–type country philosopher on a New York–based radio show that translated in short order into a regular spot as a hillbilly comedian on the popular *Rudy Vallee Show*, a gig that made him, according to a poll of radio editors, the "most outstanding new radio star" of 1935.[1]

The following January Burns took his backwoods shtick back to the West Coast for a role on the program *The Kraft Music Hall*, starring crooner

Bing Crosby. His affiliation with Crosby led to his big movie break in the 1936 film *Rhythm on the Range* (starring Crosby and Frances Farmer), the first of a dozen pictures Burns would make at Paramount over a five-year stretch during which he continued to appear regularly on Crosby's popular radio show. The end of his film career coincided with the beginning of his own radio program, *The Arkansas Traveler*, which aired on CBS, and later NBC, from 1941 to 1947. The hillbilly comedian proved to be a savvy

Bob Burns and his bazooka, an instrument he first created as a teenager in Van Buren, Arkansas. Courtesy of The Museum / Cabot High School, Cabot, Arkansas.

businessman. Having made a fortune off of real estate investments, Burns retired to his two-hundred-acre ranch northwest of Beverly Hills and was rarely heard from again until his death in 1956.[2]

Posterity and the obscurity caused by the passage of time have led us to believe that Burns's was a one-note comedy career. Though that may not be far from the truth, he nevertheless embodied the dual nature of the Arkansaw image, the divide between the dim-witted hillbilly and the noble hillman. Like a hillbilly Rohrschach test, Bob Burns elicited different reactions from different audiences. Rural listeners and viewers around the country recognized him as one of their own—or at least the nearest facsimile Hollywood could manufacture. His leisurely, folksy stories about Grandpa Snazzy, Uncle Fud, and Aunt Doody were benign enough to inspire knowing snickers from country folk, yet ridiculous enough to satisfy the stereotypes of the sophisticated and urbane. Back in his home state, Burns's countrified comedy was harmless enough to breed unwavering devotion among real Arkansawyers but insidious enough to convince self-conscious Arkansans to criticize his characters' negative impact on an already soiled state image. In the end, true to the subversive tradition of the rural rube, Burns's movie characters almost always prevailed, even in the face of seemingly superior adversaries. His Pete-Whetstone-meets-Jed-Clampett persona satisfied the dispossessed as well as their champions, and the era was full of the better sort of people lining up to fight for the downtrodden or fantasizing about their willingness to do so.

Throughout his dozen years in the limelight, Bob Burns's slow-talking, tall-tale-telling characters played into an Arkansaw image that had been under construction for more than a century. Radio audiences and moviegoers were well acquainted with it. Burns's bazooka may have been a strange new replacement for the fiddle, but his career was littered with conscious connections to the Arkansaw image—from the 1938 movie *The Arkansas Traveler* to his later radio show of the same name. The American pop-cultural landscape suffered no shortage of Arkansaw images, either. At no other time in history has the Arkansaw image—and the hillbilly in general—been such a ubiquitous part of the American cultural dialogue. Indeed, historian Anthony Harkins refers to the Depression era as the "hillbilly's cultural epicenter."[3] Americans partook of a heaping helping of Arkansaw in the years between Versailles and VJ-Day. As always, just who the Arkansawyer was and what he stood for was open to interpretation.

An Ode to Arkansas: Mencken's Minions

One person who suffered no pangs of ambivalence when it came to the Wonder State, or any other topic, was Henry Louis Mencken. A Baltimore-based writer and magazine editor, Mencken became the voice of a new mentality of modernist cynicism in postwar America. His denunciations of Arkansas—scarce as they were—are by now the stuff of legend within the state. They were also indicative of a new wave of critical, nonfiction treatments emanating from the nation's magazines and newspapers in the age of Fitzgerald and Hemingway. Young intellectuals, self-appointed spokespersons for a now-urban nation, lashed out at the narrow-minded Babbitts of rural and small-town America—the people Mencken referred to as the Booboisie, those who, in the words of Arkansas-based writer and publisher Charles J. Finger, "dare not be other than they are."[4] It was in this atmosphere that Mencken—by no means the only representative of his ilk but certainly the guru—turned on his favorite whipping boy, the South, and in the process elevated perpetuation of the negative Arkansaw image to poetic new heights.

We can rest assured that the state of Arkansas infrequently burdened the mind of H. L. Mencken, and then only in reference to its hallowed rank among the benighted states with which he so loved to joust. The old Bear State received nary a mention in "The Sahara of the Bozart," one of Mencken's earliest and best-known denunciations of Dixie. By 1921, however, the caustic scribe had worked his way across the Mississippi, finding space for a couple of anti-Arkansas remarks in "The South Begins to Mutter," an intentionally combative and provocative essay in the New York magazine of smarm and sarcasm called *The Smart Set*. Mencken pondered the existence of "trackless, unexplored" Arkansas, "a state almost fabulous. (Who, indeed, has ever been in it? I know New Yorkers who have been in Cochin China, Kafristan, Paraguay, Somaliland and West Virginia, but not one who has ever penetrated the miasmatic jungles of Arkansas.)" In all the state Mencken could find only one thing worthy of praise, Charles J. Finger's *All's Well*, a Fayetteville-based literary magazine. This publication, Mencken groaned, "must cause a great deal of lifting of eyebrows among the Arkansans, if any of them ever see it. It constantly praises authors whose books would set fire to the Carnegie libraries down there." Finished with his rapid skewering of Arkansas, Mencken moved on, flinging arrows of insult at unsuspecting targets across the South. The instant and angry reactions from the front line of Arkansas's defense, to be chronicled in the interlude following this chapter, made a mountain out of Mencken's mole hill, a not unpleasant result for the Baltimore writer.[5]

Almost a decade later he came back for a more thorough dismantling of the Wonder State. Spurred by Governor Harvey Parnell's defensiveness in the face of national reports of hunger and privation in Arkansas in the winter of 1931, Mencken unleashed his calculated vitriol on "perhaps the most shiftless and backward State in the whole galaxy. Only Mississippi offers it serious rivalry for last place in all American tables of statistics."

Taking off the gloves, Mencken decried the state's oppressive plantation system, its antievolutionist proclivities, and the "gangs of grafters" who prey upon "benighted and miserable" Arkansawyers. "Naturally enough, every youngster of any human value who grows up in such a wallow clears out as soon as possible." Of a trip through western Arkansas and eastern Oklahoma, Mencken felt "like a man emerging from a region devastated by war. Such shabby and flea-bitten villages I had never seen before, or such dreadful people." Mencken claimed to have seen "women by the road-side with their children between their knees, picking lice like mother monkeys in the zoo."[6]

Responding to impassioned replies by former governor Charles H. Brough, Mencken penned two additional Baltimore *Evening Sun* diatribes on his new favorite target. Turning to statistics, a favorite tool of Brough, Mencken illustrated Arkansas's lowly rank in just about every category other than prohibitionists, "lynchings and open-air baptisms," and he scoffed at Brough's list of Arkansas's best and brightest, calling it "too dreadful to be treated seriously." Criticizing the state's debt problems and its inability to feed and care for its "miserable, exploited, chronically half-starved share-croppers," Mencken challenged the ex-governor to "give over his vain talk of Masonic poet laureates, high-salaried auditors and other such wonders of the Arkansas sideshow and apply his great learning to the relief of his suffering State."[7]

If Mencken inflicted only a couple of glancing blows to the midsection of Arkansas in his free-for-all with Dixie, there were others who unleashed haymakers aimed right at the jaw of Arkansaw. In a 1933 *Vanity Fair* piece devoted to the "stooge of forty-seven states," Travis Y. Oliver argued that "when the tide of civilization swept westward it detoured Arkansas." In fact, mere "mention of the name Arkansas among persons from more effete regions always provokes laughter much as the risibilities of a Manhattan vaudeville audience are roused by a wise crack about Brooklyn." Condemning the state's fundamentalist religion and resistance to new ideas, Oliver waxed Menckenian in regards to the cultural barrenness of Arkansas. "Not a single artist of note ever emerged from the state," he wrote. "Pitifully few writers of first rate ability claim Arkansas as home. Search as one will, there can be found no great teacher, preacher, jurist, or scientist whose childhood was molded by an Arkansas environment."[8]

Elmer J. Bouher, a Presbyterian missionary bent on dragging the sometimes-reluctant residents of rural Madison County into the modern world, found life in the Ozarks "limited—cruelly, pitifully limited; limited by isolation, by ignorance, by paltry tasks, by uninspired toil, by barebone poverty, by the absence of beauty and joy, all passed on from father to son, from mother to daughter, generation after generation, a blasted, mildewed heritage." Another newcomer to northwestern Arkansas penned his reflections on a journey into the backcountry a year later. In a 1923 *Century* magazine feature, Charles J. Finger wrote ironically of a "Utopia in Arkansas," a place filled with unsavory backwoods characters and at least one filthy little hole-in-the-wall store. Sounding Bouher's theme, he lamented "blighted men and women who seemed never to have known youth, but only toil; people lost in solitary wilderness like the lonely ones of Chaucer."[9]

Just one month before the publication of Finger's essay, the *Nation* carried an article whose debt to Mencken was obvious. In "Arkansas: A Native Proletariat," C. L. Edson, a midwesterner who had lived for a time in the Ozarks, unleashed page after page of invective on the "morons' paradise." "A people who were willing to foot it a hundred miles through the muck to get nowhere founded Arkansas and achieved their aim," spat Edson. "Arkansas has its own popular motto and it is this: 'I've never seen nothin', I don't know nothin', I ain't got nothin', and I don't want nothin'.' These fundamental aims the people of Arkansas have achieved in every particular." Edson differentiated among three distinct types of Arkansawyers— Crackers, Pikers, and Big Smoky mountaineers—who in sum "make the Arkansas nation . . . as distinct from the other peoples in America as is a Swede from a Dane." The writer found the learned in short supply. "Few can read in Arkansas, and those who can do not. . . . Every old Southern State has produced scholars, except Arkansas, according to Mencken's dictum, and no man of first-class intellect was born in Arkansas, lived there, or even passed through the State." Little wonder then that, according to Edson, "whenever Arkansawyers appear in Kansas, California, South Carolina, or Texas the natives hold up their hands in horror, fearing that their Spartan State will be erased by the obliterating helot swarm."[10]

Three years later the *American Mercury,* edited by Mencken himself, carried an essay even more venomous than Edson's. This time the piece came from a native still living in the state he found so dissatisfying and limiting. An Ozarker by birth, former Socialist candidate for governor, and faculty member at Mena's Commonwealth College, Clay Fulks found his Ouachita Mountain neighbors every bit as unreceptive to modern science and susceptible to demagoguery as were the East Tennesseans Mencken had chronicled a year earlier during the Scopes Trial. "Arkansas has a few Jukeses, many Kallikaks, and melancholy expanses of dull mediocrity relieved here and there by strange individuals who sometimes give great offense to the general by thinking for themselves."[11] Those who possessed the capacity to think for themselves rarely did. "The State's public and professional men . . . try with amazing success to keep themselves on the intellectual level of the peasantry." The result of this atmosphere of anti-intellectualism was a land in which "the hairs on the heads of heretics are numbered, and the intelligent minority has no rights which the majority is bound to respect." In conclusion, Fulks despaired that "no man with anything worthwhile to say ever comes among us. We have to listen to scheming politicians and pulpit morons or stay at home."[12]

Though, like Mencken, Edson and Fulks made no attempt to present balanced views of Arkansas, their essays, unlike Mencken's, belie something akin to an underlying subtext of romanticism. Even amid a population of "scheming politicians and pulpit morons," Fulks argued that, in spite of their dependence on fundamentalism and tendency toward "the herd instinct," Arkansawyers were "humorous, sympathetic, honest, generous, and patient, and their hands are quick to relieve distress. They are shrewd and industrious, and have the native capacity for far more learning than they have aspired to."[13]

It would be foolish to argue that a couple of backhanded compliments suddenly render Fulks's essay a study in angst-ridden ambivalence. Edson's portrait of Arkansas, however, definitely reflects the romantic's dilemma. Behind his apparent disdain for Arkansas and the numskulls and morons who lived there lurked an envy of and appreciation for the Arkansawyers' simple and unfettered existence. "But they desire little. No ambition consumes them. . . . In the great war of man against nature, science against ignorance, Arkansas has remained a neutral." Like many a left-wing intellectual, Edson mistook his former neighbors for a premodern and unacquisitive tribe. "Here is the dictatorship of the proletariat in America. These scrub-stock people have been free to work out their own destiny under ideal conditions. . . . Capitalism has not laid a heavy hand on them." Edson also detected method in Arkansaw's madness, a winking complicity behind the yokel façade. "The trick of the Arkansawyer is to capitalize his boorishness. . . . The Arkansawyer says: 'Look, I am a buffoon. With one hand I drive my mule, with the other I toss off epigrams.' He therefore has no desire to ape gentility; he knows he is as good as anyone." In the end, Edson thought he had discovered in the Arkansawyers a people unburdened by Protestant shame and Victorian angst, an exotic tribe where none should exist. "There is no Freudian grouch in the soul of Arkansas . . . They have not in all their philosophy any complaint against anything. They are the only white tribe among us that habitually fiddles and sings."[14]

The reference to "white tribe" is a crucial element of the romantic fascination with Arkansaw and the Ozarks in the years after World War I. For Edson the inherent danger of exoticism was tempered by the color of the Arkansawyer's skin. Like the majority of whites of the era, both Edson and Fulks ignored the state's African American population in the process of contributing to the century-old Arkansaw image. One might argue that the two were simply writing about the people they knew from their experiences in the overwhelmingly white portions of the state—Edson in the Ozarks, Fulks in the Ouachitas and Ozarks—but it was not as simple as that. As we have seen, the Arkansaw image was, almost without exception, tethered to the lower orders of white society. There had not always been something romantic about this whiteness. But by the 1920s there was a conscious preoccupation not only with the color of the Arkansawyer but with his presumed ethnicity as well. It was the great age of Anglo-Saxonism, that orgy of blueblood racism.

C. L. Edson found irony in the tepid response of Nebraskan "Swedes and Teutons" toward migrant laborers from Arkansas. The "sturdy Nebraskans (from North Europe) were shocked by the general worthlessness of the Arkansawyers and were heard to declare: 'If they keep on letting that kind of people into this country, America has gone to hell.'" Anglo-Saxonism carried this burden; impoverished Arkansawyers might be the last seedbed of pure Anglo-Saxon stock, but to many they were an embarrassment to the race and a threat to the assumption of Anglo-Saxon/Teutonic superiority.[15]

Most observers, though, eschewed Edson's Anglo-Saxon ambivalence in favor of an unapologetic and only thinly veiled racist celebration of America's great white hope. The Reverend Warren Wilson, a noted Presbyterian minister and member of his denomination's Board of Home Missions, observed that, despite their "pioneer habits of gun-toting and whisky stilling," the "pure white American stock" of Kingston, Arkansas, were "intelligent and progressive . . . in high degree." Writing in *Outlook*, Lawrence F. Abbott gushed a stream of eugenics-laced praise for the "pure Anglo-Saxon strain" of the students at Clarksville's College of the Ozarks. The surrounding region, he claimed, "produces representatives of fine old American stock whose physique, crania, and profiles would not have been out of place among the Greek athletes in the stadium at Athens." Photojournalist Charles Phelps Cushing found in the Ozarks "a sturdy strong race of men —not merely 100% American but 1,000% American." "If ever you *have* thought of yourself as a genuine 'one hundred' per center," Cushing cautioned his largely northern readership, "the mountaineers, with excellent justification, regard you as a 'foreigner' in *their* United States."[16]

There was no shortage of writers, journalists, and scholars trumpeting a mixture of contemporary ancestors homage, One-hundred Percent Americanism, and Anglo-Saxonism in the Depression decade. *New York Times* book critic Edward Larocque Tinker absorbed enough of this rhetoric from the era's speight of Ozark books to proclaim that "the Ozark Mountains . . . are peopled by a thoroughly Anglo-Saxon race that jealously retains its old ways of talk, thought and life." A reporter for the *New York Times* intoned, "The Ozarker is living in the eighteenth century or earlier," while yet another book reviewer found that "the mountaineers present a faithful picture of society 300 years ago." In the Arkansas Ozarks acclaimed artist Thomas Hart Benton discovered that "a belated frontierism persists to this day and people are found whose manners and psychologies antedate those of Andrew Jackson's time." Even former Arkansas governor Charles H. Brough got in on the action, declaring in a 1932 speech in Memphis that his state could "boast of the finest strain of Anglo-Saxon blood on the North American continent." Arkansas native and ubiquitous chronicler of Depression-era Ozark life Charles Morrow Wilson found in the Ozarks "a country of Spenserian speech, Shakespearean people, and of cavaliers and curtsies. . . . Husbandmen and ploughmen of Shakespeare's England and present-day upland farmers could very likely have rubbed shoulders and swapped yarns with few misunderstandings." Magazine publisher and Ozark chronicler Otto Ernest Rayburn was so enamored with the assumed ethnic purity of the region that he devoted an entire chapter of his 1941 book, *Ozark Country*, to a discussion of the "Anglo-Saxon Seed Bed."[17]

The Ozarks Watchers

The Anglo-Saxon label was most often applied to highland southerners in the Ozarks and Appalachia. For all practical purposes in the era covered by this chapter the Arkansaw image became synonymous with a blossoming Ozark image. From the late 1920s through the World War II era, Ozarkers were about as newsworthy as a regional folk could be. As one *New York Times* writer put it in 1934: "For all his houn' dawgs, fiddle scrapin', and 'kiver' making, the Ozarkian is one of the most sought after and studied individuals in Middle America."[18] Rare was the year that didn't see at least one nonfiction Ozark book hit the shelves, and the Ozark life feature story became a staple of magazines and major newspapers around the nation. These written accounts bore a resemblance to the travel accounts of a century earlier, as an educated, urbane cadre of writers tried to encapsulate a curious and time-forgotten people for a nation of readers with an appetite for the exotic. The dual nature of the Arkansaw image spawned in part by the nineteenth-century travelers' observations shone through in the Depression-era imagery, now largely subsumed beneath the Ozark image. Some observers marveled at the Ozarker's backwardness and found in his shortcomings validation of the progressive spirit that had rendered the Ozark region a modern anachronism. Increasingly, though, Depression-era journalists and writers—like Gerstäcker in the wilds of Arkansas one hundred years before—found reasons to celebrate the region and its inhabitants. Left-leaning writers, disenchanted with a capitalistic society that seemed bent on devouring itself, found in these contemporary ancestors a premodern people on American soil, an antidote to the short-sighted materialism and greed of America. The Ozarkers' supposed resource-fulness and independence earned accolades from a variety of political persuasions. Here indeed was a people from whom other Americans could learn a great deal.

Not everything Ozarkers had to teach was suitable for polite society, however. The hillbilly remained an ever-present feature of Ozark sketches. Louis La Coss, a St. Louis journalist who chronicled the slow but steady transformation of the region in the 1920s and 1930s, expressed America's collective knowledge of Ozark people:

> The typical Ozarkian was a man who went barefoot the year-around, supported his homespun garments with a single gallus, subsisted on corn pone and fat bacon and spent his days shooting squirrels and his nights chasing coons with a houn' dog. The typical Ozarkian chewed tobacco, smoked a corncob pipe, engaged in moonshining even before there was such a thing as prohibition and had never profaned his vision with the sight of a locomotive, much less an automobile.[19]

While not a comprehensive list, La Coss's observation identified several Ozark vices that had long been associated with the Arkansaw image. A short list of these hillbilly characteristics would include a tendency toward violence, a fondness for moonshine and shining, a weakness for supersti-tion, a conscious and cussed rejection of "progress," and a general back-wardness that might foster anything from illiteracy to sexual deviancy.

Violence and clannishness held a prized position in the hall of Arkansaw and hillbilly stereotypes. The late nineteenth-century feuds in West Virginia, Kentucky, and other Appalachian states, reported widely and salaciously by a yellowing press, had long since burned themselves into the national consciousness. And if the Ozarks watchers were correct, the violence that had been part and parcel of pioneer Arkansas life still bubbled near the surface in the hills. Writing in *Outlook*, William R. Draper assured his readers that in the Ozarks "feuds of love and passion have flared and died, moonshine has been made and bartered, tie timber has been stolen, some murders have been unnecessary." "Not so long ago," one *New York Times* reporter noted, "the [Ozarks] was known for the primi-tiveness of its people and the lawlessness of its gangs." Another reported that "feuds raged for generations in the log-cabin settlements along the winding trails." According to others of the Depression-era, little had changed. "Mountain jealousy is highly inflammable and can easily lead to murder." Laura Knickerbocker of the *New York Times* found in the Missouri

Ozarks "men who shoot to kill over trifles."[20] Charles Morrow Wilson, the most prolific of all Ozark watchers of the era, discovered that "backwoods morality places a low valuation on human life . . . Homicides happen with astonishing frequency." In Wilson's hill country, even the best citizens were not immune to hot-blooded reprisals.

> The run of mankillers or feudists are neither degenerates nor mono-maniacs, but good level-headed commoners, ordinarily temperate, honest and reasonably abstemious. . . . In the main these back-country killings are wholesome, respectable affairs committed by and upon wholesome and respectable citizens . . . Land, crops, ten-ant tolls, horseshoe tournaments, pie suppers, courtroom testi-mony, horse traders, unfortunate connotations and clean corn liquor serve generally as motivation.[21]

Some may quarrel with Wilson's choice of language, and I, for one, have a newfound respect for my ancestors' ability to emerge unscathed from pie suppers and horseshoe pitchings, but it's the sentiment—or in this case, sentimentality—that counts. Wilson, like his contemporary Vance Randolph, had a way of making mud pies out of manure. Only twenty-three years old when he penned this essay for a national magazine, Wilson was about the same age that Friedrich Gerstäcker had been when he fell in love with the Arkansas backcountry. Unlike his nineteenth-century German forerunner, Wilson was a native of the region, having been born and raised in Fayetteville, but, like Gerstäcker, he was the product of a middle-class upbringing and discovered in the hills of Arkansas a people whose unfa-miliarity—whose "otherness"—exhilarated him to the bone. For Wilson, the Ozarkers were authentic people whose foibles endeared them just as much as did their Anglo-Saxonism and rusticity.[22]

The radical in Wilson appreciated the Ozarker's wide streak of individu-alism and independence, just as the southwestern humorists had reveled in the nonconformity of their Arkansaw forebears. Nowhere was this dis-cordant nature more evident than in the hillman's penchant for defying Alexander Hamilton and the oppressors of free spirits. After all, nothing says hillbilly quite like mash and a copper worm. A 1930 article in the *New York Times* informed readers that in the Ozarks "farmers spent most of their time converting their corn crops into liquid form." Four years later a writer in the same publication remarked that "canny Ozarkians have discovered the attraction of mountainside refreshment stations where mountain dew may be had without bribery."[23]

While Progressive-era Americans had demonized the distillers of illicit intoxicants, Charles Morrow Wilson's revisionist interpretation reinforced the romanticism of an "art of the hills." "Down in the hill country, a good

Charles Morrow Wilson, c. 1950. Picture Collection, number 912. Special Collections, University of Arkansas Libraries, Fayetteville.

crop of corn means just one thing—moonshine." Wilson tracked down one Ozark moonshiner, recently released from prison, whose clean-shaven mug and "conversation . . . nothing short of brilliant" seemed to defy the stereotypes affiliated with his kind, in spite of his dirt-floor log cabin. Wilson's moonshiners sported Dickensian names like Sody Bullteeter and produced "bright-eyed and well-bodied and grinning" offspring. Wilson described the son of moonshiner Alfred Saulee: "Mountain sunlight fell upon him caressingly, and he stood with the nonchalant gracefulness of an olden god." He was fortunate that young Saulee was a nonreader, lest Wilson could have added "fancy stories about supple young moonshiners" to the list of motivations for mountaineer violence. Even Ozark livestock possessed an affinity for good shine, Wilson found. "Hogs are passionately fond of the still slops and beers . . . They can trail down a still for half a dozen cross-country miles."[24]

Moonshining remained an integral element of the Ozark/Arkansaw image, though the region—nor the highland South in general, for that matter—laid no claim to exclusivity in this popular rural practice. As historian Ben F. Johnson III has shown, "other sections of the state were as remote as the northern hills and as promising for distillers." In fact, Johnson argues, "Arkansas during the moonshine era could lay claim to far fewer wildcat whiskey operations than the Appalachian regions." Whether that was indeed the case or Arkansas moonshiners were just more adept at eluding revenuers, it seems certain that moonshining in the Ozarks attracted more attention than it deserved. One chronicler of Ozark society who thought so was Vance Randolph. No stranger to exaggerating cultural peculiarities, Randolph nonetheless downplayed moonshining and bootlegging in the region. "It is a subject that does not interest me particularly," he wrote in his 1931 book, *The Ozarks: An American Survival of Primitive Society*, "since liquor seems to be made and sold everywhere nowadays, and the Ozark methods of production and distribution probably do not differ greatly from those practiced in other sparsely settled parts of the United States." Ever responsive to public demand, Randolph included a chapter on moonshining anyhow, lamenting "that almost every 'furriner' who visits us of late displays an almost morbid curiosity about this matter, and it would never do to write a book about the Ozark country without some mention of moonshine and moonshiners."[25]

Vance Randolph on one of his many folklore and folk music recording outings for the Library of Congress. Courtesy of Townsend Godsey Foundation. Photo from Lyons Memorial Library, College of the Ozarks, Point Lookout, Missouri.

Though not as inclined as Wilson to worship the rustic dwellers of the hills, Randolph was convinced that Ozark backwardness was a matter of choice. Like so many swept up in the romantic spirit, Randolph hailed from a conservative, middle-class background and early on found himself drawn to people on society's margins, people unlike anything he had known, whether they be the miners of his small Kansas hometown or the simple hill folks of the Ozarks, to which he moved in 1919. Driven by populistic political views and a contrarian nature, Randolph found in his Ozark neighbors the antithesis of the Chamber of Commerce–Rotarian Babbittry that he came to despise, and in so doing projected onto them his own conscious rejection of mainstream "progress." His characterization of the Ozarks as "the most backward and deliberately unprogressive region in the United States" was compliment, not condemnation.[26]

More than a few Ozark watchers of the 1920s and 1930s agreed with Randolph's assessment. Photojournalist Charles Phelps Cushing saw in the Ozarks a "last stand" against the encroaching world. According to Louis La Coss, "factories mean nothing" to "true Ozarkians. . . . Electricity is a thing for city folk." A *New York Times* reporter detected "the resistance of the hills to penetration by the outside world." Another reasoned that "dyed-in-the-wool Ozarkers are proudly primitive. Their isolation is a religion and their clannishness a virtue." Laura Knickerbocker found that hill people had "held to their poverty-stricken farms while the rest of the country sped toward a high-powered industrialization." Contemporary though these living ancestors might be, "they jealously retain[ed] . . . old ways of talk, thought and life."[27]

Whether it was motivated by conscious rejection of modernity or by ignorance and isolation, the region's backwardness, at least by the standards of the age, was something on which almost all Ozarks watchers could agree. Charles Phelps Cushing felt that "the very word 'Ozarks' itself has a romantic sound, implying remoteness, wild and rugged scenery, and to some extent . . . truly primitive conditions of living." Louis La Coss reiterated that idea: "For years the name of Ozarks has been synonymous with backwardness both in education of the inhabitants and in commercial and industrial development." Years of isolation and poverty had produced a land of "razor-back hogs, flea-bitten dogs, moonshiners who are deadly foes of 'revenuers' and a moronic citizenry whose progress up the social scale has been so negligible that corn pone is both staple and delicacy and shoes are something that only city dudes wear." Young Charles Morrow Wilson must have been delighted if he really "talked with hill people who never heard of the World War" more than a decade after the armistice. One *New York Times* reporter claimed that "in the deeper recesses of the mountains hill people may be found who know neither radio nor newspaper."

Laura Knickerbocker discovered that "far back in the cedar brakes unbelievable hygienic standards prevail. Bathtubs are unknown, few cabins have outhouses."[28]

Poor grooming was among the least unpleasant symptoms of Ozark backwardness, according to a few Ozarks watchers who commented on the hillman's liberal views on sex and supposed penchant for sexual deviancy. Wilson connected Ozarkers' relative lack of religious fervor with the freedom with which they struck up physical relationships. Finding at summer brush arbor revivals "more reversions to Bachus than fearful prostrations before stern-featured Jehovah," Wilson suggested that such community functions accounted for "more souls made than saved." W. R. Draper also combined religion and sex when alluding to the hillbilly stereotype of incest: "The Ozarkians . . . have lived lazy, kin marrying, morally clean, but none too God-loving lives." Folklorist Vance Randolph, whose later collections of ribald stories underscored his fascination with the obscene, suggested that inbreeding was but part of a broader culture of sexual deviancy in the hills. "Incestuous relations are common enough, and seem to arouse very little moral indignation." Jumping from the salacious to the outrageous, Randolph claimed that "sexual acts between human beings and domestic animals are rather common in the Ozarks, and nearly every native believes that these unions are sometimes fruitful."[29]

In general, though, the region's isolation and perceived uniqueness inspired a fittingly broad assessment of backwardness. In her 1941 book *Yesterday Today: Life in the Ozarks,* Catherine S. Barker gave readers a peek into "the Arkansas where the people live as your pioneering great- or great-great-grandparents lived." Barker's Ozarker was an ideal research subject:

> He offers a wonderful laboratory demonstration for students of early American history—living life today as it was lived in yesteryears. He offers an example, for the student of sociology, of the effect of almost complete isolation, with intermarriage, and with his standards and mores ingrown. For the economist he has a modified barter system and outmoded methods of production. To those interested in the moral and spiritual development of a retarded people he presents an urgent problem.[30]

In spite of the frequently negative portraits of life in the Ozarks, romanticism was never far away. After all, as Thomas Hart Benton reminded us, "it is a country lending itself readily to romantic interpretation."[31] The duality of the Arkansaw image survived, even flourished, in the years between the world wars. In fact, in the Depression-era zenith of Ozarks watching the Ozarker was more likely to be held up for praise and emulation than for derision. For some, the twentieth-century descendants of the Arkansaw squatter and the brawling frontiersman inspired ambivalent reactions ranging from disgust to celebration. For a few, there was no two ways about it—the rustic, romantic Ozarkers were just what the Depression ordered.

No writer of the era was more unapologetically romantic when it came to the Ozarks than Otto Ernest Rayburn. An Iowan by birth and Kansan by raising, young Rayburn was so moved by Harold Bell Wright's *The Shepherd of the Hills* that he moved to the southwestern Missouri backcountry in 1917. Service in World War I and a budding teaching career carried him away from the Ozarks, but he returned in 1923 and spent the next decade teaching, writing, and editing two magazines—*Ozark Life* and *Arcadian*—in northern Arkansas and southern Missouri. The necessities of making a living took him to the Ouachitas of southwestern Arkansas and eventually out of the state for most of the Depression and World War II years, but he maintained a devotion to his adopted hills and finally found his way back to Eureka Springs, where he lived out his life as a magazine publisher, bookstore owner, real estate peddler, and incessant promoter of the bucolic, arcadian Ozarks.[32]

Although his busy pen churned out hundreds of magazine and newspaper articles on Ozark life during three and a half decades of writing, Rayburn's one book-length description of the region, *Ozark Country* (1941), packaged and summarized his romantic impressions of "a modern Arcadia where one may enjoy simple happiness, innocent pleasures, and untroubled quiet." Rayburn criticized the recent flurry of books, articles, radio shows, movies, and plays that "ridiculed the native of the hills almost beyond redemption," and argued that "unbiased interpreters are needed to tell the romantic story of Ozarkland." Of course, Rayburn was just as biased in his own respectful way as were the ridiculers. *Ozark Country* presented an Ozarks of stunning natural beauty filled with contemporary ancestors, a place where one could while away the drowsy hours of summer on a store porch and spend a cold winter's night wrapped in hand-made quilts, buried in a cozy feather bed. "It is still possible in some sections of this romantic land," stressed Rayburn, "to turn back the clock and listen to the hum of the spinning wheel, the creak of the loom, the groan of the waterwheel at the mill, the rhythmic poetry of the cradle in its golden sea of grain, and to enjoy the generosity that springs from every true hillman's heart." Rayburn was smitten with every last trapping of life in the hills—from log cabins to mountain ballads and from bee hunters to folk remedies—and, like many a romantic, feared that the Ozarker's uniqueness would wilt beneath the onslaught of modernization.[33]

Rayburn's was but one in a chorus of romantic voices in the Depression era. A reporter for *National Republic* captured the nostalgic appreciation for

Otto Ernest Rayburn. Picture Collection, number 3426. Special Collections, University of Arkansas Libraries, Fayetteville.

this land of anachronism: "Yet one may still hear a pack of hounds open-up on the hot end of a fox trail and at daybreak listen to the hunter sounding his horn. Old-time fiddlers saw out 'Sally Goodin' and 'Cotton Eye Joe' at square dances in log cabins on the hillsides. Women beside their spinning wheels still walk back and forth drawing out the thread." Having read Vance Randolph's *An Ozark Anthology*, *New York Times* book critic Edward Larocque Tinker was moved to marvel at "men in those mountains who sleep on cord beds and hunt with muzzle-loading rifles; women who use spinning wheels and hand-made looms; minstrels who sing old English ballads brought over by seventeenth-century British colonists." Charles Morrow Wilson, never one to overlook the romantic charm of his hinterlanders, found the Ozarks "still a land of barter, where a bucketful of eggs may go in trade for a bottle of pink pills, three yards of calico and a new lamp chimney; or six red hens for a month's supply of sugar and coffee." Venturing into Wilson's Ozarks transported one to "another world. You can tramp for a week along woodland paths or half-forgotten roads without sighting an automobile; you find century-old villages in counties untouched by railroads and but lightly touched by wagon roads."[34]

Writers also found positive character traits among the Ozark people, such as honesty, generosity, and even native intelligence. "The backhills have their intellectual life," reminded Charles Morrow Wilson. "They hold sensitive spirits and brilliant and appreciative minds." Ozarkers also found practical outlets for this intelligence. "To say that backwoodsmen are generally ignorant of law would be far from accurate," argued Wilson. "The run of them are surprisingly well informed on legal procedures and craftiness." According to Wilson, the Ozarker's simple and unhurried lifestyle encouraged neighborly conversation. "The rural Ozarkadian has time to ponder and observe and to build friendships. He can ponder at easy random on kings, cabbages, and hog killing; on hay curing, government, and chinch bugs, on war and God and birth." Wilson also combated the perception of the Ozarks as a region of slovenliness. "Backhills homes are usually clean and tidy and possessed of dignity." Their inhabitants were likewise "painstakingly honest" folks who "wouldn't take a pin from your dresser or a hickory nut from your woodlot." Wilson commented on the Ozarkers' "unpresuming dignity" and "quiet courtliness," while another writer found them "generous and hospitable." Thomas Hart Benton found in the Ozarker a reflection of a personality that defied boundaries of space and time: "The plain people of the hills, like all plain people in lonely places, are hospitable and friendly."[35]

Perhaps most appealing during the Depression era was the Ozarker's supposed independence, a trait noted in abundance in early accounts of Arkansawyers. In a nation that had managed to trade a heritage of pioneer survivalism for modern dependency, the resourcefulness of the Ozarker seemed both anachronistic and crucial to the American psyche. A *New York Times* reporter wrote of "the free and exceedingly independent citizens of the region." Sometimes this independent spirit reflected a leathery, perhaps even sinister, individualism. Laura Knickerbocker observed that the Ozarker "looks with distrust at a cooperative community life." "Politically speaking," stressed Charles Morrow Wilson, "the run of backhillsmen are individualists. To them law and government and constitution and professional politics are vague as river mists in autumn." But community life remained strong in the region, and true independence had always depended on helpful neighbors. "I know a land of true self-sufficiency," Wilson marveled of one particularly studied Arkansas community, "a land where subsistence homesteads have flourished for a century or more, without the aid of government bureaus, administrations, or newspaper headlines."[36]

Pop-Culture Podunk

It is difficult to say just how many Americans encountered the portraits of Arkansaw and the Ozarks offered by the "nonfiction" books and articles of the Depression era. The fact that most of the period's popular national magazines featured at least one story on the Ozark region and that the country's largest newspaper, the *New York Times,* frequently printed feature stories and book reviews that focused on Ozarkers suggests that America's reading public gained a familiarity with the hill people of Arkansas and Missouri. Even more powerful in the perpetuating and shaping of an Arkansaw/Ozark image during the Depression and World War II years were the common images conveyed to the masses by radio, comic strips, sports figures, songs, and film, and to a lesser extent by the stage and novel. The popular cultural landscape of the 1930s and 1940s featured a greater number of Arkansaw/Ozark—and hillbilly, for that matter—characters and references than any other era in American history. True to the tradition of the Arkansaw image, these characters presented mixed signals to a variety of audiences spread across the continent. As usual, the response of the listeners, viewers, and readers was generally conditioned by perspective, so that the interpretations ranged from the hopelessly backward and degraded to the heroically anachronistic.

Ol' Diz and the Ballplaying Bumpkins

In the Depression years no national pastime held the public's attention quite like *the* national pastime. Baseball was big business, a valuable diversion in an often-dreary landscape. And the sport was influenced by the same romantic fascination with rural characters that gripped magazine writers and movie producers. Professional baseball had been an urban sport until the post–World War I era, played largely by immigrants and the sons of immigrants. This most pastoral of games had come late to the countryside, especially the southern countryside. But when it arrived, it produced a stable of rural players with monikers like Rube and Country or nicknamed after Podunk hometowns like Pea Ridge or Vinegar Bend. These farm boys and small-town kids intrigued big city reporters with their naivety and colorful colloquialisms; writers lined up to get the scoop on the latest hick from the sticks.

Arkansas boasted more than its share of ballplayers in the interwar years, no fewer than four of whom would be enshrined in the Hall of Fame. Waldo's Travis Jackson patrolled shortstop for the New York Giants in the 1920s and early 1930s; Joseph Floyd "Arky" Vaughan, born in Madison County, became the best in the game at that same position for the Pittsburgh Pirates in the 1930s. Bill Dickey of Kensett may have been overshadowed by teammates Babe Ruth and Lou Gehrig, but the Yankee backstop was the steady anchor of that franchise's first dynasty. Lon Warneke, the "Arkansas Hummingbird" from Mount Ida, thrilled Chicago Cubs and St. Louis Cardinals fans with his fastball on the way to 192 career victories. Lynwood "Schoolboy" Rowe, a skinny righthander from El Dorado, led the Detroit Tigers to the 1934 American League pennant before arm troubles derailed his career a couple of years later. Henry Clyde Day, nick-named "Pea Ridge" after his Benton County hometown, made up in show-manship what he lacked in pitching prowess by unleashing hog calls from the mound. But none of Arkansas's baseball stars captured the nation's attention—or exuded the Arkansaw image—like a boisterous hurler out of the hardscrabble Ouachitas.

He was Pete Whetstone in cleats. A raw-boned mountain boy for sure, but to hear him tell it he was the best there ever was. Barely literate, unbridled

Dizzy Dean. Courtesy of The Museum / Cabot High School, Cabot, Arkansas.

braggart with a right arm to back it up, he was a reporter's dream. If Mark Twain had written about baseball, this would have been his creation. And he was Arkansaw through and through. Dizzy Dean burst on the national scene in the dark, early years of the Depression. A twenty-year-old kid—at least as far as anyone could tell, for the young pitcher from the wilds of Arkansas was so windy that no one was certain what his real name was, much less his birth date—who electrified the baseball world, Diz was the most dominating pitcher of his era, a flame-thrower who shone so brightly that a career of only five full seasons catapulted him into immortality as a Hall of Famer.

Dean was a perfect embodiment of the Arkansaw image in an age when there was no shortage of Arkansaw icons. His brashness and swagger seemed straight out of the Old Southwest, his combination of naivety and cunning, of hillbilly and hero, a projection of the dual image onto the national stage. Some poked fun at the hayseed from Arkansas; others found him refreshing and saw in this former cotton picker a symbol of hope, living proof that America could still deliver on its promise to the humble and lowly.

Born in the Logan County community of Lucas in 1910, Jay Hanna Dean was raised the son of a widowed sharecropper and migrant worker. The Deans moved to Oklahoma in the 1920s and it was there that the "big and loud and friendly" teenager, barefoot and clad in overalls, began showing signs of greatness on the diamond. After a three-year stint in the army, during which "he was by every measuring stick invented the worst soldier in this or any army," "Dizzy" Dean embarked on a professional baseball career that would land him on the mound for the St. Louis Cardinals almost four months shy of his twenty-first birthday. The strapping country boy held the Pittsburgh Pirates to three hits that day, and within a couple of years his domination would extend over every lineup in the National League. His pitching may have required an additional bit of seasoning in 1930, but Diz's swagger was fully formed well before he ever donned a Cardinals uniform. Incurably boastful, Dean was what a modern sportswriter might call "walking bulletin board material." As a minor leaguer he had bragged that "beating the Birmingham Barons will be like taking candy from a baby," suggesting that he might "strap my pitching arm behind me and pitch with the other hand" just to give the other team a fighting chance. More often than not his strong right arm carried through on his predictions.[37]

By 1934, he was the best pitcher in the game, a "zany . . . belligerent buffoon" on the World Series champion Cardinals, the chief clown on the colorful Gas House Gang. He was the pride of St. Louis. As one New York sportswriter observed, "Farmers came out of the distant Ozarks and Mid-West traveling salesmen arrange their itineraries to catch him." At the pinnacle of his adulation and greatness, he was a cross between Mohammad Ali and Will Rogers—a perceptive rube dispensing braggadocio and down-home philosophy in equal measure. Diz and little brother Paul—as soft-spoken and unassuming as Dizzy was bombastic—appeared in a Broadway vaudeville revue after their heroic World Series victory, and the following season found twenty-five-year-old Diz with his own St. Louis newspaper column, ghost-written by journalist Roy Stockton.[38]

At a time when baseball was truly king of American sports, Dizzy Dean cut a figure exceeded by few. His celebrity stemmed as much from his hillbilly persona—a characterization played up by the media and by Dean himself—as from his prowess on the pitching mound. His career cut short by injury, Diz would achieve iconic status long after his playing days had ended as a plain-talking, joke-telling, English language-butchering radio and television analyst. In the 1930s, though, he embodied the Arkansaw image like no other.

Good Old Arkansaw: In Song and Story

Early in his radio career, Dean took to filling in the empty spaces of a broadcast with any number of diversions. One of those diversions became a signature of his long broadcasting career—the singing of a hillbilly song, most frequently "The Wabash Cannonball." Had he been more appreciative of his own role in perpetuating the Arkansaw image, Diz may have preferred something a little more specific to his home state, such as "Arkansas Sheik" or "Blue-Eyed Sally." Among the purveyors of the Janus-faced Arkansaw image in the era between the world wars was a bevy of popular songs depicting Arkansas, and the Ozarks in particular, as a bucolic arcadia or a haven of the hillbilly. The Arkansaw/Ozark songs of the interwar years were generally of two types—comic and sentimental—and both types "emphasize[d] the rural isolation of the area and the hospitality of its people."[39] Consequently, most of the era's songs presented Arkansas and the Ozark region in a positive light.

Two notable exceptions to that generality were "Arkansas Sheik," a comic skewering first recorded in 1928 by Clayton McMichen and Riley Puckett, and "Second Class Hotel," also known as "The Arkansas Hotel." Warning Missouri gals to avoid marrying Arkansas boys, the former describes the backwoods sheik, his run-down farmstead, and his slatternly cabin. Dressed in buckskin and an old floppy hat, the sheik was a worthy descendant of Mark Twain's "Arkansaw" and the squatter of Arkansas Traveler legend. "The first thing he does whenever he goes in / He takes a chew of tobacco and he slobbers on his chin." He had little to his name besides "an old blind mule and an old milk cow / A razorback hog and a bull-tongue plow / He had his poke salad and his sassafras tea / But the Arkansas Sheik is a mystery to me."[40] Inspired by the older "Bill Stafford," "Second Class Hotel" relates the story of one man's residency in "a crumb joint in the state of Arkansas," run by his slovenly, drunken mother-in-law whose "face would wreck a brand new model Ford." Down-home cooking was not her forte: "Oh, you should have seen the bread / It was made of glue and lead / That's the kind of grub you get in Arkansas." Only the bugs, who "come back from no-man's land with can-openers in each hand," seem interested in his mother-in-law's vittles.[41]

One song that bridged the gap between hillbilly farce and sentimentality was "Blue-Eyed Sally," written by Al Bernard and Russel Robinson, a popular minstrel duo known as the Dixie Stars. Bernard and Robinson combined the colorful dialect usually found in minstrel tunes, though a hillbilly dialect in this instance, with a light-hearted romantic theme. "Sally, dear, it's been a year / Since I left Arkansaw / Lordy knows I miss 'ya' / How I long to kiss 'ya.'" Backwoods bliss awaits the singer and his betrothed. "We'll be happy blue-eyed Sally / In a rustic shack for two / Down on that Ozark trail there'll be big do-ins' / When 'we-uns' meet with 'you-uns.'"[42]

Most Arkansas and Ozark songs of the period carried the romantic theme of "Blue-Eyed Sally" without the playfully condescending dialect—and certainly without the harsh characterizations found in "Arkansas Sheik" and "Second Class Hotel." The Ozark region was especially fertile ground for sentimentality. "My Ozark Mountain Home," "When Flowers Bloom Again in the Ozarks," "Ozark Mountain Rose," "Where the Ozarks Kiss the Sky," "Ozark Smiles," "Mystic Hills of the Ozarks," and "Little Sweetheart of the Ozarks" were among several tunes that evoked feelings of nostalgia and romance through references to arcadian countrysides and rural simplicity. "The Foothills of the Ozarks" was representative of these Depression-era sentimental pieces. "In the Foothills of the Ozarks the old folks wait for me / In the little old log cabin that's where I long to be / No matter where I wander or where I chance to be / The Foothills of the Ozarks are home sweet home to me." Even the maudlin "My Ozark Mountain Home," first recorded by Ozark, Arkansas's own George Edgin's Corndodgers in 1932, expressed a longing for a deceased mother and the "little cabin home" of the singer's childhood. "Though the house is blown away / And the fields with grass are grey / I can ne'er forget my Ozark Mountain home." Eschewing sentimentality for 1920s boosterism, James Braswell's "In the Land of a Million Smiles" nonetheless painted a rosy picture of the region. "In taking your vacation, I'll tell you where to go. A way down in the Ozarks, You'll love that place I know."[43]

Many of the songs that specified Arkansas as the location reflected this same nostalgia for the good old days back home and wonder at the work of nature. In "Somewhere in Arkansas" the narrator longs to return home after a life of roaming: "But it's down in Arkansas / That's the place that I'm in love / So I'm going back to Arkansas / And see my turtle dove." In "The Old Dinner Bell," a traveler pines for the state and the simpler life he left behind: "I must travel back to Arkansas tomorrow / I left there several months ago / 'Twas the only time that ever I was happy / When I used to beat that old banjo." Even a song about leaving the state could reflect a sentimental attachment to the life left behind. In "Going to Leave Old Arkansas," recorded in 1928 by northeastern Arkansas group A. E. Ward and His Plowboys, a man bound for the North mourns his impending journey. "My heart is awful heavy, boys / And tears are in my eyes / But tomorrow night when the sun goes down / I'm goin' to say goodbye." Other songs, anticipating Arkansas's eventual embrace of the Natural State moniker, reflected a romantic attachment to nature, among them "Song of Arkansas," "Arkansas, Our Eden," and "Arkansas Song." Representative of this lot was Maude Bethel Lewis's 1922 song "Arkansas I Love You." "I love your mountains and your wooded hills / Your rivers and your little laughing rills / Your skies so blue and all your song-birds too / My own dear Arkansas."[44]

It should be pointed out, if it's not already apparent, that the three songs in the previous paragraph—the "positive" image songs—were all performed originally by Arkansawyers, while the hillbilly image songs discussed previously were written and performed by non-Arkies. This is a phenomenon that we have witnessed elsewhere in this study, and one that makes sense enough. Arkansawyers have always been willing to poke fun at their shortcomings—and even to laugh at the fun poked by others—but they have evinced an emotional attachment to home and a willingness to defend Arkansas and her people, whether that be making the squatter the wily hero of the Arkansas Traveler legend or singing about the old homeplace in the hills. One medium that rarely offered the perspective of the Arkansawyer in the interwar years was the fictional treatment of Arkansas and the Ozarks. In spite of the outsider-dominated view of the fictional Arkansaw/Ozarks, most depictions hewed close to the romantic tradition most associated with Harold Bell Wright's *The Shepherd of the Hills*. That this should be the case is not surprising, especially when you consider the nature of novel writing. It's one thing to pen a four-stanza ditty decrying a state's hillbilly backwardness, but quite another to devote months of writing to besmirch a people in book form. That did happen, but a reader was more likely to encounter a one-dimensional hillbilly image of Arkansaw in a peripheral character, not in a novel's cast of key figures. Besides, the ridiculous success of *The Shepherd of the Hills* had already revealed the gold in them thar romantic hills.

A number of the era's most formulaic novels contributed to the developing Ozark image, which, as we have seen, would by the 1930s in large part substitute itself for the older Arkansaw image. More often than not, the writers of such novels used Wright's Missouri setting, resulting in an indirect contribution to the Arkansaw image by virtue of their Ozark source material. A. M. Haswell, a longtime resident of Springfield, Missouri, placed his romantic historical novels *A Daughter in the Ozarks* and *A Drama of the Hills* in southwestern Missouri. Another southwestern Missouri resident, Rose Wilder Lane, penned a number of Ozark-themed, Missouri-set novels, including *Hill-Billy*. Born from the same spirit of arcadian romanticism that inspired Wright's novels, *Hill-Billy* relates the story of a farm boy who moves to the "big" town and becomes a successful attorney before falling victim to a deceitful town girl. Only his eventual marriage to an authentic woman from the hills redeems this wayward young man who had been enticed by the foreign materialism of modern American life.[45] Writers based outside the Ozarks often centered their stories on the experiences of newcomers to the region, finding romantic quaintness in, though infrequently acceptance of, the apparently primitive lifestyles of the natives. Such was the case with novelist Louise Platt Hauck, whose novels —such as *Wild Grape* and *Rainbow Glory*—pictured an Ozarks "glamorous with romance and steeped in the superstitions of the ignorant people who live there."[46]

Among the novelists to relate stories of the Arkansas Ozarks were Charles Morrow Wilson and Vance Randolph. Wilson's first Ozark novel, *Acres of Sky,* falls squarely within the romantic tradition of Harold Bell Wright, though Wilson possessed a flair for words conspicuous for its absence in Wright's work. Wilson's novel, which would be turned into a dramatic musical that premiered at the University of Arkansas a generation later, dabbled in the most recognizable stereotypes of backcountry life. Key characters in the book included moonshiners (not surprisingly, given our earlier discussion of Wilson's take on this art, among the noblest figures in his fictional Arkansas), a withered old conjurewoman and her comely, seductive daughter, shady itinerant, brush-arbor preachers reeking of snake oil, and the Dyes and Mistons, two families who've been feuding for so long that no one seems to remember what all the fuss is about.[47]

The young protagonist of the story, Hal Duncan, "like the scion of an olden god," leaves Hawg Eye to be educated, with plans of returning home one day "in friendship to teach and preach." He does so, only to lose his farm to the greedy banker in town and his best friend, pint-sized bee-hunter-turned-moonshiner Elijah Shrum, to the state penitentiary. Ultimately, young Hal is saved from a life of work-a-day toil only when the banker dies and his widow, whom the virile, handsome, and idealistic young hillman had bedded some years earlier, decides to give the farm back to her one-time lover. *Acres of Sky* is not great literature, but as the work of a young man with a romantic fascination with the people of the

Arkansas backcountry it is representative of the era's rather positive and nostalgic interpretation of the Ozarks and of Arkansas. In the final estimation, Wilson's Arkansas towns are populated by the same boorish, weak-willed, pudgy-soft characters that inhabit all of hyper-civilized America; only in the backcountry will one find the antidote to modernization. As Elijah tells Hal, "for plain open livin' the hills teach folks a mighty lot, if you give 'em time."[48]

The best of the Ozark novels of the interwar period—and the closest the Ozarks would come to the Southern Renascence—was Thames Williamson's *The Woods Colt*. The reviewer for *Time* thought it good enough to vie for a Pulitzer Prize. As in *Acres of Sky,* moonshine and the divide and animosity between town folks and "hill billies" play important roles in Williamson's novel. The character to whom the title (a backwoods euphemism for bastard child) refers is Clint Morgan, a wild young buck from Possum Holler who takes a shine to the local seductress, Tillie Starbuck. In a jealous rage, Clint thrashes another of Tillie's would-be suitors, uppity and conniving mail carrier and moonshine distributor Ed Prather, and the woods colt's destruction of the post office in the melee lands him in federal handcuffs. Clint eventually escapes from the federal officer, who derides him as a "hill billy" and "brush ape." After later killing the fed, Clint takes to the remote hills, where he uses his considerable outdoorsman skills to live off the land, sleeps with his slow-minded teenage cousin, and gets mixed up with a clan of unsavory backwoods denizens before being trapped and killed in a moonshiner's cave.[49]

Though not the unbridled romantic depiction found in *Acres of Sky*—even Wilson may have struggled to find the silver lining in the kissing cousins arc—*The Woods Colt* was by no means a simple denunciation of Ozarks backwoods culture. In Williamson's telling of the tale, the Ozarks backwoodsman is both noble and uncivilized. Clint may be a hot-headed hillbilly bastard, but there is a certain nobility in his ability to survive in the wilderness and to outfox his greenhorn pursuers. And his final soliloquy reveals his own appreciation for his natural environment and its centrality to his existence: "They're mighty purty right this minute, they shore are. The leaves is all red an' yaller, an' they're a-movin' gentle-like, back an' forth, jest enough to let you know they're there. . . . The days is gittin' late. Purty soon it'll be time to git out the old houn'-dog an' start out after coons, some o' these frosty nights, or maybe git a possum up a persimmon tree."[50]

Undoubtedly more influential than the scant shelf of novels in the development and perpetuation of the Arkansaw/Ozark image in the Depression era was the newspaper comic strip—specifically a trio of comic strips that emerged almost simultaneously in 1934. Paul Webb's *The*

Mountain Boys, Billy DeBeck's *Snuffy Smith,* and Al Capp's *Li'l Abner* "mir-rored the complex mix of emotions and attitudes of Depression-era audiences," according to historian Anthony Harkins. Among the various concerns reflected in the popular comic strips were "the public fear of systemic economic and social collapse," the era's obsession with the rural, "benighted" South, and a hopeful "vision of the durability of the American people and the American spirit in the face of adversity." The cartoons were at the very least dual purpose, offering the more cynical "the pleasure of laughing at the misfortune of others," the more optimistic the "cheering reassurance that rural poverty was not as bleak as it appeared in news accounts."[51] But the comic strips didn't do all these things in equal measure.

Of the three, only *Lil' Abner* would come to be directly tied to the Arkansas Ozarks. Conversely, Paul Webb's *The Mountain Boys* was the least geographically specific and the most culturally dismissive. Appearing for the better part of a decade and a half in *Esquire,* Webb's cartoons focused on the mythical community of lazy, filthy, ignorant hillbillies who revolved around three brothers whose long beards, bare feet, and ever-present moonshine jug made for the perfect portrayal of an already iconic figure. A native of Pennsylvania who had never set foot in the highland South before hatching *The Mountain Boys,* Webb dabbled in the crudest of hillbilly stereotypes: hyper-sexuality, bestiality, inbreeding, sloth, and an overwhelming animality. For the most part, according to Harkins, Webb's hillbillies were "ignorant and hopelessly inept but basically gentle souls who calmly accept their fate." Yet, as Harkins observes, in spite of the exaggerated ridiculousness of *The Mountain Boys* cartoons, they appealed to audiences "as models of human endurance."[52]

While it is indeed a stretch to find a silver lining in the dark hillbilly cloud of Webb's cartoons, *Snuffy Smith* emerged as a more balanced character, a truer representative of the dualistic imagery of a Jim Doggett or a Pete Whetstone. Like all of the hillbilly men created by the Chicagoan DeBeck, Snuffy was an ignorant, lazy, gun-toting, and sometimes thieving moonshiner whose life of leisure was built upon the overworked back of his subordinate, long-suffering wife. Yet, "he also represents the antielite attitudes, rugged independence, and physical prowess of the mythic frontiersman" who so enamored young romantics like Albert Pike and Friedrich Gerstäcker. By highlighting Snuffy's independence, egalitarianism, and rejection of modernity, DeBeck presented "a more upbeat countervision of rural southerners," such as that championed by Ozark watchers like Vance Randolph, Charles Morrow Wilson, and Otto Ernest Rayburn.[53]

Snuffy Smith's Hootin' Holler was ostensibly in the North Carolina mountains, although references to Little Rock and Crystal Springs, Arkansas, contributed to the melding of the Appalachians, Ozarks, and Ouachitas into a "single mythical geographic location," a generic highland South that housed Webb's *Mountain Boys* and many other pop-cultural hillbillies of the era. Influenced by this fuzzy geography, Al Capp at first located his mythical Dogpatch in Kentucky but later shifted it to the Ozarks (by endorsing the theme park discussed in chapter 4), and to this day the imagery of this most famous hillbilly comic strip is tied to the Ozark region in general and to the Arkansas Ozarks more specifically. Saddled with an inveterate outsider's mentality, likely the product of his working-class, Jewish upbringing in New England, Capp (né Alfred Gerald Caplin) did not share the romantics' infatuation with rural simplicity and traditionalism. In the early years, however, his comic strips "extol[led] the virtues of the common folk and represented a strongly felt class-consciousness and hostility toward the wealthy."[54]

The central characters in Capp's comic world were the Yokums (Mammy, Pappy, and Lil' Abner) and Lil' Abner's love interest, Daisy Mae, a buxom bumpkin beauty who inexplicably sprang from the primitively backward and brutal Scragg family. Over time, the population of Dogpatch grew to include dozens of colorful characters, from Moonshine McSwine and his daughter Moonbeam to Earthquake McGoon and Hairless Joe. Debuting *Lil' Abner* just two months after *The Mountain Boys* first greeted *Esquire* readers, Capp made no more effort than had Webb to portray something akin to real hill people. In fact, the Yokums' geographic origination and cultural characteristics were usually of secondary importance to the fundamental aim of skewering the pomposity and myopic ignorance of the wealthy and well born. Close to half of the episodes in the early years took place outside of Dogpatch. A favorite locale was New York City, where Capp mined hilarity and satire from the fish-out-of-water experiences of the Yokums amid Manhattan high society. The Yokums frequently came off as simple-minded and ridiculous, but Capp obviously favored their naivety, authenticity, and lack of acquisitiveness over the greed and prevarication of the gluttonous elite. The combination of Lil' Abner and Mammy Yokum lends the comic strip its grounding in morality and country cunning. Lil' Abner's good looks and strapping physique reflect a naive wholesomeness, while, like Jed Clampett of a later generation of hillbilly characters, according to Anthony Harkins, "Mammy alone among the Dogpatchers possesses an unalloyed common sense that can cut through the duplicity and confidence scams of city slickers."[55]

Although *Lil' Abner* reflects a glimmer of romanticism by holding the Yokums and Daisy Mae up "as the human embodiment of a primitive but pure natural world," Capp's comic strip was no paean to the virtues of life in the Ozarks. Other than these four main characters, Harkins notes, the "inhabitants of Dogpatch are physically grotesque and little better than wild animals" and prone to the same stereotypical vices that occupy the lives of Paul Webb's *Mountain Boys*. Ultimately, the cynical Capp dismissed practically everyone, suggesting "that while the poor need to be pitied, definitive uplift is impossible, for they remain ignorant, backward and uneducable." By the mid-1940s, Dogpatch would devolve into "a pure fantasy realm of sexually charged grotesques and monsters," and with this transformation would dissolve any pretext of this mountain community's role as an alternative to the materialism and greed of mainstream American life.[56]

Good Ole Arkansaw: On the Air, Stage, and Screen

The comic strips and cartoons of Webb, DeBeck, and Capp reached an audience far larger than the one exposed to the Arkansaw/Ozarks image through the novel or the nonfiction feature story. But even a comic strip with as wide a distribution and readership as *Lil' Abner* could not match the popularity and influence of the era's most powerful purveyor of the Arkansaw image—radio. At no other time in history has Arkansas been so prominently featured in the nation's most popular medium as was the case with national radio programming in the 1930s and 1940s. *Lum and Abner* and Bob Burns brought Arkansas into millions of parlors and onto front porches with a cast of characters whose obvious exaggerations did nothing to loosen their grip on the hearts and minds of rural and small-town Americans. Although defensive Arkansans of succeeding generations have often read back into these personalities, or at least Burns, an opportunistic willingness to exploit the state's longstanding negative image for fame and fortune, the overriding spirit of the radio shows was one of gentle self-deprecation mixed with sincere reverence and nostalgia for a way of life in danger of succumbing to the onslaught of the modern world. In other words, the romantic Arkansaw image was alive and well on the airwaves of radio's golden age.

Lum and Abner was the most successful Arkansas-affiliated program and one of the longest-running shows on the air. During its run of almost a quarter of a century, the show attracted an audience second only to that of *Amos 'n Andy*. *Lum and Abner* was the creation of Chester Lauck and Norris Goff, two young men from the Ouachita Mountains town of Mena. Having earned a reputation for performing blackface comedy routines, "Chet" Lauck and "Tuffy" Goff were invited to appear on a Hot Springs radio broadcast sponsored by the Mena Lions Club in April 1931. Intending to reprise a black dialect routine that had recently brought down the house in Mena, the duo changed their minds on the drive to Hot Springs and decided instead to create two rural white characters, hastily adopting the names Lum Edwards (Lauck) and Abner Peabody (Goff). This drive-time brainstorming launched a partnership that would keep them together until the Eisenhower years. Their volunteer appearance turned into a weekly show on the station, KTHS, but the program's popularity and the stars' talent quickly outgrew their southwestern Arkansas audience. After a couple of months Lauck and Goff found a bigger stage, and *Lum and Abner*'s fifteen-minute skits began airing five mornings a week as a summer replacement show on a Chicago NBC affiliate. The program experienced enough success to earn a succession of sponsors and short contracts until catching on with NBC affiliate WTAM in Cleveland in late 1932, a move that would land *Lum and Abner* in national syndication within a year under the sponsorship of the Ford Motor Company. In succeeding years, like many radio acts of the era, Norris and Goff took their show to a number of different cities in the employ of various sponsors and networks, eventually settling in Hollywood in 1937.[57]

Although *Lum and Abner* were farmers, justices of the peace, and frequent general store loafers in the earliest incarnation of the show, by February 1933 the characters had assumed their familiar roles as proprietors of their own country mercantile, which with the help of a listener write-in contest soon became known as the Jot 'em Down Store. The store served the often-eccentric citizens of fictional Pine Ridge, Arkansas, which the actors had based on a tiny Montgomery County crossroads hamlet called Waters.[58] Although Lauck was only twenty-nine when the show started and Goff just twenty-four, their alter egos were slow-talking and slow-moving old men whose compassion and concern for their neighbors hamstrung their business efforts but endeared them to many a listener. As the show matured, Lauck and Goff developed and voiced a panoply of supporting characters, such as Cedric Weehunt, Grandpappy Spears, Squire Skimp, Mousey Gray, Snake Hogan, and Mose Moots.[59]

Lum and Abner was not cut from the mold of Capp's and Webb's exploitative cartoons. The humor of Lauck and Goff was gentle and character-driven and never mean-spirited. Like the comedy of Bob Burns, *Lum and Abner* possessed that gestalt quality usually evident in humor mined from ethnic and cultural sources. Rural and small-town listeners heard familiar voices and grew attached to colorful, mythical neighbors whose foibles and eccentricities, unlike those of their flesh-and-blood neighbors, resulted in nothing more than a little mayhem for Pine Ridge's storekeepers. Chet Lauck was likely thinking of those other listeners, a more contemptuous crowd who might find in the shortcomings of Pine Ridge's residents evidence of their own cultural superiority, when he told a *New York Times* reporter: "'Make the audience think they are smarter than you and ten to one you will click in a sketch such as ours.'" In the tradition of

"Lum and Abner," Chester Lauck and Norris Goff. Courtesy of
National Lum and Abner Society Collection.

the best sitcoms, *Lum and Abner* found its laughs by placing believable and likable characters in a variety of predicaments. As Lauck explained to *Radio Guide* magazine, "We try to make our program amusing through the situations we build up rather than through the ignorance or obtuseness of any character."[60]

Lum and Abner was one of several shows of the 1930s and 1940s—along with classics like *Amos 'n Andy, Ma Perkins,* and *Fibber McGee and Molly*— whose comedy emanated from the rural and small-town wellspring of self-deprecation and appreciation for modest eccentricity. In that sense, *Lum and Abner* was no hillbilly program. And Lauck and Goff, despite their small-town Arkansas upbringings, were no more hillbilly than were the actors on any typical network show. Both came from prominent, business-owning families in Mena, and both had attended the University of Arkansas before returning to the Ouachitas to take up careers in business. (Lauck had even followed up his two years at the university with a stint at Chicago's Academy of Fine Arts.) Goff's travels for his father's wholesale company had taken him into countless country mercantiles like the Jot 'em Down Store and had introduced him to enough colorful personalities to populate multiple radio show communities. The stars' blending of their own middle-class sensibilities with the rural romanticism of the age likely rendered *Lum and Abner* palatable to a larger American audience. "Lauck and Goff fashioned their work with an awareness of longtime nostalgia for the rural past," historian Randal L. Hall suggests, "but they wholeheartedly endorsed a forward-looking focus on economic progress."[61]

But as far as millions of listeners were concerned, Lauck and Goff were the genuine items. Their familiarity with the kinds of characters they were inhabiting did indeed lend *Lum and Abner* a verisimilitude that generic hillbilly entertainment of the era lacked and a sincere belief in the value, if not the superiority, of the simple life portrayed on the show that couldn't be faked. They never wavered in their belief "that the simple philosophy of the Arkansas hills, genuine and unadorned, is very interesting."[62] By the end of the Depression decade the duo had parlayed their growing radio fame into a movie career, in part a result of the show's move to Hollywood, where it would remain for the final sixteen years of its remarkable twenty-three-year run.

The longevity of Bob Burns's radio career could not match that of Lauck's and Goff's, but at the height of his success his star shone brighter than that of *Lum and Abner,* and arguably brighter than that of any rural comedian of his era. Burns's legacy has proven more ambiguous and problematic than *Lum and Abner*'s as well. Whereas *Lum and Abner* remains a favorite of nostalgic Old-Time Radio devotees and stands as a symbol of a kinder, cleaner comedy from a bygone era, Bob Burns generally finds his way into modern discussions only as a comedian/actor willing to conform to Hollywood's notion of hinterland buffoonishness in exchange for fame and riches—at least until he was willing no more—and as a crucial link in the chain of contributors to an image problem that continues to plague his home state more than half a century after his death. But this assessment of Burns's career and his complicity in the tarnishing of Arkansas's image lacks nuance—and thus fairness—and reflects a modern reliance on the claims of a few contemporaries of Burns who overreacted to his mostly innocuous comedy or who, ironically, had no intention of defending Arkansas in the first place.

To be sure, the comedy of stereotyping—racial and cultural—played a central role in the career of Bob Burns. Burns spent more than a decade as a blackface and hillbilly performer before receiving a one-year contract to play blackface parts for Fox Studios in 1930. When his year in Hollywood led to nothing of a more permanent nature, Burns fell on hard times and eventually turned to nightclub and radio work to support his family. Dropping blackface for a routine that was part hillbilly corniness, part Will Rogers-style rural philosophizing, he came up with an idea for a radio show that he called *Gawkin' Around* and that would feature the comedian playing a little music and telling stories—essentially what he would eventually do on radio—but found no takers. After knocking around Los Angeles on a succession of low-paying, and occasionally no-paying, radio gigs, Burns, now sneaking up on middle-age, decided to take his cornpone comedy to the Big Apple. A successful audition earned him a string of guest spots on *The Fleischmann Hour* (a.k.a. *The Rudy Vallee Show*) and on *The Kraft Music Hall* with Paul Whiteman in 1935, with Burns doing his best Will Rogers-country-political-satirist imitation until Rogers's death in a plane crash late that summer made such imitation more cloying than flattering.[63]

This was the big break he had been looking for, and, even after trading in his Will Rogers routine for the rural raconteur he had worked up in Los Angeles, his down-home style was appealing enough to earn Burns a six-month contract as Bing Crosby's comic sidekick on the new West Coast version of *The Kraft Music Hall,* which debuted in January 1936. By the time he left Crosby's show in 1941—reportedly because Kraft's management felt his five-thousand-dollar-per-week salary was too rich for a second fiddle—Burns had become a national celebrity and an enduring symbol of the Arkansaw image. For a time in the latter part of the 1930s, Burns had even penned a horse-sense musings column, "Well, I'll Tell You," for *Esquire,* the same magazine that brought Paul Webb's *The Mountain Boys* into parlors and offices around the country. In the summer of 1941, CBS offered Burns his own radio show, *The Arkansas Traveler* (later renamed *The*

Bob Burns Show), and for the next five and a half years Arkansas's most famous comedian played "a backwoods sage who roamed the land doing good deeds" and weaving for listeners far-fetched, though never mean-spirited, yarns about fictitious relatives back in Van Buren.[64]

In general, the comic tone of *The Arkansas Traveler* was similar to that of *Lum and Abner*. Sure, the introduction, which featured such Burns ruminations as "My folks down there are tall and lean, They look just like a big string bean, And some of 'em are just as green" spoken to the accompaniment of the chorus to "Down in Arkansas," suggested that the show to follow would likely disparage the Arkansas Traveler's home state. In general, though, the introduction was as close as Burns came to poking fun at the folks back home. The segments that followed—from the star's folksy monologue to the weekly story of the "Arkansas Traveler," the editor of the Van Buren newspaper—tended to be as reverent toward small-town values and country smarts as any episode of *Lum and Abner*. *Radio Life* magazine noted the mostly respectful mood of the show in the absence of a "strained effort to make funny 'hillbilly' clothes, bare feet, or props do the work of characterizations."[65]

Like Lauck and Goff, Burns was no simple hillbilly, and the fact that reporters occasionally commented on the dichotomy between the man born Robin Burn and the stage persona named Bob Burns likely contributed to suspicions that Burns might be a charlatan. The son of an engineer, and university-trained for an engineering career himself, Burns had experienced a thoroughly middle-class raising in his family's two-story, main-street house. This rather hayseedless background was no secret to folks back home. Even the hometown paper noted that "Bob never lived a day in the country in his life except when he was working one summer for his Uncle Bob Cook on his prairie fields of Oklahoma and then hit it back for the sidewalks when the sun went down." The airwaves and movie screens of the Depression era overflowed with hillbillies, most of them of the fully fabricated variety. One astute observer of Hollywood hillbillies argued that most radio rubes "couldn't tell a piece of corn pone from a rifle ball" and that on the big screen "the rarinest hillbillies have come from places like New York, Edinburgh, and Portland, Me." Of New York "radio hillbilly" Zeke Manners, another writer quipped: "As for living in the Ozarks, Zeke dwells in a penthouse apartment and is waited upon by a valet." That Burns, in spite of his small-town, edge-of-the-Ozarks heritage, might be just as articulate and intelligent as most of his Hollywood peers when off stage and away from the microphone likely challenged the very stereotypes that his act was purported to exacerbate. As one *New York Times* reporter discovered, Burns "is no more homespun than anybody else. . . . Not unlike the late Will Rogers, he has had more schooling than it is discreet for a homespun comedian to admit having." Later, *Radio Life* found "nothing slapstick about" Burns and noted that "he dresses conservatively for his broadcasts."[66]

In spite of their similar subject matter and the common, winking tone of their humor, Lauck and Goff received warm fan letters—fifteen thousand per week by 1933—while Burns faced criticism for maligning the state of Arkansas. Or did he? It is true that Burns's comedy spurred occasional backlashes and outbursts of defensiveness in his home state—a few letters to the editor and nonspecific testimonials, such as a WPA writer's claim that "some Arkansans feel that Burns does the State a disservice in helping to perpetuate the fable of the hill-billy in connection with it." But, as Burns informed an *Arkansas Gazette* reporter, "the plaintiffs were a small minority." It seems quite possible that historians and the defenders of Arkansas have exaggerated not only the offensiveness of Burns's humor but the level of acrimony it generated. By the turn of the twenty-first century, appraisals of Bob Burns such as this one from historian Ben F. Johnson III had become commonplace among the chroniclers of Arkansas: "Arkansas listeners thought that Lum and Abner were salutary representations of rural Arkansas, while they censured Burns for peopling his tales with dimwitted hillbillies." Likewise, Randal L. Hall observes that Burns, unlike Chester Lauck and Norris Goff, "earned cheap laughs by playing up the negative vision of hillbillies." In *The Jungles of Arkansas,* journalist Bob Lancaster noted that Burns "stirred a considerable amount of criticism and resentment . . . [for] perpetuating the old slow-train stereotype of the Arkansas hillbilly."[67]

In spite of the occasional letter to the editor, Burns's radio comedy was popular in Arkansas, especially among rural and small-town listeners, and most of his movies were warmly received in his home state. For the premiere of *Rhythm on the Range,* the 1936 film that gave Burns his first big movie role, Little Rock staged Bob Burns's Day, complete with a parade and a cavalcade of state "celebrities," including Senator Joseph T. Robinson and Arkansas tycoon Harvey Couch. Like a few defenders of Arkansas's honor at the time, Lancaster exaggerated the opposition to Burns. The "flurry of letters to the editor in the *Gazette* in 1936" that the journalist used to bolster his assessment of displeasure with Burns—if taken as a referendum— was actually a vote of confidence for the comedian. Sparked by an "Arkansan by adoption" who expressed her disdain for "any humor that makes light of this state and the people living within its boundaries," the "flurry" of responses that followed over the next two weeks eventually grew to eight letters. Six of the *Gazette* readers defended Burns's comedy; only two took exception with his treatment of Arkansas people, and one of those admitted to never having listened to Burns on the radio.[68]

The fact that a few listeners and watchers reacted negatively to Burns's humor but that almost no one objected to *Lum and Abner* stemmed mainly from the differing styles and presentations of the performers. As Lancaster described it, "Burns did comedy while Lauck and Goff did humor."[69] Lauck and Goff inhabited the characters they created; Burns told windy stories about his. The distance between first- and second-person comic narratives wouldn't seem to be a significant one, but in the court of public perception it could be. Furthermore, the world of *Lum and Abner* remained neatly enclosed in mythical Pine Ridge, while the freer association of the name "Arkansas" with Bob Burns tended to bring the whole state more fully underneath the comedy microscope. For educated and urban listeners in Arkansas, those most likely to express their dissatisfaction in writing, this could be a crucial distinction.

But the fact is that Bob Burns and his comedy never lost their appeal among the country folk and small-town residents who were the bread-and-butter audience for shows like *Lum and Abner* and *The Arkansas Traveler*. The fact is that people with no pretensions often find it easy to laugh at things at which their social betters believe it's better not to laugh. The years between the wars were rife with examples of such entertainments aimed at, but seemingly and simultaneously poking fun at, audiences of supposed hayseeds and yokels. Among them were live shows, whether of the vaudeville, carnival, or playhouse variety, that highlighted and exaggerated the peculiarities of rustics. Bob Burns was no stranger to such entertainment, having honed his skills on the blackface/hillbilly circuit in the 1910s and 1920s. Perhaps the best-known vaudeville-type show of the era that consciously tapped into the Arkansaw image was the group known as the Arkansas Travelers.

The Arkansas Travelers were the creation of Leon and Frank Weaver, brothers from rural Christian County, Missouri, who, according to one historian of Ozark musical acts, likely adopted the name of their neighboring state out of a belief that their audiences "equated Arkansas with the 'hillbilly' Ozarks!" The widespread recognition and cultural resonance of the Arkansas Traveler must have played a role as well. The older of the two, Leon, had begun his show business career as a hillbilly musician in a traveling medicine show—earning some renown for his ability to coax recognizable notes out of a handsaw—and after World War I teamed up with little brother Frank to form a hillbilly music and comedy act. The brothers adopted stage names with a rustic, minstrel ring to them—Abner and Cicero—and eventually built the Arkansas Travelers into a troupe of more than twenty musicians and performers. The most significant addition was Leon's wife, June, who as Elviry played a domineering, shrill-voiced leader of the cast, and who off-stage divorced Leon and married his brother Frank, all the while staying on as a key member of the show. Audiences in New York, Chicago, London, and Paris would have appreciated this bit of real-life hillbilly generosity, but it's unclear if the Weavers and Elviry ever made use of their personal lives in their act. By the 1930s, the Arkansas Travelers were a major success, appearing on stage in London for six weeks before touring France, Sweden, and Denmark. Like the squatter in the Arkansas Traveler legend, the Weaver Brothers' troupe gave urban audiences "the rube comedy they expected from backwoodsmen," but both onstage and at the ticket booth the hillbillies usually emerged triumphant.[70]

Theater audiences in the 1930s and 1940s caught occasional glimpses of the Arkansaw image, and these were often more over the top than the antics of the Weaver Brothers and Elviry. In many respects this Arkansaw comedy was simply an extension of a more generic hillbilly comedy, which itself was part and parcel of the era's ethnic and regional Vaudeville comedic style.[71] So it is not surprising that, as with other forms of entertainment during this era, stage productions increasingly carried the Arkansaw image through their treatments of but one of the state's geographic subregions, the Ozarks. Among the acts appearing at New York City's Hippodrome in 1928 were the "Hill Billies, five hulking backwoodsmen right out of the Ozarks." Over the next two decades, three Ozark-set plays

The Weaver Brothers and Elviry. Courtesy of History Museum for Springfield-Greene County, Missouri.

made it to Broadway. The first, *Swing Your Lady,* started its brief run at the Booth Theatre in October 1936. Set in southern Missouri, it told the story of a female blacksmith-turned-wrestler, and did so with enough corncob pipes, off-kilter dialect, bare feet, and blackened teeth to jeopardize future job prospects for any of the key players. Still, Warner Brothers thought enough of it to put it on the screen two years later, a move that the movie's star, Humphrey Bogart, would forever regret. The screen version of *Swing Your Lady* featured the film debuts of the Weaver Brothers and Elviry—as well as one of the earliest appearances of Ronald Reagan—but not even such surefire numbers as "Mountain Swingaroo" and "Hillbilly from Tenth Avenue" could save this musical from a critical spanking.[72]

It may have been bad, but *Swing Your Lady* outperformed *The First Million,* a play about a thieving clan of Ozark bank robbers that lasted all of five performances at the Ritz. Critically panned, this "crude and feeble hillbilly comedy" was noteworthy only for the novelty of its teenaged producer. By most accounts the Arkansas/Ozarks play that found the most eager audiences as it toured the country in the 1940s made *Swing Your Lady* look like the spawn of Eugene O'Neill by comparison. Billed as "the worst play in the world" and "The Show that Makes 'Tobacco Road' Blush," *Maid in the Ozarks* was a "fifth-rate hill-billy burlesque" that mixed images of the benighted South with every hillbilly trope imaginable. Taglined "life among the Arkansas hillbillies," the show featured such stock characters as the stern granny, the moonshining grandson and his philandering waitress fiancé from Little Rock, a gossiping neighbor, randy teenagers, a Klansman, a "rat-faced truancy officer," and a "moronic imbecile of 15 who dangles earthworms over his brow and nose." The plot, as one might expect, was beside the point.[73]

With low-brow humor and high-cut dresses, *Maid in the Ozarks* confounded critics as it titillated audiences from coast to coast, beginning with an eighty-six-week run in Los Angeles. A critic who saw the play soon after its 1942 arrival in Chicago, where it would remain for more than fourteen months, chalked up the improbable success of this "eternal parade of hillbilly goatishness" to its generous quotient of skin and its appeal to newcomers to the city "who never before laid eyes upon live actors, and yet who, now, in war-work prosperity, have plenty of cash and little to spend it on." The Great Northern Theatre, in an effort to eliminate the "snooty" trappings that might turn away the paying riff-raff, even arranged for "red-shirted hillbilly singers [to] pop up in the orchestra pit as soon as curtains fall" at intermission. "After reducing the stage to the level of urchins eating angle-worms," *Maid in the Ozarks* made its way through the major cities of the Midwest before getting its shot at Broadway audiences in the Belasco Theatre in July 1946. Producer Jules Pfeiffer's prediction that "the general,

"MAID IN THE OZARKS"

BY CLAIRE PARRISH

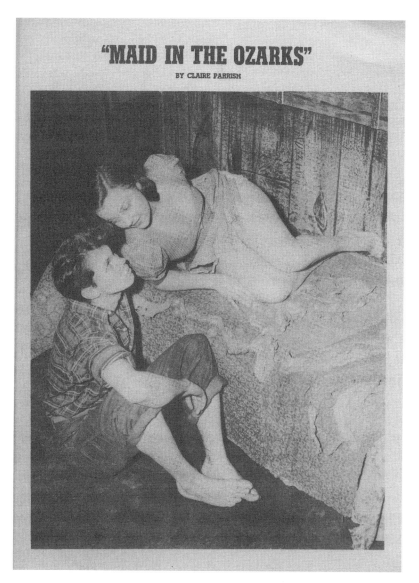

Photograph from a program for *Maid in the Ozarks,* Great Northern Theatre, Chicago, Illinois. Courtesy of Great Northern Theatre.

critical consensus will be that this play is the worst that has ever hit Broadway" turned into a self-fulfilling prophecy. Critics who weren't dumbstruck by the inanity of it all dismissed the play only slightly quicker than did theater-goers. "To recount the half-wit plot, or list the names of cast members trapped in this odoriferous curio, would constitute a waste of the typesetter's (and reader's) valuable time." *Maid in the Ozarks*'s run on Broadway was short-lived, but the producers, who would have turned Mel Brooks's Max Bialystock green with envy, could at least strike the set in the knowledge that they bested *Swing Your Lady* by two performances.[74]

Critics who lambasted plays like *Maid in the Ozarks* and the various hillbilly movies of the era did so not because their subjects were offensive but because they were bad theater, or bad cinema. Critics despised the hillbilly characters just as much as they disapproved of the actors playing them and of the scripts enlivening them. And, like the critic who suffered through *Maid in the Ozarks* in Chicago, they sometimes leveled their contempt on the crowds who kept producers churning out such drivel. And the movie world of the era was full of producers willing to court this market with a wagonload of hillbilly films, most of them of a quality only slightly better than that of *Maid in the Ozarks*.

So let us wrap up this survey of the heyday of the hillbilly with a look at motion pictures that played off the Arkansaw/Ozarks image. Stage productions highlighted the more negative, hillbilly side of the Arkansaw image, almost without exception. But films, like the era's other media, tended to promote the full spectrum of Arkansaw imagery, from the romantically noble to the comically, occasionally even ominously, backward, with various gradations in between. Though Arkansawyers were rarely taken seriously in these pictures, more often than not their naivety, genuineness, and fundamental country goodness triumphed in the end, reaffirming the romantic's faith in the natural man and distrust for the modern.

If one word could sum up the bevy of Arkansas and Ozark movies of the interwar years, it would probably be "forgettable." At least that's the one printable word that comes to mind. But just because Arkansas's big screen fare lacked quality doesn't mean the movies exercised no impact on the perpetuation of the Arkansaw image. From the condescending hayseed farce of *I'm From Arkansas* to the bucolic melodrama of *The Shepherd of the Hills*, the films about and set in Arkansas and the Ozarks carried the by now familiar and thoroughly ambivalent notions of life in the backwoods. Comedies dominated, and more than a few were musicals. After all, who doesn't prefer their hillbillies jovial and musical? Besides, *The Grapes of Wrath* was solemn enough to balance the jocularity of fifty hillbilly flicks.

Films set in Arkansas or in the Ozarks remained rare before the mid-1930s, at least in comparison with the dozens of pictures set in Appalachia.

The earliest films, such as *A Romance of the Ozarks, Billie—The Hill Billy,* and *An Ozark Romance,* followed the popular formula of the outsider who falls for and/or rescues a beautiful mountain girl who has inexplicably sprung from a backward and in some cases sinister family—a precursor to Al Capp's Daisy Mae Scragg. Post–World War I movies gravitated toward extremes, with the land of feuding and fighting hillbillies represented in *The Rebellious Bride* and *The Big Killing* (a comedy despite the title) and the more melodrama-prone, soul-rejuvenating hill country depicted in *Shepherd of the Hills* (1941) and *The Bishop of the Ozarks.*[75]

Hollywood found Arkansas and the Ozark region during the heart of the Depression, however, and the years between the mid-1930s and the Truman administration introduced moviegoers to Arkansaw/Ozark imagery both disdainful and romantic on more than two dozen films. Occasionally these films ventured into the familiar territory of melodrama. Such was the case with *Pilgrimage* (1933), the story of a bitter farm woman in mythical Three Cedars, Arkansas, who, after the death of her son in World War I, temporarily turns her back on the young widow and baby the son left behind. A critically acclaimed picture by legendary auteur John Ford, *Pilgrimage,* alas, had little to do with Arkansas per se. Another melodramatic film that could have been set anywhere in rural America was the 1936 movie *Girl of the Ozarks,* a tale based on nineteenth-century novelist Martha Finley's "Elsie Dinsmore" stories about a plucky little girl left to her own devices, and the kindness of strangers, after her mother's death. But the serious tone of *Pilgrimage* and *Girl of the Ozarks* was unusual among the Arkansaw/Ozarks films.[76]

Conversely, the backwoods comedy treatment of *I'm From Arkansas* (1944) was not out of the ordinary, but its relentlessly ridiculous tone was. Set in mythical Pitchfork, Arkansas, the plot (using the term loosely) concerned the efforts of a conniving industrial butcher to snooker Ma Alden out of her land after the discovery of boiling spring water that causes extreme fertility in hogs—it is, after all, a sow's nationally publicized litter of eighteen piglets that attracts a showgirl troupe to town and provides the excuse for this musical variety show that masqueraded as a movie. At one point the famous sow, Esmerelda, disappears and the townsfolk take time about trying to call her up. Most of the characters in Pitchfork are unredeemed caricatures—father and son Juniper and Efus Jenkins are *The Mountain Boys* without beards and sexual fecundity—or strange misfits from the vaudeville stage—El Brendel as a half-wit with a Swedish accent—and even songs by two now-obscure Arkansas-born singers, Carolina Cotton and Jimmy Wakely, couldn't rescue *I'm From Arkansas* from the B-movie junk heap.[77]

Although almost all the Arkansas- and Ozark-set movies of the era in question were comedies, almost none exhibited the condescension of *I'm*

From Arkansas. And almost all of them starred one of four individuals or acting teams, most of whom we've already become acquainted with. The films of the Weaver Brothers and Elviry came the closest to tipping in the direction of *I'm From Arkansas*–style buffoonery, but even in the midst of their cornpone slapstick Vaudeville's former Arkansas Travelers displayed a modicum of country dignity and maintained the high ground of rural honesty and morality.

The Weaver Brothers and Elviry made their big screen debut in the over-the-top Ozark hillbilly picture *Swing Your Lady* in 1938. Although the movie was critically panned, by the time of its release the Weaver trio had already signed on with Republic Pictures, a young studio that specialized in B-grade movies and westerns. Over the next four years Republic released eleven films starring the Weaver Brothers and Elviry. Formulaic and riddled with stereotypes, the low-budget pictures targeted a growing audience of rural Americans with access to movie houses and urbanites only recently removed from the farm. Almost all the Weavers' movies were musicals, or at the least featured a couple of hillbilly performances, and all were set in the Ozarks or among rural southerners. The plots found the Weavers inhabiting a variety of circumstances familiar to poor southerners of the late Depression era: sharecroppers oppressed by a wealthy landlord in *In Old Missouri* (1940), migrant workers in southern California in *Tuxedo Junction* (1941), landless drought victims in *Friendly Neighbors* (1940), and musicians-turned-politicians in *Grand Ole Opry* (1940). At least two of the films of the Weaver Brothers and Elviry were set in Arkansas, including their first Republic release, *Down in Arkansaw* (1938). In this film, the federal government pressures the Weavers to sell their land for a dam-building project. But what at first promises to be a defense of backcountry traditionalism gives way to budding romance and the rationality of "progress" when the Weavers' attractive daughter falls for the dam engineer, prompting the Arkansawyers to relinquish their property rights. For the 1941 film *Arkansas Judge,* the Weavers temporarily abandoned their cornpone schtick for a more dramatic story of petty theft and crime solving in fictional Peaceful Valley. With few exceptions the hillbilly antics and free play with stereotypes in the Weavers' movies were balanced by their generosity and compassion for neighbors and strangers alike, and, like the Clampetts a generation later, they somehow emerged triumphant from the most daunting circumstances.[78]

The same could be said for *Lum and Abner,* both on the radio and in the theater. After their relocation to Hollywood, Chet Lauck and Norris Goff starred in six films for RKO Pictures between 1940 and 1946. Aiming for the same audience that Republic enticed with the Weaver Brothers movies, the *Lum and Abner* pictures gave viewers the opportunity to see the two old storekeepers and their Pine Ridge neighbors whom they had gotten to know in the 1930s. The movies rarely strayed too far from the tried-and-true radio formula built on the repartee between Lum Edwards and Abner Peabody. Consequently, the *Lum and Abner* films eschewed blatant hillbilly hilarity for a gentler cracker-barrel comedy, with the proprietors of the Jot 'em Down Store getting themselves into and out of major predicaments in little more than an hour's time. After the uncharacteristically maudlin first movie, *Dreaming Out Loud,* in which a sweet girl is killed by a spoiled pretty boy in a hit-and-run accident on the dusty road in front of the Jot 'em Down Store, Lum and Abner returned to more familiar territory with 1942's *The Bashful Bachelor,* a picture with no deaths but a few brushes with the hereafter as Abner tries to help his partner land a sweetheart by placing himself in harm's way so that Lum can come to the rescue. Three of the six Lum and Abner films turned to the ever-popular bumpkins-in-the-city formula by taking the storekeepers to Chicago twice and to Washington, D.C. The final picture, *Partners in Time,* brought the old fellows back to Pine Ridge for a sometimes-sentimental look at the backstory of radio's favorite small-town entrepreneurs.

The people of Arkansas seem to have appreciated Mena's favorite sons on film, just as they adored them on radio. Little Rock rolled out the red

Lobby card from the "Lum and Abner" movie *Dreaming Out Loud.*
Courtesy of National Lum and Abner Society Collection.

carpet for Chet Lauck and Tuffy Goff when the capital city hosted the premiere of *Dreaming Out Loud* in September 1940—complete with the secretary of state's greeting at Adams Field followed by a reception at the Albert Pike Hotel hosted by Governor Homer Bailey. At a Rotary Club / Chamber of Commerce luncheon that attracted a "record attendance," the governor, coming off a recent defeat in the Democratic primary, seemed more intent on discussing politics than on celebrating the visiting celebrities. But Secretary of State C. G. Hall, an acquaintance of Lauck and Goff during their college days in Fayetteville, noted that "one reason why people love them is that they portray people we all know," and Rotary president R. A. Kern, an old road engineer, recounted eating sardines and crackers at Dick Huddleston's store—the model for Jot 'em Down—"many a time."[79]

Familiarity was a major factor in the popularity of Lum and Abner on radio and in the movies. While Arkansawyers couldn't relate to another movie star of the era, Judy Canova, in the same sense that they could to Lauck and Goff, her radio popularity gave her a familiar name and voice that found their way into a number of hillbilly movies in the 1940s. Canova, who fashioned a long show business career as a cornpone comedienne, was not from the Ozarks but was often associated with the region because of a number of Ozark-set movies. Born and raised in Florida, Canova was groomed from an early age for her career in country comedy. Touring with her siblings as the Three Georgia Crackers or Three Canovas, she sang, yodeled, and joked her way to New York and a guest spot on Rudy Vallee's *Fleischmann Hour* in 1933, which led to regular roles on shows hosted by Paul Whiteman and Edgar Bergen. A co-starring turn in the 1939 Broadway musical *Yokel Boy* and small parts in a number of Depression-era movies landed Canova a contract with Republic Pictures that would result in eighteen films between 1940 and 1955. Like Republic stable mates the Weaver Brothers and Elviry, Canova found herself forever typecast as a naive, musically inclined rube, usually in pigtails and calico, and the Florida native played some variation of this character, located somewhere in the mythical rural South, in successful, hyper comedies like *Sis Hopkins* (1941), *Sleepytime Gal* (1942), *Oklahoma Annie* (1946), *Honeychile* (1951), and *Carolina Cannonball* (1955). A number of her films were set in the Ozarks of Arkansas or Missouri. In *Scatterbrain* (1940), Canova's hillbilly girl gets discovered by a Hollywood producer and whisked off, along with her family, to southern California, where the fish-out-of-water antics proceed. Like a lot of hillbilly comedy, *Scatterbrain* is as much satire of the pretensions and veiled ignorance of Hollywood's elite as it is countrified farce. Such was also the case with *Puddin' Head* (1941) and *Joan of Ozark* (1942). In the former, Judy and her father, storekeepers named Goober in mythical Withering Heights, Arkansas, inherit a mansion in New York City; their experiences in the big city prove similar to those of the Yocums in *Lil' Abner,* with the genuine guilelessness of the bumpkins exposing the pretensions and pomposity of the elite. *Joan of Ozark* also finds its way to New York as hillbilly Judy Hull is discovered by a nightclub talent agent and once in New York brings down the house with a hillbilly musical number while foiling a Nazi spy ring. As usual, the Hulls are stereotypical hillbillies, but Judy manages to rise to the challenge of the urban world, even if by accident.

From 1943 to 1955, Canova maintained a successful dual career as a B-movie mainstay and as a popular radio personality on *The Judy Canova Show.* She may have learned a thing or two about Hollywood multitasking from her one-time radio co-star, Bob Burns, who launched his own career as a leading man on the big screen in the latter half of the Depression decade. After his success in supporting roles in *Rhythm on the Range* and *The Big Broadcast of 1937* (both released in 1936), Burns received a multi-picture contract from Paramount. Over the next four years he headlined eleven films—all of them comedies—in which he played some slight variation of his hillbilly philosopher radio persona. Whether playing a hillbilly musician trying to save a small-town Tennessee radio station in *Comin' Round the Mountain* (1940), a Missouri mule trader who gets caught up in the world of the British aristocracy in *I'm From Missouri* (1939), or a drifting gambler disguised as a man of the cloth but possessed of a heart of gold in *Alias the Deacon* (1940), Burns's roles were extensions of his folksy radio character on *The Kraft Music Hall.*

Although Burns was in no danger of being overwhelmed by Academy of Motion Pictures adulation, his work on screen rarely received unfavorable responses from audiences or critics. The fact that few if any of Burns's films approached the over-the-top hysteria of the hillbilly romps of Judy

Lobby card from the film *Joan of Ozark.* Courtesy of Paramount Pictures.

Canova and the Weavers certainly made the movies more palatable to reviewers. *New York Times* critic Bosley Crowther described *Alias the Deacon* as "an undistinguished but thoroughly genial little farce-comedy" and offered slight praise for "the blank expressions and dry wit of Mr. Burns as the royal dodger." Another *Times* film critic, Frank S. Nugent, found *I'm From Missouri* to be "a pleasant variation on the commonplace folksiness-vs.-social-ambition theme" and, without mock sincerity, "an occasionally hilarious example of a type of Western which we can only classify as mule opera." The critic described the movie's star as "that genial and character-istically asymmetrical map of the Southwest Territory" and claimed that Burns had played the role of mule trader Sweeney Bliss to "perfection." Nugent was pleasantly surprised by *The Arkansas Traveler*—"an amusing bit of homespun, much in the manner of the old Will Rogers films"—and its strapping country star. "Mr. Burns does rather well, too, in spite of his vaudeville-wise wait for the laugh," Nugent surmised, "and with a bit of practice, he may become a first-rate character man, possibly the one to restore rural America to the fond place it had when Mr. Rogers was being its poet."[80]

It is the latter film that best represents the romantic, even sentimen-tal, side of the Arkansaw image. In *The Arkansas Traveler* Burns plays a name-less "hobo ex machina" who arrives in a small town and within a matter of days saves the struggling newspaper, starts a radio station, plays match-maker between two attractive youngsters from rival families, and brings the town's most dastardly citizen to justice. If not great theater, it was nonetheless "pleasant homespun comedy" devoid of the baser stereotyp-ing found in most hillbilly stage presentations and many big-screen come-dies. Arkansas's official reaction to *The Arkansas Traveler* suggested no sore feelings. The film's world premiere in Little Rock attracted a standing-room-only crowd of eleven hundred to the Pulaski Theater on 6 October 1938, even without the picture's star in attendance. In declaring "Arkansas Traveler Day," Little Rock's mayor lauded Burns as "one of [Arkansas's] most outstanding native sons" and his movie as "a project that will bring credit and favorable comment to the state." The *Arkansas Gazette* praised the movie as "one of the few, and perhaps the first, which casts no ridicule on Burns' home state."[81]

But in true Arkansaw fashion, Burns's films reflected a wider range of imagery. In *Radio City Revels* (1938), he plays an inept Arkansas hillbilly who tramps to New York City to pursue a songwriting career but whose musical muse comes to visit only in his dreams. And Burns would end his movie career with the unfortunate *Comin' Round the Mountain,* a story of a hillbilly musician who returns home to Monotony, Tennessee, after strik-ing out in the big city. Carrying the tagline "Hillbilly Howler of the Year," it was Burns's most exploitative film. Likely still stinging from criticism for *Comin' Round the Mountain,* the "Arkansas Philosopher" surprised everyone when he refused to honor his contract for a proposed movie titled "Joan of Arkansas" due to its "disgusting" script that impugned Burns's fellow Arkansawyers. "All they know at the studio about Arkansas is what they see in the cartoons of a magazine that sells for 50 cents," Burns quipped.[82]

Burns's sudden shift to defender of his home state may have caught some people off guard, but only because his comedy was frequently viewed as more pandering to an urbane crowd than it actually was. But the fact that someone would take on Arkansas's detractors was nothing new by 1941. In the first half of the twentieth century, especially, the defenders of the Wonder State were just as vocal as the anti-Arkansas pundits and producers they challenged. As our survey has shown thus far, it would seem that the romantically positive, or at least innocuous, interpretations of Arkansas were as numerous as the more negative portrayals, and probably more so. Defensive Arkansans honed in on the negative imagery, however, and through their vociferous attacks—and the gleeful counterattacks these prompted—managed to saddle the state with a dual opprobrium as not only a hillbilly state, but a hillbilly state with no sense of humor.

THIRD INTERLUDE

Getting Defensive

Charles H. Brough loved Arkansas. He truly did. And he told anyone who would listen. He trotted out tables of statistics to laud Arkansas's farmers. He quoted from her poets and historians. He trumpeted the beauty of her hills and streams. He scanned the pages of *Who's Who* for the names of successful businessmen and military officers who divulged even the most tenuous link with the Wonder State. Few people ever embraced an American state with as much passion and purpose as Brough embraced Arkansas. Despite the fact that Arkansas was his adopted home state—or perhaps because of it—Brough also proudly assumed the mantle as the old Bear State's number-one defender.

If the state of Arkansas had dispatched a search party to track down an ideal defender, a leader whose qualifications and mindset flew in the face of everything a scoffing national public thought it knew about Arkansas, it would have brought back someone very much like Charles Hillman Brough. He was in almost every sense the antithesis of the nineteenth-century Arkansawyer. Born to well-to-do Yankee parents in Utah and raised by an uncle and aunt, idealistic carpetbagger educators in Mississippi, Brough was a precocious boy who graduated at the top of his Mississippi College class at the age of seventeen. By the time he turned twenty-six, Brough had earned a Ph.D. in economics, history, and jurisprudence from the Johns Hopkins University and a law degree from the University of Mississippi, sandwiching between these two academic forays a three-year stint as a college professor during which he published his dissertation and other studies and lectured extensively across the state of Mississippi. One year later, in 1903, a faculty position at the University of Arkansas brought Brough to the state that he would make his home for the next three decades.[1]

In the annals of Arkansas, Charles H. Brough is best remembered as the state's most progressive governor, an intellectual with the political skill to shepherd through a conservative and decidedly less intellectual statehouse a variety of reforms and progressive statutes and the bipartisan appeal to receive the endorsement of the Republicans in his reelection campaign of 1918. For our purposes, his activities after leaving the governor's mansion are even more important. During the first half of the 1920s, Brough toured the nation as both a chautauqua speaker and as the publicity agent for an organization attempting to boost economic development in Arkansas. In both roles the former governor became a "'walking advertisement for Arkansas.'"[2] As his adopted state's self-appointed defender, Brough took on Arkansas's detractors, challenging anyone who would dispute his glowing account of the Wonder State. He met the H. L. Menckens of the world with wagging finger and self-righteous indignation and, in so doing, highlighted a crucial element in the evolution and perpetuation of the Arkansaw image. Brough was only the most prominent in a long line of Arkansas defenders, a group whose earnest and sometimes shrill attacks on the state's ridiculers served, ironically, to highlight the more negative aspects of the Arkansaw image over the positive ones and to underscore the inferiority complex of a self-conscious and defensive element of Arkansas's better sort.

Brough in no way resembled the Arkansawyer of legend. He may not have been a typical Arkansawyer, but his substantial education and even his status as an Arkansan-by-choice made Brough a good candidate for Arkansas's defense. Only rarely did the Arkansawyers who were the targets of derision and condescension—the rural and small-town folk who, many (including Arkansans) thought, lived lives circumscribed by backwardness, illiteracy, and spiritual barrenness—challenge the Arkansaw image in a

Charles H. Brough. Courtesy of Old State House Museum, Little Rock, Arkansas.

public forum. This is not surprising. These were the very people whose lack of education and low socioeconomic standing rendered them the least likely to have access to the means of public protest, even when they were aware of the negative stereotypes that dogged their state. But protesting negative stereotypes was far down the list of priorities for the vast majority of Arkansawyers; the business of surviving and providing for one's family relegated such a self-conscious exercise as image cultivation and defense to the category of luxury, and few people in Arkansas could afford such a luxury. Furthermore, Arkansawyers' comparative isolation resulted in fewer contacts with outsiders and with the accounts of Arkansas life and Arkansawyers sometimes generated by these outsiders. Consequently, the Arkansaw image was nothing more than an afterthought for most of the people it supposedly represented.

This is not to suggest that the common people of Arkansas possessed no understanding of the Arkansaw image, however. To the contrary, most Arkansawyers recognized more thoroughly than did their social and economic betters the multifaceted nature of the image and the ease with which one could co-opt that image. The "Arkansas Traveler" dialogue and songs of Arkansas, both humorous and romantic, were ensconced in the folk tradition by the time of Brough's boosterism. One of Brough's predecessors in the governor's house, Jeff Davis, had fashioned the state's most successful political career to date by casting himself as a champion of the kind of fellow the high-collared roosters of Little Rock found unsavory. Though the product of a thoroughly middle-class raising himself and college educated to boot, Davis gladly co-opted the Arkansaw image. "If you red-necks or hill-billies ever come to Little Rock," the governor was reported to have drawled, "be sure and come to see me—come to my house. . . . If I am not at home tell my wife who you are; tell her you are my friend and that you belong to the sun-burned sons of toil."[3] Unlike his adversaries in Little Rock, Davis understood that his supporters had a different take on the Arkansaw image. These Arkansawyers, who like most powerless people did not shy away from laughing at their own shortcomings, both real and perceived, focused on the winking wiliness of the fiddling squatter, the cunning independence of the moonshiner, and the frontier ingenuity of the backwoodsman.

The self-deprecation that has so long infused the humor of the powerless and penniless was in short supply among the defenders of Arkansas. As members of, and more likely spokespersons for, the socioeconomic establishment, the defenders came to the realization that the Arkansaw image was costing the state and its business leaders money. This was no laughing matter. The hardscrabble farmer in the Ozarks or the Ouachitas or the piney woods may not have appreciated the image's deleterious economic impact, however one might go about measuring it, but the chambers of commerce and the civic clubs and the champions of industry and the pushers of "progress" most certainly did.

Given this, it's not surprising that the first official defense of Arkansas emerged during Reconstruction, an era marked by an aggressive infusion of industrial capitalism and a conscious and progressive attempt to distance the state from its Bear State past. In 1872 and 1873, Arkansas's Reconstruction Republican government sponsored the publication of two books designed to attract industry and immigrants to the state. Typical of Reconstruction-era booster pieces, the books, both written by Arkansas newcomer and businessman James P. Henry, painted a rosy portrait of "the most inviting portion of the American continent." But, mindful of his new state's reputation around the country, Henry had to temper his exaggerated boosterism with assurances of the dawning of a new day in Arkansas. Although he admitted that "the vast interior country, between the navigable rivers . . . in times past, furnished a safe retreat for those who had reason to fear the law," Henry promised potential investors and settlers that "this state of things has passed away. Ruffianism has seen its day here."[4]

As we have seen, Arkansas's reputation for violence and lawlessness was well established before the Civil War, and boosters such as Henry had their work cut out for them if they were to convince readers that the Bear State was both civilized and safe. "It should be borne in mind," wrote Henry, "that the emigrant to Arkansas does not take up his home in a wilderness, but in a country possessed of towns and cities, schools, churches, railroads and lines of water transportation." Furthermore, "the inhabitants comprise people from all the States, and are as moral and law-abiding as anywhere." Lest anyone doubt the veracity of the statements of a man paid to brag on the state, Henry quoted a clergyman to the same effect: "'I have traveled over a large portion of the State, and have seen no approach to lawlessness in the inhabitants, and in no portion of the land is there a better observance of the laws on the part of the people.'" But even amid talk of "smiling landscapes of water, timber, and varied scenery," the image occasionally peeked out from behind the mountain of booster speak. "This is a good country for a lazy man," warned Henry, "but we have quite enough of that class already. We want immigrants that will go to work with an earnestness to accomplish something for themselves."[5]

In spite of a little laziness and some past ruffianism, James P. Henry was convinced that "Arkansas is destined to become one of the greatest states in the Union in population, production and wealth." Henry and his Republican cohorts would not maintain power long enough to ensure Arkansas's rise to greatness, but their combination of boosterism, historical revisionism, and selective reporting lived on in the rhetoric and capitalist-minded promotions of the peddlers of the New South philosophy. Two years after Democrats and Conservatives "redeemed" Arkansas from Republican rule, Little Rock realtor T. B. Mills & Company sponsored an excursion of dozens of midwestern newspaper editors by rail through "the least known, and the most systematically misrepresented State, of the entire Union" and then published a detailed account of the skillfully chaperoned journey of these "new Arkansas travelers," along with the many praises they sent north to be published in their papers. Like Henry, the Mills Company admitted that early "Arkansas *was* a wilderness, farther removed, to all practical intents, from the centers of civilization, than Alaska now is" and that "from that day to this it has been the fashion [among reporters] to locate every apocryphal back-woods story in Arkansas, and to fill up the foot of a column with a scurvy jest at her expense." But the newspapermen from Kokomo, Peoria, Elyria, and Topeka would find a verdant land bursting with fruits, fibers, timber, and minerals, a "vast area . . . [that] affords such variety of products as California alone can equal." Peopled by "brave men of necessity . . . [who] have proved as orderly and law-abiding a community as honors the soil of any sister commonwealth," Arkansas and its leaders were blessed with "an energy and progressive spirit which encourages and protects that immigration which alone is needed in order to raise her to the full measure of her deserved prosperity."[6]

Though he might not have shared Henry's carpetbagger condescension or the Mills Company's desire to put on a good face for skeptical midwesterners, George W. Donaghey maintained a New South optimism two generations later: "Among these Southern States I am firmly convinced that Arkansas will lead the rest, both in varied resources and productivity." Arkansas's first Progressive governor, Donaghey was, before Brough, her most outspoken champion. In a 1910 article in *Collier's* magazine, "Arkansas: The Only State That Produces Diamonds," Donaghey laid out the booster blueprint that Brough would later perfect: mention a couple of unique facts about the state, mix in some statistics that would seem to refute Arkansas's negative image, and cap it off with a hyperbolic prediction, such as "Arkansas will be the center of the manufacturing States of the South."[7]

Unlike Brough, Donaghey had been raised in Arkansas and could claim only the slimmest exposure to higher education. But he shared his fellow progressive's disdain for those who would impugn the name of Arkansas. Donaghey was a wealthy businessman who had seen a good deal of the country, and, like many successful Arkansans, he chafed at the state's portrayal in the national media. As governor he began keeping a file of "every article from the New York papers that contained cause for wounding the pride of every Arkansan who read it." So incensed was he over the *New York Times*'s treatment of Theodore Roosevelt's visit to Hot

George W. Donaghey with Theodore Roosevelt, 1910. George Washington Donaghey Papers (MS D714m), loc. 233, box 1, folder 2, number 42. Special Collections, University of Arkansas Libraries, Fayetteville.

Springs in 1910, in which the *Times* reporter devoted considerable energy
to describing the local dignitaries who shed their shoes and socks upon the
former president's departure, that Donaghey reprinted the piece in his
autobiography. "Such articles did Arkansas incalculable harm," lamented
Donaghey, but, as have many Arkansans over the years, the governor
found cause for action in the perceived slight, admitting that the *New York
Times* article and pieces like it served as "'inspiration for the school legislation'" that he sponsored during his four years in office.[8]

Compared with Brough, however, Donaghey was only dabbling in
defensiveness and boosterism. While still in the governor's mansion,
Brough contributed a lengthy article on the state to the journal of a traveling salesmen's fraternal society; it would offer a hint of things to come
in his post-gubernatorial career. Part history and part boosterish propaganda, the article chronicled recent road building and other modernization efforts in Arkansas, with ruminations on bauxite, peaches, diamonds,
and anything else that Arkansas could claim in greater supply than other
states. "Arkansas, once cartooned . . . , has come into her own," promised
Brough. "Her face is toward the rising sun; her shibboleth is progress; and
she is pressing forward toward the goal of the prize of the high calling of
her manifest destiny as a great American commonwealth." Upon leaving
the governor's mansion in 1921, Brough took his boosterism on the road.
Perhaps it was the ex-governor on one of his journeys who inspired a
stanza of Robert Frost's poem, "New Hampshire": "I met a traveler from
Arkansas / Who boasted of his state as beautiful / For diamonds and apples."
Not one to suffer an eager booster aboard a train—it being "evening in the
Pullman"—Frost's narrator observes, hopefully, "I see the porter's made
your bed."[9]

Once on the lecturer's circuit Brough regaled, and likely bored, audiences around the nation with pages of statistics touting everything from
rice acreage to college- and university-enrollment in Arkansas, with lists of
Arkansans who made good (which they almost always did somewhere far
away from the Wonder State), and with musings on the merits of his state's
usually obscure writers and historians. In a 1929 radio address, and subsequent *Arkansas Democrat* composition, Brough escorted listeners and readers on a tour of the state, praising the sights, sounds, and resources of each
region, from Little Rock, the "City of Roses," to Lake Chicot, the "Lake
Lucerne of Arkansas." So enraptured was Brough with his own state that
he perhaps failed to notice granting the sobriquet "Athens of Arkansas" to
both Fayetteville and Arkadelphia.[10]

Like his predecessors in the Arkansas defense department, Brough frequently tried to turn the tables on what he felt to be popular misconcep-
tions about Arkansas and its regions. "Hitherto characterized as a rendevous

[*sic*] of illiteracy, a hiding place for desperate criminals, and an asylum for the indigent of society," he informed an audience of writers in Missouri, "the Ozarks, as a matter of fact, constitute a veritable paradise of educational achievement and literary genius of the highest order." The ex-governor, whose audiences were generally made up of Protestants with long lineages in the United States, also tapped into the age's xenophobic romanticism as a way to herald his state's sturdy citizens—at least those of a certain hue and heritage. "My commonwealth . . . can boast of the finest strain of Anglo-Saxon blood on the North American continent," he assured an audience of teachers in Memphis.[11]

Although it is unclear if he followed Donaghey's example in studiously maintaining a file of anti-Arkansiana churned out by eastern newspapers and magazines, it is apparent that Brough was quick to chastise those who, he felt, unjustly criticized Arkansas and her citizens. In 1930 he wrote to the editor of *Collier's Weekly* to protest an article in which the late governor and senator James P. Clarke had been portrayed as an "illiterate buffoon." "Arkansas has been cartooned and caricatured long enough," claimed Brough. "Our statesmen and citizens are as a rule cultured and refined, and proverbially patriotic."[12]

The former governor's most notable defense of Arkansas came a year later, however, and in reaction to the provocative statements of the era's best-known Arkansas-basher. H. L. Mencken's 1931 column in the Baltimore *Evening Sun* (chronicled in the previous chapter) inspired an impassioned rebuttal from the watchdog of the Wonder State. By the time their learned tête-à-tête was finished, each man had contributed three columns to the paper. In rare and florid form, Brough, operating on mere reflex after years of boosterism, attempted in his initial letter to buttress Arkansas's claims to respectability by referring to her as the "twin sister of Michigan in the galaxy of American States" and by extolling the great businessmen and literary figures produced by Arkansas. Calling the Michigan comparison a "lamentable dialectical blunder," Mencken shot back by marshaling his own mountain of statistical evidence to reveal the gulf between the two states, with Michigan emerging the clear victor. As to Brough's catalog of his state's notables, Mencken dismissed it as "too dreadful to be treated seriously." In spite of Mencken's patronizing praise for his adversary— where Arkansas was concerned, he felt that Brough was, next to Senator Joseph T. Robinson, "the best of the whole boiling"—the ex-governor shot back. Dismissing Mencken's "personal flattery of my own limited abilities," Brough continued to challenge the "grave injustices that . . . you have done the commonwealth which has so signally honored me" and expressed regret "that such a brilliant, trenchant pen as yours should be employed in the ignoble task of grossly magligning [*sic*] one of the suffering commonwealths of the American Union."[13]

Had Brough remained true to the final thought of his second letter—"So far as I am concerned, however, this will close the chapter"—he may have walked away from his war with Mencken with dignity and something akin to a moral victory. Mencken's attacks on Arkansas and the rural South in the early 1930s were little more than calculated attempts to boost a flagging readership and to recapture the cultural relevance he had left behind in the 1920s. The American intelligentsia was drifting toward an appreciation for, if not outright love affair with, the downtrodden southern masses in the Depression era, and criticisms like Mencken's seemed unnecessarily mean-spirited and out of step. But Brough, like most defenders of Arkansas, never mastered the graceful exit; and Mencken was counting on it. To Mencken's charge that "Dr. Brough give over his vain talk of Masonic poet laureates, high-salaried auditors and other such wonders of the Arkansas sideshow and apply his great learning to the relief of his suffering State," Brough replied with yet another list of facts and figures, a weak and inaccurate description of the transformation of the cotton plantation system into truck farms, and a defense of the Mencken-despised Bible Belt anchored by an oddly chosen quote from that noted scholar and religious figure President Andrew Jackson. Once again sincerity and defensiveness had caused a well-intentioned person to wonder too far into the web of Mencken's opportunism and disdainfulness.[14]

The Case against the Case for Arkansas

A decade earlier, though, Mencken had been at the top of his game. In the previous chapter we read his dismissal of "trackless and unexplored" Arkansas tucked inside an antisouthern diatribe entitled "The South Begins to Mutter." Although the totality of the Baltimore iconoclast's treatment of lowly Arkansas wouldn't have constituted a solid paragraph, the furor generated by "The South Begins to Mutter" would render Brough's later sparring with Mencken a trivial affair by comparison. Rarely has a state's establishmentarians lashed out so vehemently and uniformly in reaction to such a peripheral insult. In doing so, the Mencken bashers laid claim to exhibit A in the resolution that informs this little interlude: that the defenders of Arkansas have proven themselves more irritating than the detractors.

No sooner had Mencken lambasted the "miasmatic jungles" of Arkansas than he came under fire from angry Arkansas writers, editors, and civic leaders. Little Rock's *Arkansas Democrat* and the *Little Rock Daily News* led the print media charge, the latter calling "Menneken" a "poor, ignorant, misguided fool" and an "infernal and ignorant mountebank!" In his study of Mencken and the South, Fred C. Hobson Jr. observes that after the publication of his first and best-remembered antisouthern essay, "The Sahara of the Bozart," Mencken "assumed the allegorical role of Satan." But the word Arkansas was nowhere to be found in Mencken's Bozart—more from the state's invisibility and inconsequentiality than from its ineptitude—and it was his "The South Begins to Mutter" that fitted him with horns and hooves in the Wonder State. The editor of the *Little Rock Daily News* puzzled over the blather of Arkansas's new worst enemy. "Why this tirade on the South, and particularly on Arkansas, we do not know; why he picked out this state to slander we cannot conceive." But there was no doubt that Mencken's denunciations had been misinformed. "Upon this soil there have lived and moved more men of superior intellect than have trod the earth since Cataline conspired and Caesar fought; more men of character and destiny than have been in this world since Moses trod with weary feet the dreary way from Egypt to Canaan."[15]

No publication devoted more print to denunciations of "Herr Mencken" and subsequent impassioned defenses of Arkansas than did *The Arkansas Writer*, a young literary magazine emanating from Little Rock. Editor Clio Harper, Little Rock politician and businessman-turned-poet, denounced Mencken as "an insufferable excrescence on the body of American litera-ture. . . . an intellectual anarchist, a literary Bolshevik." "It is my purpose to bring these slanders to the attention of every prominent newspaper and civic organization through the South," announced Harper. And harangues like the following would have had the desired effect if not for the magazine's limited readership. "It is difficult to do justice to his pestiferous slanders in the brief space of a short review, and the full offensiveness of his asinine effluvia can be comprehended only by reading all of the seven pages; . . . Some poor, weak champions may be overcome by his Mephistophelian lance, but the war is on, and, other champions will arise who will never leave the field until the Black Knight of Slander is unhorsed!" It is difficult to do justice to Harper's condemnation in such a brief account as well. Suffice it to say that Mencken's incendiary comments lit a fire under Arkansas's boosters and literati, a flame that continued to burn in the pages of *The Arkansas Writer* for several more months. Subsequent issues carried letters from readers endorsing Harper's skewering of Mencken, boosterish features such as "Arkansans Who Have Made Good" and "Telling the North About the Successful Writers of Arkansas," and a poem called "The Philosophy of an Arkansas Farmer," a lengthy ode to Clio Harper and two other defenders of Arkansas, Charles H. Brough and Arkansas Advance-ment Association president Virgil C. Pettie:

> An' that is why he changed his mind, an' said he'd been a thinkin'
> The best thing fer our State to do—jes' send fer this man Menkin,
> An show him round about the State, and let the booger see

This land o' milk an' honey, where folks from care are free;
If we can get him down here—if it's only fer a day,
Purty soon he'll be a-lookin' fer a place to live an' stay.[16]

Which brings us to exhibit B and smoking-gun candidates Virgil C. Pettie and the Arkansas Advancement Association. Organized about the time of the publication of Mencken's "The South Begins to Mutter," the AAA's brand of over-the-top, self-affirming boosterism was enough to transform even the most glad-handing Rotarian into a cynical Sinclair Lewis. Pettie and his Arkansas Advancement Association pursued several avenues in their attempt to defend Arkansas from Mencken and like-minded modernists. The AAA put out a call for essays and songs that "tell Arkansas' wonderful story to the world." *The Arkansas Writer* must have agreed with the AAA's pronouncement that "no subject calls for greater effort than the uplift of Arkansas. . . . In it every Arkansas writer must see a call and almost a divine inspiration." Not content to simply return volley, the AAA was well aware of the old dictum that the best defense is a good offense. In that vein the organization made plans to persuade every Arkansan venturing beyond the state's borders to wear a button stating, "I am Proud of Arkansas," and to arm these Arkansas travelers with cards listing "twenty or more reasons why Arkansas is the greatest state." To make sure that some Arkansans did indeed make it beyond the borders, the AAA sent a special train bearing Arkansas products, speakers, and even beauty queens on a tour through the North. And in case this wasn't irritating enough, the AAA promised "to place on every visitor and traveling salesman possible, a button, 'I Have Been to Arkansas and I Like It.'" Among the AAA's goals:

To prepare a series of catechisms which will be taught in the public schools, and read by all people of the state.
To have an Arkansas Day in New York during the winter.
To combat outside agencies which seek to discountenance Arkansas enterprises, by meeting their propaganda at its source.
To influence the popular song writers to occasionally insert the word Arkansas in their effusions.[17]

Such boosterism run amok must have looked to Mencken like a thigh-high, seventy-five-mile-an-hour gopher ball. It was too easy, apparently, for Mencken passed it up—perhaps the best evidence that Arkansas remained an afterthought. But Mencken certainly couldn't ignore the AAA's more ambitious goal of having him kicked out of the country. Mistaking the Baltimore-born writer for a "former subject of the German kaiser," Pettie believed "that Mencken has made himself sufficiently obnoxious to a majority of American people to warrant deportation" and asked the Arkansas delegation in Congress to introduce legislation to that effect. Although Mencken would undoubtedly have cherished the publicity generated by such an undertaking, cooler heads prevailed and anti-Mencken hysteria eventually subsided. Cooler heads inside Arkansas had already smelled a rat. The *Arkansas Gazette* remained conspicuously silent on the matter of Mencken, while the editor of the *Arkansas Democrat* got "the feeling that perhaps we have been paying too much attention to Mr. Mencken, and in so doing, 'playing his game' for him in just the way that he desires." He urged his readers and his fellow media members in Arkansas to meet Mencken with "the silence which he hates above all things else."[18] Fine advice, but hard to follow—as Governor Brough would later prove.

As literature Bernie Babcock's *The Man Who Lied on Arkansas and What It Got Him* leaves a lot to be desired. As a historical document, though, it makes for a strong Exhibit C in the case against Arkansas's defenders. Like Brough, Julia Burnelle Smade Babcock was of hearty midwestern stock and came to be one of the great promoters of all things Arkansas. Long before Brough sang Arkansas's praises on the chautauqua circuit and prior to the creation of *The Arkansas Writer,* Babcock's *Sketch Book* published the work of the state's poets and photographers, and her effort to found Little Rock's Museum of Natural History and Antiquities in the 1920s was motivated in part by a desire to "'belie the state's reputation as a cultural backwater.'" But her most overt defense of the state she had called home since her Ohio family moved south in her childhood was *The Man Who Lied on Arkansas and What It Got Him,* which she published in 1909 in response to the spate of joke books and comic novels that greeted the new century. With all the subtlety of a thirteen-pound maul, Babcock's story relates the tale of the "Liar Man" who "took up with Arkansas people, received every courtesy at their hand, and for their kindness made them appear ridiculous." Though the very personal nature of the booklet suggests that Babcock—fictionalized as "the Girl" in the story—was personally charmed and snookered by Charles Hibler or some other flim-flam, Arkansas defiler, the Liar Man ultimately becomes a composite of all those who, in the author's estimation, soiled the good name of Arkansas, from Sandy Faulkner and Thomas Bangs Thorpe to Opie Read and Thomas W. Jackson. To counteract the image of Arkansas set forth in the Liar Man's "Podunk in Arkansas," Babcock locates the Girl in a "magnificent Colonial style" home in Little Rock, where a lavishly furnished "Arkansas Room" boasted shelves of books by Arkansas writers and where the Girl performed for the Liar Man an elegant song by an Arkansas composer.[19]

The impassioned defenses set forth by Babcock, Harper, Pettie, and others illustrate the sincere affection many Arkansans felt for their state, as well

Bernie Babcock.
Courtesy of Marcia
Camp.

as the collective inferiority complex that motivated these defenses. For every H. L. Mencken and C. L. Edson there was a writer or promoter, or two, willing to find progress and hope in the Wonder State. Alexander Johnson discovered in Arkansas a "hearty, wholesome, intelligent, warm-hearted people" overseeing progressive farms and blessed with virgin timber and mineral resources. Sherman Rogers, recruited by the Arkansas Bankers' Association to counteract the negative press the state received due to its controversial and depreciating road bonds in the early 1920s, not surprisingly praised Arkansas as a land of bountiful natural resources and defended her fiscal integrity in an article entitled simply "A Defense of Arkansas." According to Lawrence F. Abbott, "The people of Arkansas certainly have faith in their state; they are progressive; they are looking to the future." Kansas City newspaperman W. G. Clugston was "willing to stand up in any crowd and defend" Arkansas, whose people "display less religious intolerance, less hate-hokum, than the inhabitants of any other state west of the Mississippi." And a generation later, if *National Geographic* was to be believed, Arkansas was on the doorstep of modernization and transformation. "But louder than hounds or fiddles are the challenging voices of this born-again Arkansas as it shouts to make itself heard above the roar of new paper mills and aluminum factories."[20]

The final quote captured the optimism that pervaded Arkansas boosterism after World War II. As had been the case since Reconstruction, however, much of this boosterish braggadocio continued to come couched in familiarly defensive rhetoric. Rivaling the Arkansas Advancement Association as the smoking gun of our little inquest is exhibit D—Avantus Green's *With This We Challenge,* a cheap booklet published near the end of World War II that combined the usual manipulative statistical defense of Arkansas with a fifth-grader's knack for insult deflection. Green's master plan seems to have been to elevate Arkansas by taking pot shots at every other state in the union. The result, one fears in retrospect, was not quite what Green and other defenders of the state were shooting for. Breathless trumpeting of the annual values of various Arkansas industries was accompanied by lusty celebrations of such products as watermelons, rice, cotton, ducks, oil, timber, diamonds, and strawberries, "the most luscious morsel of delectable juicy soul-food in the cornucopia of the gods!"[21]

But Green was torn between two loves—talking up Arkansas and denigrating everything and everybody not from Arkansas. He criticized current celebrities such as Bob Burns and Cole Porter for their contributions to the Arkansaw image and condemned even more egregious offenders such as Thomas W. Jackson. Most curious were his frequent reactions to the state's hillbilly image, which he attempted to refute not by denying the existence of hillbillies but by locating them in "Tennessee, Kentucky, Essex County (N.Y.) and Southern Missouri," or just about anywhere besides Arkansas. "Everything was all right in Arkansas until in the middle of the 19th Century some hillbillies from Tennessee and Kentucky passed through on their way to discover and settle California and Oregon. They were seen crossing the state and were mistaken (by a couple of Neanderthal men from Boston) for natives." Such statements represented the pinnacle of wit in *With This We Challenge,* and Green's slightly revised 1966 edition maintained the original's lofty discourse. Referring to the Arkansas State Symphony Orchestra as "the greatest . . . musical organization in the world, although some diehards of Boston and Cincinnati may not even accept that fact just yet," Green expanded the territory of the hillbilly to include "Clinton county, New York, Orange county, Vermont, Litchfield county, Connecticut, northern Pennsylvania, eastern California, and the state of West Virginia," and this time blamed Arkansas's image not on Kentuckians and Tennesseans but on "a group of Yale men from the Green Mountains [who] rode across our State on mule back."[22]

Exhibit E—Karr Shannon's *On a Fast Train Through Arkansas*—gets bonus points for being both comprehensible and comprehensive in its chronicling of more than half a century of Arkansaw imagery, but its defensive/boosterish attitude and penchant for hyperbole differ little from the spirit of *With This We Challenge*. Shannon was almost unique among the defenders of Arkansas, for unlike Brough, Babcock, Harper, and most others he was a product of the rural hill country that had come to dominate the Arkansaw image in the twentieth century. Born and raised on an Izard County farm, Shannon, a self-proclaimed hillbilly, worked as a teacher and small-town newspaper editor before becoming a columnist for the *Arkansas Democrat* in 1944. Although he took up the cause of crusading for his native state once he reached the capital city—not a great leap from the localized boosterism practiced by every small-town newspaperman of the era—his background in the hardscrabble Ozarks differentiated his brand of defense. Whereas the Arkansas literati and chamber of commerce crowds preferred to deny the existence of an underclass of caricature-ready rustics, or even to blame them for the negative Arkansaw image in tones as condescending as those of the Arkansas bashers, Shannon, like the romantics who populate these pages, reveled in the anachronism and unpretentiousness of his former neighbors in the Arkansas backcountry, an appreciation reflected in his collection of folklore and rural humor published as *Hillbilly Philosophy* in 1932.[23]

Shannon took his place in the pantheon of Arkansas's self-appointed defenders with his 1948 book, *On a Fast Train Through Arkansas*. Subtitled "A Rebuke to Thomas Jackson's *On a Slow Train*," Shannon's book featured a forward by post–World War II Arkansas's most active economic booster, C. Hamilton Moses, president of the Arkansas Economic Council / State Chamber of Commerce. "You can't estimate the great damage to Arkansas caused by the book *On a Slow Train Through Arkansaw*. . . . [I]t will take years to live over the bad effects of this book." If Arkansas still could not shake the *Slow Train* legacy forty-five years after the joke book's first appearance, Shannon's belated rebuttal wasn't likely to banish the Arkansaw image, especially with its avowed purpose of praising Arkansas's modern rail system even as it rode into irrelevance in the wake of the automobile age. Shannon also found the *Slow Train* image a tough one to shake, lamenting that "thousands up East . . . actually believe that Arkansas today is just as Jackson portrayed it." And like Brough and others who came before him, Shannon found plenty of offenders on which to place blame, from Mark Twain and Opie Read to the Weaver Brothers and Elviry, who played the "natives of Arkansas as ignorant, hook-wormy and hayseedy." For most defenders of Arkansas, the defensiveness was tinged with deflection, as if to say: "The Arkansawyers you're speaking of don't represent the *real* Arkansas; they aren't us." But for Karr Shannon, the derisive magazine articles and media caricatures hit close to home, quite literally.[24]

Exhibit F reflects what might best be termed the "Hillbillies Ain't Us" defense. Though nothing in the past couple of generations has approached the ridiculousness of *With This We Challenge,* Arkansans' knee-jerk defensiveness hasn't disappeared. Especially hard to swallow for Rotarians and the state's self-appointed arbiters of high culture was the nation's fascination with mountain music and culture in the wake of the 1960s' folk revival. Perhaps even more galling has been the state's increasing willingness—more often than not for financial reasons—to endorse and propagate the less savory images accompanying the spotlight on hillbilly Arkansas. In his popular *Arkansas Gazette* column "Our Town," Richard Allin questioned the State Parks, Recreation and Travel Commission's decision to provide more than half the funds needed to send ballad singers and Ozark musicians to appear on stage at the Smithsonian's National Folk Festival in the summer of 1970. He echoed the concerns of more than a few Arkansans when he asked "why federal funds earmarked for the enrichment of our cultural life at home should be diverted to extend Arkansas's stereotyped backwoods character before the eyes of the nation." Allin quoted one anonymous grumbler who complained that "'Arkansas has more symphony orchestras, theater groups, chamber orchestras, and choral groups than it has sorghum mills. And who in hell admits to eating chitlins?'"[25]

The state's ambivalent relationship with a backwoods image that held cash-cow potential was at no time better evident than in January 1976. Despite the inclusion of interviews with Senator Dale Bumpers and two University of Arkansas scientists and segments on desegregation at Central High and Vietnamese refugees at Fort Chaffee, the *Today Show*'s bicentennial salute to Arkansas featured just enough of Jimmy Driftwood and banjo players at the Ozark Folk Center State Park to make chamber of commerce presidents around the state squirm in discomfort. So incensed with the morning show's "slanted, biased, and sarcastic techniques to depict Arkansas in a degrading, hillbilly image" was state representative Ode Maddox, a Montgomery County country boy pulling a Karr Shannon by overzealously defending the interests of the cultural and economic elite, that he introduced a house resolution censuring NBC for its "deliberate misrepresentation of Arkansas." Maddox's resolution, a Charles H. Brough chautauqua speech folded into house-bill form, ticked off a familiar list of institutions and developments ignored by the *Today Show,* from the Arkansas Symphony Orchestra to the state's progress in manufacturing, from the magnificent architecture of the state capitol to Little Rock's Arts Center. In a case of strange coincidence, the very morning that the *Today Show* blasphemed the Land of Opportunity with its puzzling concentration on the nationally unique Ozark Folk Center to the exclusion of paeans to the intriguing Mar-Bax shirt factory and an orchestra almost on par with the

Toledo Symphony, the Little Rock Chamber of Commerce held a press conference to introduce two representatives from the New York public relations firm of Dudley-Anderson-Yutzy (DAY). Taking a page out of Atlanta's playbook for beating the Jim Crow / Civil Rights Movement negativity rap a decade earlier, "fantastic," "tremendous," "incredible," "superb," "marvelous" Little Rock had decided to go on the offensive against the city's "admittedly poor reputation." If the rest of the state was beyond salvation, at least the City of Roses might be able to save herself. "You've got a great story to tell," intoned one of the DAY visitors, "and we're going to try to tell it." When the state house of representatives later that day passed Maddox's resolution overwhelmingly, somewhere Charles H. Brough smiled —and Mencken grinned like the Cheshire cat.[26]

Arkansans will likely never completely abandon their fortresses of defensiveness, but even by the time that Shannon and Green were manning the turrets, the sense of urgency was in decline. The Arkansaw image, maintaining its dual nature after all these years, would live on in manifestations both familiar and unexpected, but the hillbilly craze that so thoroughly kept the image before the public's eye faded rapidly, leaving little trace by the post–World War II years. The Arkansaw image would eventually come roaring back. The state's inferiority complex would not have to come roaring back, for it never went away.

✧ CHAPTER FOUR ✧

All Roads Lead to Bubba

George Fisher caricatured dozens of prominent figures during his long career as a political cartoonist, and I would bet that almost none of his subjects offered the cartoonish possibilities of Orval Eugene Faubus. What a face! That beak of a nose that seemed to originate mid-forehead and flowed ski-slope style on and on, too great a distance for anatomical discreteness. That chin that jutted out in search of sunshine as if to escape the shadow of the powerful proboscis. Those droopy eyes that might pull double duty as sleepy or beady, depending on one's estimation of the thoughts behind them. Those satellite-dish ears that framed the kind of face that rarely finds its way to a governor's mansion. Faubus looked as if someone had walloped him flush in the face with a skillet and the force of the smack had found its outlet in his ears. And these were just his physical characteristics. Faubus's long career in Arkansas politics and his 1957 starring turn as the embodiment of massive resistance to school desegregation provided the social and psychological underpinnings essential for ideal caricaturehood.

It wasn't inevitable that the mare of the benighted South would find herself in a chute with the Arkansaw hillbilly jackass after World War II. But it happened, and the offspring was a mule named Orval. Two of the major postwar contributors to the Arkansaw image found Orval Faubus. Americans know about his role in the crisis at Little Rock's Central High; his tenure with the Dogpatch, U.S.A. theme park is more obscure. The first introduced Arkansas to the world in a way to which Arkansans were not accustomed, and in so doing threatened to forever alter the Arkansaw image. In September 1957, Arkansas paraded before the world's eyes clothed in the raiment of the racist, reactionary South, the South of marble Confederate generals and marbled plantation bosses. South Carolina or Alabama or Mississippi generally led the charge on this field. John C. Calhoun, Jefferson Davis, and William Alexander Percy hadn't given a rat's ass about Arkansas, yet here she was for all the world to see, standard-bearer of southern white defiance—with Arkansas's one genuine hillbilly governor front and center.

Little Rock's and Arkansas's and Faubus's sudden infamy in cold war America created a storm that loosed the Arkansaw image from its familiar moorings in hillbilly harbor. For a time it looked as if Arkansas might take her place alongside her sister states in the benighted and bigoted South and watch her generations-old backwoods Arkansaw image eclipsed by a more sinister image, one in which the antiprogressive spirit emanated not from dogged independence and hillbilly cussedness but from hatred and cultural rot. But, as Faubus proved, the hillbilly is nothing if not persistent. A series of developments in the 1960s and 1970s—the folk music craze, the return of the ambivalent Arkansaw image in popular entertainment, and even Dogpatch, U.S.A.—reminded people that Arkansas, though not as naive and innocent as it once had been, remained at heart a place where the good old boys were still basically good, where moonlight was for moonshiners, not magnolias, and where one could find refuge from a life that civilization had gotten the best of.

Arkansaw Intermission

The heyday of the hillbilly, and of Arkansaw's time on center stage, had passed by the end of World War II. The nation's intense fascination with the hillbilly had drawn to an end some time between Midway and Iwo Jima. It was almost as if the atomic age was incompatible with the rube. The United States emerged from the war the world's greatest power, an outward-looking nation that would soon plunge headlong into the half-century standoff with the Soviet Union we know as the Cold War. Gone was the isolationism long bred by practicality as much as by idealism. Gone as well was the intense national self-scrutiny of the Depression era, that national pastime in which no ethnic group, religious sect, or regional anomaly escaped ridicule and/or praise. As the United States began to identify itself by contrast and comparison with the rest of the world, Americans' fascination with regional and ethnic stereotypes and the entertainment based on those stereotypes faded into the background. As modern developments in the fields of communication, transportation, and entertainment hastened the march toward cultural and economic homogeneity, the real regional and ethnic differences that bolstered the old stereotypes became less pronounced and in some cases altogether insignificant. This is not to suggest that cultural and regional stereotyping for purposes of entertainment or anything else came to an end in the post–World War II years. Americans' fascination with ethnic, cultural, and regional imagery would survive in one form or another into the twenty-first century, but it would never again enjoy the spot on center stage that it had occupied in an earlier era.

The Arkansaw image, specifically, was nowhere near as prevalent after the war as before it. But that didn't mean that the Arkansaw image or the hillbilly disappeared from the American scene. The old standbys from the Depression decade—*Lil' Abner,* Bob Burns, *Lum and Abner,* Judy Canova— would survive into the postwar era for periods ranging from a couple of years to a few decades. The *Bob Burns Show* went off the air in 1947. *Lum and Abner* brought Pine Ridge into living rooms and parlors until 1954. Judy Canova also found steady film and radio work into the mid-1950s, though her cornpone grew stale and increasingly less popular in the Truman and Eisenhower years.[1]

On the big screen the frequency of hillbilly portrayals decreased steadily into the 1950s, meaning that American moviegoers were more likely than ever before to see Arkansas characters with little or no connection to the Arkansaw image. Among the most widely viewed big-screen representations of Arkansans in the 1950s were Lorelei and Dorothy, Marilyn Monroe's and Jane Russell's showgirls from Little Rock in *Gentlemen Prefer Blondes* (1953) who had apparently managed to leave accents and all behind when they escaped Arkansas. Hollywood tended to smooth the rougher edges of the backwoods denizens who survived in the postwar entertainment minefield. The most popular rustic movie clan of the 1950s, the Kettles, typified the domestication of the hillbilly. First introduced in the 1947 film *The Egg and I,* adapted from the 1945 Betty MacDonald novel, the Kettles, starring veteran character actors Marjorie Main and Percy Kilbride as Ma and Pa, appeared in a dozen movies over the course of a decade. The Kettles did not live in Arkansas, but the fictional family's tenuous link with the Ozarks, including a film called *The Kettles of the Ozarks,* connected the characters at least indirectly to the Arkansaw image. Like earlier fictional bumpkins, the Kettles "elicited a mixture of ridicule and empathy," according to historian Anthony Harkins. Pa Kettle was lazy and improvident, Ma was ill mannered, and their noisy brood of fifteen children was proof enough that their values and lifestyle were not those of the average American family. Nevertheless, the Kettles' struggles to come to grips with the modern world—as they were often forced to do in urban or suburban settings depicting the formulaic fish-out-of-water story— struck a chord with audiences whose "own unfamiliarity and unease with an increasingly mechanized and standardized postwar America" left them puzzled and nostalgic for a simpler time.[2]

The Kettles' film odyssey spanned the first decade of television, and this new medium, like film and radio before it, came to present a mixed bag of backwoods portrayals, from a romanticized tale of West Virginia migrants in southern California in *The Real McCoys* to the more farcical, if in some ways no less adoring, story of Jed Clampett and his newly wealthy

Ozark family. Among the most negatively stereotypical portrayals of the Arkansaw image in the early days of television was a 1958 episode of *The Jack Benny Show* in which the star flashed back to his fictional early days in Arkansas as the fiddler for "Zeke Benny and his Ozark Hillbillies." Decked out in longjohns *and* overalls, Benny mixed fiddling with "comedy routines about child brides and ignorant hicks who stomp the ground like a horse when they count to four."[3] Harkins attributes the rediscovery of the hillbilly in the late 1950s and early 1960s to the nation's sudden interest in, and often alarm over, the postwar migration of hundreds of thousands of southern mountaineers into the North and West. Coinciding with the civil rights era, this rediscovery could also link the hillbilly South with the racist South or, alternatively and more commonly, could serve as a reminder that there still existed a funny and fundamentally harmless (and homogenously white) hillbilly South somewhere beyond the demonized region burning hot on the evening news.

What Orval Done Gone and Wrought

In the hand-wringing aftermath of the display of massive resistance at Little Rock's Central High a number of defensive Arkansans attempted to remind critics that Arkansas (or at least Little Rock) had not been the paragon of Deep South racial oppression that revisionists might be tempted to find as they sought to explain the events of September 1957. As it became increasingly apparent—to the shapers and interpreters of the Little Rock saga at least—that this catastrophe of historic proportions was the work of one politically motivated and soft-spined governor, the capital city's pre-1957 moderation became integral to the telling of the tale. Two generations of commentators and historians would use Little Rock's "progressivism" as a preamble to the story of racism, weak leadership, and the courage of the Little Rock Nine. Certainly, the idea that what happened in Little Rock shouldn't have happened in Little Rock, given the city's and state's recent efforts to desegregate busses and the police force, universities, and even a few schools, bolsters the notion that Arkansas owed its Eisenhower-era infamy to Orval Faubus. But one catches a whiff of that old defensive desperation in this cut-and-dried version of the saga. As journalist Roy Reed and historian Elizabeth Jacoway have shown us, things are never as simple as they may seem, as we may want them to be.[4] The events of 1957 threatened to alter permanently the image of Arkansas in the national and international consciousness. Yet, the willingness of the better sort in Little Rock to deny their own racist complicity in the affair and to saddle Faubus with sole blame for the state's darkest moment ultimately served as a diversionary tactic that would allow for the gradual recovery of the essentially harmless and often appealing ambivalent Arkansaw image.

While we can debate the level of progressivism and racial moderation of post–World War II Little Rock, one thing that is certain is that the imagery of pre-Faubus Arkansas skewed toward the hillbilly end of the spectrum of southern stereotypes. By the mid-twentieth century the overwhelmingly white highland half of the state had long dominated the Arkansaw image, and, as we have seen, this Arkansaw/Ozark image had grown increasingly indistinguishable from a broader hillbilly image in American popular culture. Hillbillies seemed to occupy some mythical, lily-white South, and blacks remained invisible or at best peripheral in Arkansaw. The essential whiteness of the Arkansaw image tended to obscure any connection Arkansas might claim to the benighted South or the gothic South, despite the Bear State's active participation in the development of the Jim Crow system, its turn-of-the-century per capita lynching rate second only to Mississippi's, and its claim on what may have been the nation's worst race-related massacre of the bloody days following World War I in the rural delta community of Elaine. But that changed in 1957. Suddenly Little Rock seemed closer, culturally if not geographically, to Jackson and Memphis and Montgomery and Birmingham. People were reminded that the Mississippi River Delta made up the eastern third of this hillbilly state, that this flat, fertile stretch of sharecropper shacks and porticoed big houses covered more land in Arkansas than did the Ozarks.

The events in Little Rock would forever link Arkansas with the reactionary and racist South. The integration of Central High remains the event most likely to land Arkansas in the history books, the one piece of the Arkansas story that practically every American knows. It peeled away, temporarily at least, the veneer of hillbilly ridiculousness and backwoods rusticity that had long rendered the state worthy of derision, sometimes worthy of adulation, but never capable of any real harm. It revealed a cultural and social complexity in Arkansas heretofore masked by the pigeon-holing tendencies of stereotyping. It paved the way for subsequent first-hand examinations of Arkansas racism, such as Daisy Bates's *The Long Shadow of Little Rock* and Maya Angelou's *I Know Why the Caged Bird Sings,* the works of "tortured souls," in the words of historian Michael B. Dougan, who carried out a transition from bumpkins to bigots in the literature about Arkansas.[5]

The story of benighted Arkansas found other outlets as well. One of the more interesting and critically acclaimed portraits of something akin to a gothic Arkansas was *A Face in the Crowd,* Elia Kazan's motion picture about the rise and fall of an Arkansas entertainer. Based on Budd Schulberg's short story, "Your Arkansas Traveler"—which had been inspired by a frank, late-night conversation in which a drunken Will Rogers Jr. blasted his late father as a phony, as well as the controversial career of radio and television star Arthur Godfrey—*A Face in the Crowd* follows the meteoric rise to fame of singer and storyteller Lonesome Rhodes (played by Andy Griffith) after he is discovered sleeping one off in the county jail at Piggott, Arkansas.[6] As his career takes him to Memphis and then to New York, the mercurial, charismatic, and increasingly hubristic Rhodes alienates everyone around him and engages in self-destructive behavior until an on-air incident reveals his true character, or lack thereof, to millions of adoring fans. His downfall is swift and complete. Lonesome Rhodes's story is no aw-shucks tale of country-boy-makes-good in the tradition of romantic, rural Arkansaw. This Arkansawyer is rotten to the core, the complete and utter charlatan demagogue, and finally gets his comeuppance. In fact, Kazan's and Schulberg's ham-handed story passes up numerous opportunities to indict the forces of corruption, greed, and phoniness that create and support Rhodes and will, one suspects, find an endless supply of replacements after his fall. Instead, *A Face in the Crowd* becomes the story of one bad apple, a man so drunken with ambition and power that he destroys himself. But the fact that this bad apple was an Arkansas hayseed presented a stark departure from popular culture's usual cast of rustic or buffoonish Arkansaw characters, an alternative that seemed wholly believable to American audiences in the fall of 1957.

Movie poster, *A Face in the Crowd*, 1957. Courtesy of
Warner Brothers Entertainment, Inc.

A decade later a real-life event rekindled Arkansas's smoldering benighted South embers. The state's late 1960s prison scandal—in which new warden Thomas O. Murton, backed by information from a couple of prisoners, reported a laundry list of abuses ranging from putrid food and prisoner-on-prisoner violence to the infamous "Tucker telephone" and the murder and secret burial of inmates—produced a scathing *Time* magazine article titled "Hell in Arkansas" and a tell-all book by Murton and Joe Hyams after the former was fired in 1968. The story resurfaced more than a decade later when 20th Century Fox released the motion picture *Brubaker,* a piece of sweaty southern cinema starring Robert Redford as the idealistic and heroic outsider who tries and ultimately fails to reform Arkansas's primitive prison system.[7]

But a few good ole boy prison guards with thuggish tendencies and the stain of Little Rock would ultimately not be enough to hold Arkansas's seat at the table of Deep South devilry. The South was full of prisons more notorious than Tucker or Cummins, and *Brubaker* couldn't hold a candle to Florida's *Cool Hand Luke* when it came to Dixieland correctional cinema. And even Little Rock would find itself eclipsed in the contest for epicenter of massive resistance. Events of the early 1960s vaulted Jackson and Albany and Philadelphia and Montgomery and especially Birmingham past Little Rock in this competition. But it wasn't just that Arkansas had never quite measured up to the Deep South—there was always something a bit waffly about those post-Sumter seceders. Arkansas would find its way back toward the old Arkansaw image at least in part with the help of the governor whom most blamed for causing the mess in the first place.

In a perverse sense, it was a handy coincidence that Orval Faubus just happened to be a bona fide hillbilly. Not that he was a plain hillbilly, for, as Roy Reed reminds us, "the man was anything but ordinary." But it might be safe to say that a fellow from Greasy Creek isn't likely to get above his raising, and Faubus, like many of his Ozark and Ouachita brethren, wore his hillbilliness—the cussed, shrewd, independent brand—like a badge of honor. The governor's hardscrabble heritage in the hills of Madison County appeared to his detractors in Little Rock and beyond a crucial element to the saga unfolding around him in the autumn of 1957. "The high-collared men of the Little Rock establishment . . . looking down their noses at the hillbilly governor"—these representatives of a class often defensive of Arkansas's dignity and resentful toward the hinterlanders and ridge runners who sullied her reputation—found in Faubus an anxious but not unwilling scapegoat who with just a little nudge bounded off toward the wilderness bearing the sins of a state's systemic racism and narrow-minded traditionalism.[8] For the powerful of Little Rock and the Arkansas Delta, the bull's eye on Faubus's ample forehead deflected scrutiny away from the

underpinnings of massive resistance and racism and onto the new embodiment of the Arkansaw image. The fact that the governor was from the
same Boston Mountains that likely gave the world the squatter and his
encounter with the Arkansas Traveler paved the way for the fusion of hillbilly Arkansaw and the benighted South.

Some media outlets were quick to seize on Faubus's—and by extension
Arkansas's—cornpone rusticity. Years later Faubus recalled one particularly
combative television interview during which a young and cocky Mike
Wallace had called him "a hillbilly from Greasy Creek." *Time* magazine
referred to the governor as "the slightly sophisticated hillbilly from near

Orval Faubus and Donna Douglas, a.k.a. Elly May Clampett.
Orval Faubus Papers (MS F27 301), box 868, number 93. Special
Collections, University of Arkansas Libraries, Fayetteville.

Greasy Creek" and described Arkansas as "part delta and part mountain, part magnolia and part moonshine, where a horse is a 'critter' and a heifer a 'cow brute.'" (Faubus may have gotten some satisfaction out of the big city reporter's bovine nomenclatural faux pas, for everyone back in Madison County would have known that a "cow brute" had a tally-whacker.) Robert Sherrill of the *Nation* gleefully commented on the hick jokes that once circulated around the staff of Sid McMath after then-governor McMath appointed Faubus as his administrative assistant. Sherrill, evincing that patronizing incredulity with which the well bred and well educated almost by nature confront those who have risen in life without benefit of either, credited Faubus with "the kind of stubbornness that serves impoverished, untutored hillbillies as the extra evolutionary gene needed to pull them out of the mud and onto the sunlit shore of civilization."[9]

Little Rock had the potential to draw Arkansas fully into the Deep South, to replace the traditional Arkansaw/Ozark image with stereotypes of racist rednecks and pudgy, pasty plantation patroons. Faubus's role in the affair, combined with the persistence and popularity of the Arkansaw image, created a temporary tug-of-war between these two southern images. Two nationally distributed editorial cartoons in the summer of 1958 offered competing images of Arkansas's white population, illustrating the suddenly shifting place the state occupied in the national consciousness. Reacting to Orval Faubus's victory in the 1958 Democratic gubernatorial primary, a victory sealed in no small part by the governor's defiance of the federal government, the *Philadelphia Evening Bulletin* carried a cartoon that evoked imagery of the plantation South. Striding by a trash can containing "Federal Enforcement of Law in Arkansas" is "Massa Resistance," a southern dandy in seersucker suit who holds a cane and smokes a long-tipped cigarette while saying to no one in particular, "By gad, suh . . . We won!" Not to be outdone, the *Philadelphia Inquirer* found in the same story a different angle. That paper's editorial cartoon featured a hillbilly with floppy hat and long, bushy beard hoisting a moonshine jug labeled "Faubus Vote" and vowing, "H'yars to never, never, never—!"[10] This wasn't the first instance of dueling southern tropes, and it wouldn't be the last. But the hillbilly in homespun would outlast the planter in Colonel Sanders duds, at least as far as the image of Arkansas was concerned, and would reemerge in the 1960s as the face of Arkansaw.

Rekindling the Romance

The strange collision of Orval Faubus and massive resistance exercised a lasting impact on Arkansas's place in American history, but its long-term effect on the state's image proved remarkably negligible. Faubus's hillbillyness and the long-running popularity of the Arkansaw image may have helped Arkansas avoid a more permanent and damning association with the Deep South, but there were other forces at work that were equally influential in the reemergence of the ambivalent hillbilly/rustic image in the 1960s. The growing interest in American roots music in the late 1950s blossomed into an expansive folk revival in the 1960s. The Ozarks, and by extension Arkansas, attracted national attention for the survival of European and American ballads and folk tunes long forgotten in less isolated parts of the country. Although the blues occupied an integral position on the national folk scene and constituted a crucial piece in Arkansas's musical quilt, folk music in the state, as in much of the South, came to mean white mountain music. The national folk revival built on an earlier tradition of folk music collecting to spawn a regional revival in the Ozarks, and the popularity of this movement helped restore the old whites-only Arkansaw image. In its nostalgic folk revival manifestation, this image tended to champion the resourcefulness and independence of an "authentic" folk. In the dueling images tradition, however, the era would also find room for the comical hillbilly.

The romantic spirit that had inspired back-to-the-land anticapitalism in the Depression years and appreciation for anachronistic vestiges of American frontier life in the Appalachian ranges even earlier in the century underwent a serious reanimation near the end of the Eisenhower era. The post–World War II years—with their Levittowns and television and interstate highway system and McDonald's and gazillion labor-saving gadgets and gizmos—threatened to blanket the nation beneath a haze of homogeneity. For a growing number of young Americans deprived of regional and temporal diversity the exotic and palpably authentic sound of early blues and hillbilly recordings was intoxicating. Here were people, the records suggested, who were rooted in the soil and history of some *real* place. The attempt to commune with a fleeting and denied authenticity led many people into the same sleepy crossroads and dying countrysides that had been hemorrhaging population for the previous two decades, places whose comparative isolation rendered them valuable repositories of a lost way of life—and of those blues and hillbilly songs.

Arkansas, and the Ozark region specifically, received its share of attention during the folk revival. But even before this rediscovery collectors had for many years scoured the hills and hollows for Child ballads and Americana's variety of desperado songs and play party ditties. Vance Randolph, Mary Parler (Randolph), Clement Benson, Theodore Garrison, John Gould Fletcher, John Quincy Wolf Jr., and Max Hunter were only the most noteworthy of the many who sought to record and preserve the remnants of a once-common musical heritage in rural Arkansas. Due to the efforts of Randolph, Parler, and Wolf, especially, Alan Lomax made his way into the Ozarks in 1959, where he made several recordings in Stone County, Arkansas, that were later released on an album in his *Southern Journey* series.

One of Lomax's subjects was a colorful old singer and guitar picker named Neal Morris, whose son, Jimmy Driftwood, was by 1959 the closest thing north-central Arkansas could claim to a national household name. Driftwood's first album, *Newly Discovered Early American Folk Songs*, debuted in the powerful wake of the Kingston Trio's "Tom Dooley," the folk-pop hybrid that more than any other song launched the folk revival of the late 1950s and early 1960s. Driftwood's limited vocal skills kept him from achieving stardom as a recording artist, but other singers' renditions of his catchy faux-folk ballads—most notably Johnny Horton's 1959 recording of "The Battle of New Orleans"—won the Stone County native a Grammy and made him a celebrity of the folk circuit. Attempting to generate economic activity for Stone County, one of Arkansas's most isolated and impoverished, local leaders enlisted the help of their famous neighbor to create the Arkansas Folk Festival in 1963. By Driftwood's design the musical portion of the festival featured local singers and musicians—"timber cutters, farmers, housewives, and all plain people of the hills," in his words—and the handicraft portion of the festival boasted items ranging from corn-shuck dolls and walking sticks to quilts and white-oak baskets, all made by residents of northern Arkansas. Within a few years the Arkansas Folk Festival was the state's number-one tourist event, attracting tens of thousands of visitors each April to remote Mountain View.[11]

Festival goers appreciated every granny's version of "Barbara Allen" and "The Blind Child" and clapped and stomped every time a fiddler sheared down on "Soldier's Joy," to be sure. Many also found this celebration of a lily-white South a welcomed diversion from otherwise constant media reminders that there was currently little to celebrate in the real South. At the very moment Jimmy Driftwood stepped to the microphone to announce the inaugural act on the spring night of that first festival, some 475 miles away Martin Luther King Jr. and dozens of his fellow marchers sat locked up in the city jail in Birmingham, Alabama. Not that the Arkansas Folk Festival offered a disingenuous, segregated version of the locale's traditional music scene. Stone County was in fact one of the Ozark region's all-white counties. But many Arkansans from corner to corner were eager to endorse this particular genre of roots music as *Arkansas* folk music, an implicit ethnocentrism that ignored the dynamic musical traditions of black Arkansans and hearkened back to post–World War I celebrations of America's supposed Anglo-Saxon seedbeds in Appalachia and the Ozarks. It was, after all, Cecil Sharp's quest for British relics in Appalachian

Legendary Arkansas folk singer Almeda Riddle at Mountain View's
Arkansas Folk Festival, c. 1963. Courtesy of Ernie Deane Collection,
Arkansas History Commission, Little Rock.

balladry during World War I that had sparked ballad hunting in America and had implied that true American folk culture was something to be found in the racially undefiled highland South.

The folk revival helped reestablish the Ozark/Arkansaw image of the pre–World War II era. The nostalgia for the simplicity of an agrarian America and the romantic appreciation for the assumed premodern lifestyles of Ozarkers generated other institutions that lauded the once-common skills of the folk. Branson's Silver Dollar City capitalized on this rustic, frontier image when it opened for business in 1960, though it later dabbled in hillbilly stereotype as well. In Arkansas the momentum generated by the Arkansas Folk Festival eventually resulted in the Ozark Folk Center, which opened as a state park in 1973. The folk revival didn't limit its influence to the realm of the festival and the living museum, however. The interest in the folk—in our case the Arkansawyer—extended into the public arena in ways both official and serious, such as the debate over poverty in the early 1960s, and not so serious, such as the reemergence of the Arkansaw hillbilly in popular culture.

Coinciding with the folk revival—though in reality more a product of presidential electioneering and concern over migration out of the South than of romanticism—was a renewed interest in the plight of the rural poor. Appalachia especially attracted the attention of the national media and the federal government. Television networks and national magazines chronicled the depressing poverty left behind as extractive industries downsized or abandoned the mountains altogether, and the Kennedy administration responded with the creation of the Appalachian Regional Commission. The smaller and less politically crucial Ozarks underwent little of this proletarian scrutiny, though poverty was as much a part of the fabric in the region as in Appalachia. On rare occasions the national media shone the spotlight on economic challenges in the Arkansas Ozarks. In 1961, Baxter County in northern Arkansas became the first recipient of grant money from the Area Redevelopment Administration, a Kennedy administration creation designed to pump life into moribund regional economies. Covering the story for the *New York Times,* Peter Braestrup found that "surface prosperity . . . masks the poverty and underemployment" of Baxter and Marion counties. In this "poor area in a poor state . . . sit ramshackle shacks, even a log cabin or two, as prime examples of what Washington calls 'rural slums.'"[12]

When the Johnson administration responded to Ozark poverty with the creation of the Ozarks Regional Commission (ORC) four years later, *Wall Street Journal* reporter James C. Tanner visited impoverished Newton County and discovered "a land where the washing machine still can be found on the front porch of jerry-built backwoods cabins." Tanner believed that the Ozark region suffered "greater economic distress than the much-publicized Appalachia." "While Appalachia draws the headlines and massive doses of federal aid the economic situation in the Ozarks continues to deteriorate."[13] Ultimately, the ORC accomplished little in the Arkansas Ozarks, reflecting not so much an economic rejuvenation in the Ozarks as both a lack of "sexy" poverty—abandoned coal towns make for better photo ops than back roads dotted with mobile homes—and the stubborn allure of other images more readily associated with Arkansas and the Ozarks, such as the rustic quaintness of its inhabitants and the rugged beauty of its great outdoors, an important theme to which we shall return directly.

By the mid-1960s Appalachia found itself in the vortex of the country's war on poverty, and this development marked a divergence in the perceptions of the two southern highland regions. Heretofore, the imagery associated with the Ozarks and Appalachia in the American consciousness had been practically indistinguishable. To most Americans a hillbilly was a hillbilly and a noble mountaineer was a noble mountaineer, whether his log cabin was in the Boston Mountains or the Smokies. The constant media coverage of and government hand-wringing over the rural slums and company-town plight of Appalachia, however, helped politicize and mobilize a segment of the mountain population and sparked a rise in academic interest in the region that would highlight a history of victimization and exploitation that seemed suddenly more tragic than comic. To be sure, vast stretches of the Appalachians were as unaffected by the scars of coal mining and the proletarianization of textile mills as was the Ozarks, but in the public's eye Appalachia's inhabitants ceased to conform to the simplistic, dual image of the noble mountaineer and hillbilly simpleton. The Ozarks, which maintained a lower profile in the poverty wars of the decade, maintained its dichotomous, mythical image even as Appalachia's grew more nuanced. Gatlinburg and Boone and other places continued to peddle the premodern Appalachia, but *Newsweek, Time,* and other national media and the highly publicized Appalachian Regional Commission had exposed the region's long experience with modern, exploitative capitalism. America wasn't convinced just yet that the Ozarks had come into contact with modernity.

This static image of the Ozarks and of Arkansas was evident in other nonfictional treatments of the post–World War II era, and in Arkansaw tradition these observations tended to range from the derisive to the romantic. In a book chronicling the past and present of the forty-eight states, John Gunther resurrected a jaundiced vision of Arkansas and its most infamous region. Calling the Ozarks the "Poor White Trash citadel of America," he dismissed the region's inhabitants as "undeveloped, suspicious, and inert."

"There are children aged fifteen who have never seen a toothbrush." The state fared little better, though Gunther did enumerate a small list of redeeming features, including J. William Fulbright, Hot Springs, and gambling. "Arkansas is a highly curious and interesting community," intoned Gunther, as he moved in for the condemnation. "It is one of the most impoverished of all American states, with an intermontane backwoods inaccessible and primitive in the extreme." In a similar undertaking almost four decades later—the span of years underscoring the static nature of the Arkansaw image—Neal R. Peirce and Jerry Hagstrom found Arkansas "touched less by ways of industrialized society than any of its neighbors, a place obdurately independent and hopelessly provincial . . . It was an island set apart, a civilization primitive and poor."[14]

Though stereotypes ran rampant, few post–World War II journalists and travel writers emulated the unabashed condemnation of Gunther. Even Peirce and Hagstrom proved susceptible to the tradition of romanticism that flows through these pages. Trotting out tropes so reminiscent of a bygone era that they had begun to smell of political incorrectness, the authors discovered in the Arkansas Ozarks, at least as it greeted the 1970s, "one of the few frontier areas left in America, where the physical and cultural isolation preserved the centuries-old lifestyles, including vestiges of Elizabethan speech and the ballads of the people's English and Scotch-Irish forebears." Peirce and Hagstrom marveled over the "isolated hamlets where men still turned the soil with a horse- or mule-drawn plow," and their subsequent laments over the arrival of "mobile retirees and footloose industry" belied a romantic nostalgia that flavored the accounts of many writers.[15]

Among the major reasons for the perseverance of the static and romantic Arkansaw image in journalistic accounts of the state were the exaggerated influence of folklorists and travel writers, especially when it came to relaying images of the Ozarks, and the continuation of the synonymity of the images of Arkansas and the Ozarks in the minds of many people. Vance Randolph's accounts of folk life in the Ozarks and his collections of folk tales—such as *We Always Lie to Strangers* and *Who Blowed Up the Church House?*—reached a growing audience. Otto Ernest Rayburn's *Ozark Guide* found readers eager to read about and visit an exotic American locale. Both men became unofficial spokesmen for the highland half of Arkansas, and both perpetuated popular perceptions of a region forgotten by time—Rayburn through his nostalgic romanticism and Randolph by his iconoclastic embrace of a lifestyle that seemed to reject a modern American brand of "progress." Rayburn and Randolph were convinced, and saddened, that visitors to the region were witnessing the final days of a way of living that had long ago been obliterated in most other parts of the country.

Journalists and travel writers carried the theme. A *New York Times* reporter who ventured to north-central Arkansas to chronicle the early days of construction on Bull Shoals Dam believed that life for the locals was "much the same as that of the pioneers who first settled here. They have barn dances, candy pullings, pie socials, box suppers, hog-calling contests, 'possum hunts . . . They sing songs like 'The Three Rogues,' 'The Oxford Girl' and 'Houn' Dog.'" A dozen years later another writer for the *New York Times* evinced a nostalgic, if sometimes patronizing, appreciation for the survival of old ways in the face of new developments in the Ozarks, a region "about as close as one gets these days to old-fashioned America." "Many of the natives still depend for subsistence on a scrawny patch of corn and 'taters and black-eyed peas, a few hogs and an infallible trigger finger," observed the reporter. "In summer they wear sun bonnets and go barefooted. They say 'cain't' and 'her'n,' 'his'n' and 'kiver,' 'your'n' and 'winder' and 'piller' and 'fust.' . . . They believe in snake charms and they plant trees and dehorn cattle by the sign of the moon." Such nostalgic depictions of the region survived into the post-Watergate era. A 1981 *Reader's Digest* piece stressed that "life in the Ozarks is notably like life in the rural past. Stacked beside cabins with wood stoves for heating rise hand-hewn walls of cordwood. Few of those cabins have phones; some have only kerosene lanterns for light." Photographers contributed to the static image as well. The most notable of several photographic accounts of the Ozarks published in the 1970s and 1980s was Roger and Bob Minick's *Hills of Home,* a sentimental and nostalgic evocation of a land of anachronism.[16]

The landscape was as integral to the Minicks' Arkansas Ozarks as were the Ozarkers. For many others who chronicled the Ozarks and Arkansas, the natural world became the focus. The uninitiated who happened upon a pictorial essay that appeared in *American Heritage* would have found scant evidence that human life abounded in the Ozarks, as colorful mountain hillside vistas and green rivers dominated the magazine's pages.[17] As the post–World War II era wore on environmental issues came to the fore in Arkansas, resulting in a more central role for the natural world in the evolving image of Arkansas.

Whether it was Orval Faubus's sense of a shift in the winds of public opinion or the Luddite streak of an old country boy, one of the most significant acts of his final year as governor was his decision to take a stand against the Army Corps of Engineers' plans to dam the Buffalo River. The governor had friends on both sides of the issue. Those who held out hope that a lake on the Buffalo would bring economic prosperity to a depressed cranny of the state must have been a little surprised that the old politician would unabashedly throw his considerable clout behind one team in this controversial struggle in the Ozarks. But Faubus, this governor so many believed had never quite cleaned the creek mud from between his toes, possessed a sincere appreciation for his state's natural beauty and wilderness, an appreciation that could even impel him to wax poetic and nostalgic: "In many places the giant power-driven machines of man are flattening the hedges, fence rows, and nooks, where the song birds nested, and timid rabbits reared their young; . . . filling up the beautiful pools which furnished a home for the wary bass and the brilliant golden-hued sun fish."[18] Many in Arkansas shared his sentiments.

Naturalness had always been fundamental to Arkansas and the Arkansaw image. Writers and entertainers had long celebrated or denigrated the fact that Arkansawyers tended to live close to nature. And Arkansas's sparse settlement and rural nature was integral to the style of life associated with the state. By the mid-twentieth century, observers of and visitors to Arkansas were inclined to react more favorably to the scenery than to the humans who often despoiled the view. As transportation improvements allowed greater numbers of people to view the Arkansas countrysides from the Delta to the Ozarks, Arkansas gained a reputation as a good place for recreation and sight-seeing, just wild enough to appeal to romantic longings but civilized and modern enough to preclude any real hardship or danger. The Ozark region, in particular, attracted attention from magazines and newspapers across the nation. Beginning in the early 1950s, the *New York Times* ran annual, summer features on outdoor recreation in the region. Magazines such as *Life* and *National Geographic* published pictorials on the Ozarks and Arkansas. The people of the Ozarks and Arkansas tended to yield the spotlight to photographs of misty morning ridges and rushing streams.

The state of Arkansas would gradually come to appreciate the potential for marketing the natural environment—or, in the case of the many man-made reservoirs, the unnatural environment. The Department of Parks and Tourism adopted the slogan, "Arkansas Is a Natural," in the 1970s, and in 1989 Governor Clinton proclaimed June 17 "Natural State Appreciation Day." Five years later the general assembly officially changed the state's nickname to "The Natural State," ending the forty-eight-year run of "The Land of Opportunity."[19] As we have seen, the term "natural state" carries more than one connotation in regard to the Arkansaw image. It is clear that state officials were thinking of water and air and earth when they adopted the new cognomen, but the old notion of the Arkansawyer as natural man survived in both nonfictional and fictional accounts of Arkansas in the years following World War II. The most popular of these fictional accounts might have run contrary to the marketing ideas of Arkansas officials, but they reflected the familiar admire-and-despise duality of the Arkansaw image.

Jethro and Abner: An Arkansaw Counterculture

Given the perseverance of the Arkansaw/Ozark image into the 1960s and beyond, it is fitting that the era's (and perhaps twentieth-century America's) most famous comic hillbilly characters came from the Ozarks and not Appalachia. *The Beverly Hillbillies* arrived on the pop-cultural scene in 1962, at the height of the folk revival and just five years removed from the beginning of the Little Rock crisis. Created by Paul Henning, *The Beverly Hillbillies* became the nation's most-watched television program within a few weeks of its debut. Although the 1960s never seriously challenged the 1930s for the title of "heyday of the hillbilly," it wasn't for lack of effort on Henning's part. The Independence, Missouri, native almost single-handedly created a cornpone comedy empire with such long-running sitcoms as *Petticoat Junction* and *Green Acres*. But the undisputed anchor of his enterprise was the beloved and critically panned *Hillbillies*, whose eight seasons on CBS transported Americans from Camelot to the Nixon Whitehouse.[20]

Like fellow midwesterner Vance Randolph, Paul Henning had been fascinated with the backcountry people of the Ozarks since his childhood trips into southwestern Missouri. But instead of settling among them, "going native," as Randolph had done, Henning used his impressions of hill people to craft comical characters for radio and television, and ultimately as sounding boards for social commentary. Although the two approached their subjects and expressed their philosophies in very different ways, Randolph and Henning shared a romantic appreciation for what they saw as genuine people free of the corrupting influences of a modern society consumed with vacuous materialism. American audiences had seen this sort of hillbilly-flavored critique of shallow consumerism and snobbery before, from Bob Burns to the Weaver Brothers and Elviry and from *Lil' Abner* to Ma and Pa Kettle. And it wasn't difficult to recognize any of these past acts in the lineage of *The Beverly Hillbillies*.

The storyline for the show was something that Steinbeck might have concocted had he been a vaudevillian instead of a fellow traveler in the Depression years, for in Henning's universe the jalopy heading for California carried not the battered and luckless Joads but the Clampetts, a clan of naive and backward Ozarkers made filthy rich by the discovery of oil on their farm. As critics frothed to point out, each of the Clampetts represented a stock character in the rural humor stable: Granny, the straight-shooting and resourceful old woman who prefers traditional ways over the newfangled practices she finds in Beverly Hills; Elly May, the curvaceous young woman who looks like she just stepped out of an Al Capp strip but approaches life with the wide-eyed amazement and unsophistication of the nearest third-grader; and Jethro Bodine, a strapping young-ster so clueless that he makes Lil' Abner look like a Rhodes Scholar by comparison. In the tradition of Jim Doggett, the Arkansas squatter (at least in his wilier incarnation), and Bob Burns's "Arkansas Traveler," Clampett patriarch Jed possesses the kind of horse sense that only a man close to nature and completely at home in his own skin can possess, the kind that gives him the edge over a more-educated and urbane but ill-intentioned adversary every time. By the end of each episode, Jed's com-mon sense, Granny's pluck, and the Clampetts' good-hearted integrity—with an ample dose of plain dumb luck—saves the family from whatever calamity had once appeared imminent, in the process exposing the high-falutin Angelenos for the greedy, shallow frauds that they are. It was a timeless formula that had long appealed to a nation that shunned defer-ence and primogeniture and championed egalitarianism. As director Richard Whorf, a former Shakespearean actor, observed: "The picture of the hayseed triumphant is part of our tradition."[21]

The Beverly Hillbillies was a lightning rod for critics who saw in its sophomoric plots and corny comedy the sure signs of the takeover of tele-vision by the rude masses, maybe even the evidence of the decline of west-ern civilization. The bone of contention was never the show's stereotypical portrayal of poor southern whites, even though the sitcom's decidedly nonsouthern cast (excepting Louisiana native Donna Douglas) left it open to such criticism. Instead, critics decried the show's unsophisticated, plebian humor, its obvious efforts to appeal to the lowest common denom-inator of comedy. One *New York Times* critic, in a piece defending the show for its clear-eyed assessment of society, noted that detractors in his line of business had referred to *The Beverly Hillbillies* as "an esthetic regression, mindless, stupid, a striking demonstration of cultural Neanderthalism." Another found the sitcom so inane and revolting that "even the hillbillies should take umbrage."[22] But that wasn't likely to happen, for hillbillies and their fellow commoners across the country formed the core audience for *The Beverly Hillbillies* and Henning's other rural sitcoms. These were the same people who had flabbergasted northeastern sophisticates with their love of Bob Burns and had spun the turnstiles to catch the Weaver Brothers and Elviry and Ma and Pa Kettle on the big screen. Some of them couldn't discern a coon from a possum; many if not most had eaten a helping of both. But they all recognized a side of themselves in the Clampetts, some-thing of the common man in a world operated by the privileged. They all sensed something in the Clampetts that spoke to the American dream, that respected the egalitarian traditions of a nation of democrats.

In spite of the obvious mental shortcomings of Jethro and the family's naivety, the Clampetts fall squarely into the category of romantic backwoods

Coming home. Three stars of *The Beverly Hillbillies* headlined the 1963 Arkansas Livestock Exposition. Courtesy of the Arkansas Livestock Show Association.

folk. Henning may have been more concerned with fleecing the better sort of Americans of their pretentiousness than exalting the virtues of salt-of-the-earth Ozarkers, but the product of his vision was a major contribution to the romantic side of the Arkansaw/Ozark image, and yet a contribution that, like the monologues of Bob Burns or the tale of Jim Doggett, could be misconstrued by a set of eyes fronting a less tolerant notion of the rural poor.

The tremendous popularity of *The Beverly Hillbillies* undoubtedly and ironically contributed to the reemergence of the more ambiguous Arkansaw/

Ozark image in the 1960s, and even to the stereotypical buffoon unredeemed by the Clampetts' fundamental goodness and common sense. Animation studio Hanna-Barbera, building on a long tradition of cartoon hillbilly stereotyping going back to Bugs Bunny's and Woody Woodpecker's visits to the feuding Ozarks and "The Martins and the Coys" from the Walt Disney feature film *Make Mine Music,* introduced Saturday morning audiences to a steady stream of hillbilly characters, beginning in 1964 with a backcountry version of *Tom and Jerry* in *Punkin' Puss and Mushmouse.* Like *Punkin' Puss and Mushmouse,* Hanna-Barbera's *Hillbilly Bears* inhabit a mythical southern highland region free of geographical specificity but full of cultural stereotype. The studio's *Wacky Races,* which aired from 1968 to 1970, offers up a human hillbilly and, not surprisingly, identifies him with Arkansas. One of ten racing teams featured on this animated paean to *The Great Race,* Luke (whose partner was a bear named Blubber) is a lazy, floppy hat-wearing hillbilly who steers his wooden-bodied, coal-fired jalopy, the Arkansas Chuggabug, with his bare feet, all the while reclining, and often sleeping, in a rocking chair. As anyone remotely familiar with Hanna-Barbera animation can surmise, *Wacky Races* wasn't burdened with subtextual cultural commentary, so Arkansawyer Luke pretty much is what he is, a mostly worthless but equally harmless (other than the obvious navigational narcolepsy issue) hillbilly who, like many hillbillies we know, is quite resourceful and not half bad in a car race.[23]

By the time Luke and Blubber Bear debuted in September 1968, Arkansas had already gotten a taste of the oddest and most perversely entertaining symbol of the enduring Arkansaw image to grace the last half of the twentieth century. Just four months earlier Dogpatch, U.S.A. had opened for business in a little hollow just off scenic route seven in Newton County. The sprawling theme park was, of course, based on Al Capp's comic strip, by now an iconic three and a half decades old. The New Englander Capp had never located his mythical Dogpatch in a specific state or region, but his millions of daily readers likely agreed with him that the Ozarks was as fitting as anywhere, and the fact that a group of Harrison, Arkansas, investors was willing to supply Capp with a generous cut of the gate sealed the deal. By 1967, when construction began on the $2.2 million park, *Lil' Abner* and his neighbors had become part of America's pop-cultural fabric and had found their way into a variety of media and promotional products. Long before the Yokums and Scraggs found their way to the Ozarks, Sadie Hawkins Day races—derived from a Dogpatch ritual whereby young women tried to catch and marry eligible but bashful bachelors—had become annual fall events on college campuses around the nation. A popular 1956 Broadway musical starring Peter Palmer and Edie Adams as Abner and Daisy Mae (as well as future Elly May Clampett, Donna Douglas, in a small role) spawned a 1959 feature film, in which Palmer reprised his title role alongside Adams's replacement Leslie Parrish. By the mid-1960s, the pilot for a *Lil' Abner* sitcom (featuring Judy Canova among others) was in the works, and an Atlanta soft drink company had begun marketing Kickapoo Joy Juice, a carbonated take-off on a decidedly stronger beverage churned out by Hairless Joe and Lonesome Polecat in Dogpatch Cave.[24]

But Dogpatch, U.S.A. was a different kind of animal. Whereas the brightly colored costumes, faux-shabby sets, and Hollywood South accents that ranged from *Lum and Abner* to *Amos 'n Andy* lent a certain winking, bicoastal artificiality to the play and movie, the theme park offered a novel venue for Capp's hillbilly schtick. *Lil' Abner* was the most prominent representative of what might be called the New York–L.A. version of hillbilly

Souvenir tray from Dogpatch, U.S.A., one of dozens of trinkets and knick-knacks marketed by the park during its twenty-five-year existence.
© Capp Enterprises, Inc. Used by permission.

comedy, the brand concocted by urban outsiders and marketed to urban outsiders, the kind most likely to peddle buffoonish caricatures or, in Capp's case, to utilize one-dimensional characters as ciphers in service of social criticism. This wasn't the homegrown slapstick of the Weaver Brothers and Elviry or the store porch monologues of Bob Burns. And though similar in execution to *The Beverly Hillbillies, Lil' Abner,* infused as it was with Capp's detached cynicism, differed in spirit from Henning's romantic creation. Arkansawyers, and poor southern folk in general, have long been recognized for their self-deprecation. It is quite likely that many if not most who patronized the park or found seasonal work dressing up like the denizens of Dogpatch and parading around with corncob pipes and exaggerated drawls approached this curiosity with the usual willingness to take the stereotyping in stride. But there was still a surreal quality to the whole enterprise—a passel of mostly Arkansawyers and Ozarkers gallivanting in the remote Boston Mountains as hillbilly characters dreamed up by a cartoonist whose knowledge of the southern backcountry would not have filled a thimble.

In this sense Dogpatch, U.S.A. was a sort of postmodern experiment on the hillbilly stereotype in general and the Arkansaw image in particular. Cultural scholar Rodger Brown notes the labyrinth of irony and paradox in this "100-acre basket of cornpone and hillbilly hokum." In an effort to emulate the Branson, Missouri, area's popular Silver Dollar City theme park and to cash in on the era's folk revival-inspired appreciation for regional heritage, Dogpatch, U.S.A.'s management insisted on blending Capp's comedy with displays and performances by real Ozark craftspeople and musicians. This relayed mixed messages to patrons and rendered the crafters and musicians "'authentic' people in an 'inauthentic' stereotyped context of moonshine, overalls and feudists." Local residents were among the first to detect the irony in the West Po'k Chop Speshul, the park's miniature train that stood as the first and only railroad ever built in Newton County. Whereas the railroad had once been the premier symbol of progress and commerce and the link to a wider world, the Speshul only went around and around in a circle. Furthermore, the fact that Dogpatch, U.S.A. was built on the actual site of an abandoned and dilapidated Arkansas village called Marble Falls (originally Wilcockson) inspired more confusion between the "real" Ozarks and the region of popular imagination. "This masterful blurring of the lines between the authentic, the replica and the hegemonic lampoon is," argues Brown, tongue firmly in cheek, "Dogpatch's claim to a place on the National Register. Restored to its original condition, it could easily serve as a living classroom illustrating lessons for schoolkids in the dynamics of cultural politics and internal colonialism."[25]

In his ruminations on the Ozark holler that once had been Marble Falls before Abner and Daisy Mae came a calling, Donald Harington chronicled locals' disdain for Dogpatch, U.S.A. One Newton Countian, quoted in Harington's lone work of "nonfiction," *Let Us Build Us a City,* dismissed the theme park as a "nuisance," while another wanted someone to "tear all them ole crazy buildings down, and put some decent roofs on 'em and put 'em all on there straight instead of all *humped-up*-like." The *humped-up* buildings, some adorned with statues of goats, were more accurate reflections of pop-cultural hillbillydom than of old-timey Ozark architecture. Many were indeed "authentic," having been hunted down in the region, taken apart, and reassembled in the park, all "obviously selected with an eye for their 'quaint' and impoverished rusticity." When authentic didn't equate to hillbilly rustic, management decreed that the old cabins "'needed to be sway-backed,'" recalled one local hired for his native craftsmanship, and called out the work crew "to smash the ridgepoles and make the roofs look slovenly."[26]

Perhaps it's fitting that our best literary account of the marriage of image and reality in the remote Arkansas Ozarks comes from the state's premier postmodernist writer. Just as visitors to Dogpatch, U.S.A. might have struggled to differentiate Ozark heritage from Arkansaw stereotype, readers of *Let Us Build Us a City* find themselves (usually unwittingly) in a world where fact and fiction overlap and flow into one another like the confluence of two meandering streams. Though it's Harington's displeasure with the theme park and its flaunting of stereotype that seasons the locals' dialogue, the novelist does seem to share the philosophy of reality underlying the work of Capp and his fellow hillbilly popularizers: the truth is a good thing, as long as it doesn't get in the way of a good story. As he admitted to an interviewer more than a dozen years after the publication of *Let Us Build Us a City,* "All of that stuff that Harrigan supposedly found with Kim in those various towns—all of that was made up and presented as the history of these towns of Arkansas." So we really don't know if local work crews had to come back in and slouch up their craftsmanship or if locals really objected to the fun that Al Capp and a group of Harrison businessmen were having at their expense. The former sounds improbable, and, unless salt-of-the-earth Arkansawyers' devil-may-care attitudes toward the Arkansaw image had altered dramatically by the Reagan era, the latter seems unlikely. And Abner Yokum himself wouldn't be gullible enough to believe that a certain peanut-chomping former governor just happened to show up at the closed-for-the-season theme park at the very moment that the curious traveler of rural Arkansas stood in the parking lot.

There is no sense getting bent out of shape over Harington's creative nonfiction, though. He, like many an erudite observer, obviously thought that the locals should be offended by the goings-on at Dogpatch, U.S.A., even if it wasn't as easy as the book implies to find someone to articulate a disdain for hillbilly hawking. Besides, maybe the only sane way to lay siege to the perpetrators of cultural slander is through the armature of creative license. A surreal and unintentionally postmodern entity like Dogpatch, U.S.A. deserves a surreal and intentionally postmodern critique by a proud Arkansawyer. But Harington didn't have to imagine the most surreal addition to the story of Arkansas's hillbilly theme park, for the real Orval Faubus, with or without his goober peas, showed up to run the place in early 1969.

Just two years removed from the governor's mansion, Faubus was hired to run Dogpatch, U.S.A. by the new owner, Little Rock millionaire Jess Odom. What a red-letter day for the Arkansaw image this was—the

Orval Faubus and wife Beth in front of the statue of Dogpatch's Civil War hero, Gen. Jubilation T. Cornpone, Dogpatch, U.S.A., 1969. Orval E. Faubus Papers (MC 922), box 54, file 4, number 1747. Special Collections, University of Arkansas Libraries, Fayetteville.

state's most infamous, real-life hillbilly running herd over a small army of faux hillbillies. Maybe Faubus was a sucker for irony, or maybe he just liked to picture editorial cartoonists falling all over themselves in a mad dash for their desks. Perhaps he appreciated the impact of his showdown with the Eisenhower administration on the image of Arkansas, realized just how close the state came to donning permanently the robe of reactionary racism, and sought to restore equilibrium by forging a bond between the real hillbilly and his Dogpatch doppelgänger. More likely, it was something more mundane, like the financial problems created by his recent construction of a hilltop mansion and his subsequent divorce. Whatever his motivation, Faubus's tenure at Dogpatch, U.S.A. proved brief and unsatisfying. He soon abandoned the Yokums and Scraggs and McSwines to reenter the political arena, where he would never again experience success. When pressed on the comparative significance of the old governor's stint at Dogpatch, the Faubus who appears in *Let Us Build Us a City* suggests that only "about a paragraph" of his eventual biography should be devoted to his theme park detour. Roy Reed would do him one better and sum it up in a sentence.[27] But the symbolic resonance remains inescapable. Arkansas's last hillbilly governor would ultimately outlive Dogpatch, U.S.A.; he would not outlive the Arkansaw image it promoted, however, and he would never live down his own scarred reputation.

Given the gusto with which the defenders of Arkansas's honor had carried out their missions throughout the century, it may seem surprising that the development of Dogpatch, U.S.A. wasn't greeted with an uproar befitting the memory of Bernie Babcock or Charles H. Brough. Certainly not everyone was excited that Capp's crew was coming to Arkansas. The *Arkansas Gazette* printed a letter from a North Little Rock man who claimed that Dogpatch, U.S.A. would "make Arkansas the laughing stock of the nation." When plans were first unveiled, Lou Oberste, associate director of publicity for the state Publicity and Parks Commission, expressed reservations that the theme park would revive Arkansas's "Bob Burns type image." His boss, Parks and Publicity Commission director Bob Evans, shared Oberste's concerns and feared that Dogpatch, U.S.A. would threaten the progressive image that the state had been cultivating in recent years.[28] This progressive image was perhaps best reflected by Winthrop Rockefeller, the former director of the Arkansas Industrial Development Commission who was busy settling into the governor's mansion as the state's first Republican chief executive since Reconstruction at the same time that the Dogpatch story broke.

With this story and plenty of other real news to cover, Little Rock's media ultimately gave little thought to the cultural implications of Dogpatch. Even the trepidation of Publicity and Parks Commission spokesmen was assuaged before the winter was over, thanks to a tour of the theme park site hosted by two members of the commission, one of whom, a newspaper publisher and business promoter from neighboring Searcy County, claimed that Dogpatch, U.S.A. would prove to be a good thing for the Arkansas image. By the time the park opened in May 1968, the state's official publicity machine was happily touting Dogpatch as "Arkansas's first super-duper commercial tourist attraction," though its euphemism-laced efforts to put a positive spin on the Newton County development proved (unintentionally) funnier than anything coming out of Capp's stale pen in the Vietnam era. Focusing primarily on the area's scenic beauty and natural wonders and the theme park's artisans and state-of-the-art equipment, the Publicity and Parks Commission's official press release praised "the nicely landscaped main building" and "rest rooms so swanky that they belie the pseudo pioneer impression Dogpatch is supposed to give." Lest visitors fear venturing into the rustic Ozarks or Arkansawyers sense something unsettling about the walking and talking hillbilly caricatures and the pageantry of the moonshiner-revenuer chase and shootout, the press release reminded readers that "Dogpatch U.S.A. is a lot of fun in a dignified sort of way and will undoubtedly be a credit to Arkansas both culturally and economically."[29]

The game had not changed considerably since the days of Brough and Babcock, when educated defenders argued not so much "Arkansans are not hillbillies" as "Not all Arkansans are hillbillies." This Arkansas of shoe and shirt factories, of tax breaks and industrial incentives, was more willing than ever to trade whatever dignity it might have left for a mess of pottage. Arkansans had bought into the nation's critique of their state; now the thought of sacrificing potential economic benefits was a much scarier proposition than the thought of being ridiculed. Besides, the location of Dogpatch, U.S.A. in an isolated hollow in the Ozarks might serve as a lightning rod to focus and absorb all the bolts of stereotype flung by a critical public, a sort of containment policy against the spread of the negative hillbilly image into parts of the state where it was most unwelcome. After all, if Arkansas had a Dogpatch, reasoned suburban Arkansans, it would likely show up in a place like Newton County. Let folks up in the hills degrade their heritage all they want, argued one letter writer to the *Arkansas Gazette,* "but tainting the entire state with their shame is a different matter."[30]

We could debate the level of cultural degradation served up by Dogpatch, U.S.A., as well as the complicity of Harrison businessmen and locals and college kids who made a buck or two cavorting around as cartoon characters. But the fiscal health of the park seems rather more cut and dried. Dogpatch, U.S.A. never achieved the economic success and national notoriety envisioned by its founders. *Lil' Abner* had suffered a decline in popularity for some time before Al Capp, whose own image had been transformed from leftist iconoclast to reactionary humbug, hung up his pen for good in 1977. It wasn't long afterward that the park began to hemorrhage money, and the decreasing relevance and familiarity of the Dogpatch characters with each passing year meant that the economic prospects weren't likely to turn around. In the final estimation, it seems likely that a major reason for the park's failure was location. Rugged and remote Newton County might have seemed the ideal setting for a place like Dogpatch, but there is a fine line between rusticity and just plain old too far off the beaten path. Orval Faubus's decision to jump off this wagon not long after jumping on it should have been a warning to the park's owner- ship, for the old governor always had a good sniffer for trends and popular crusades.

Box Office and Black Oak

The same combination of fascination and revulsion that inspired Dogpatch, U.S.A. informed the obsession with the rural, nonconformist South in the 1970s. Best represented by the dozens of good-ole-boy/outlaw movies and the bands behind the rise of southern rock music, this South was a post–Jim Crow, pre-Walmart and strip mall land in transition. The end of de jure segregation and the subsequent emergence of racial tensions, riot- ing, and violence outside the region made it safe to again romanticize the rural South. Furthermore, the "successful, optimistic, prosperous, and bland" region that emerged as a sort of "Americanized 'No South'" in the 1970s inspired nostalgia for the old countercultural South, sans overt racism, of course.[31] The nation's lingering appreciation for a nebulous folk culture supposed to be in its waning days contributed another element to the curiosity with the southern underclass. The South on the big screen in the 1970s was a rural, sweaty place, a land of cotton fields, bayous, and moun- tains (often in proximities that defied geography) and a place that appar- ently hadn't gotten the memo on air-conditioning. It was also still a white man's South. Demographics skewed heavily Caucasian, even in the deep- est of Souths, and black characters rarely ascended passivity. The good guys, whether southern liberal types (*Conrack*) or law-and-order heroes (Sheriff Buford T. Pusser in *Walking Tall*), were unstintingly fair to African Americans, however, if occasionally paternalistic. Most of the sweaty South films shied away from outright defenses of southern society—after all, the bad guys were usually southerners, too—but southern rock bands found a wider berth for their mixture of counterculture couture, hard-partying, conservatively populistic politics, and conscious defensiveness.

Given the overabundance of Arkansas movies in the 1930s and 1940s, it is a little surprising that Arkansas received comparatively scant attention by filmmakers in the sweaty South genre. But the few films set in Arkansas summoned the spirit of the Arkansaw image. Among the stealthier set in the old Bear State were two early Roger Corman-produced proletarian efforts from now-legendary auteurs: *Boxcar Bertha* and *Fighting Mad. Boxcar Bertha* (1972), the "true" story of a fictional, Depression-era heroine and her band of pro-labor, anti-corporation robbers, is best remembered today as one of Martin Scorsese's early films. Likewise, the significance of *Fighting Mad* (1976), an otherwise forgettable tale of salt-of-the-earth Arkansas farmers battling a greedy and evil strip mine owner and his minions, stems in large part from the future Oscar-winner at its helm, Jonathan Demme. In neither film does Arkansas serve as anything more than a stand-in for the generic, Hollywood South.

By far the best of the sweaty South pictures set in Arkansas was *White Lightning,* a 1973 movie that stands as one of the genre's most successful films. Like *Boxcar Bertha, White Lightning* could have been set just about anywhere in the Deep South, and because Burt Reynolds starred in the film most people today assume that it was set in his stomping grounds in the Southeast. Reynolds plays Bobby "Gator" McCluskey, a young bootlegger released from prison to help the feds nab a crooked sheriff who's running an illicit whiskey/bootlegging ring with a backwoods moonshiner. Gator has his own reasons for going after Sheriff Connors (Ned Beatty); it is rumored that the sheriff, a one-dimensional villain who in addition to being a law breaker is also a racist reactionary who blames all his problems on communists, was responsible for the death of Gator's younger brother, a college student who had disappeared while protesting in Connors's Bogan County. Gator, ever the folk hero, is reluctant to turn over the names of moonshiners and bootleggers (his people) to federal authorities and finally manages to take down the sheriff on his terms, "a source of pride," writes historian Jack Temple Kirby, "for southern whites who would rather do it themselves." Gator McCluskey fits the mold of the good old boy, a southern type popular in movies and other media in the 1970s because he was in essence, according to John Shelton Reed, "an authentic, indigenous working-class hero."[32]

The Arkansas Delta of *White Lightning* is oddly devoid of African Americans; with the exception of a brief scene in a backstreet juke joint, the only black faces in Bogan County belong to the children playing in the background of some shots. But Gator seems to harbor no ill will against blacks and even establishes an easy rapport with the one black character with a line or two of dialogue. The fact that *White Lightning*'s demographics are more Ozark than Delta is not surprising. The movie is, after all, about small-town corruption and the internal struggle for the control of the South's destiny, not about race relations per se. More important, the near absence of blacks helps reestablish the mythical white South as a sort of regional exotic and reaffirms the essential whiteness of the Arkansaw image.

This white South of Arkansaw legend was much easier to recreate in a demographically accurate sense in the 1974 low-budget film *Bootleggers*. Filmed and set in the Ozarks of north-central Arkansas, *Bootleggers* is the story of an ongoing feud between two backwoods families of bootlegging moonshiners. As in *White Lightning*, stereotypes abound in *Bootleggers*. Nevertheless, director and producer Charles B. Pierce, an Arkansas native and "regionalist" moviemaker who had his greatest success with a couple of cult horror flicks, obviously views the Arkansas hills and their inhabitants through a romantic lens. His contrast of the bad Woodalls, makers of rotgut whiskey and apparent cold-blooded instigators of the feud, with the good Pruitts, whose high-quality craftsmanship earns them a lucrative trade in Memphis, invokes the stories of a young Charles Morrow Wilson two generations earlier. Pierce's admiring shots of the White River and receding rows of ridgetops and his liberal use of locals in ancillary roles, undoubtedly the result more of a shoestring budget than any effort at realism, give *Bootleggers* a decidedly stronger Arkansas vibe than anything in the superior *White Lightning*.[33]

Pierce revealed romantic tendencies in another Arkansas-set movie, *The Legend of Boggy Creek* (1972). Using a docudrama style, Pierce related the legend of a Sasquatch-like creature that many locals believed inhabited the swampy Sulphur River bottoms near the town of Fouke in southwestern Arkansas. A cult classic that reportedly earned a fortune for Pierce, a former salesman from nearby Texarkana, *The Legend of Boggy Creek* was far from good filmmaking—though it was superior to the dreadful 1985 sequel *Boggy Creek II*. Unintentionally hilarious at times and featuring a series of dramatic recreations involving both real locals and actors—though telling which is which is no easy task, and that's not a testament to Foukian thespianism—the film nevertheless conveys Pierce's romantic vision of rural Arkansas and its people. Modern suburban viewers might misinterpret Pierce's depictions of such backwoods characters as Herb Jones, a hunter and trapper filmed at his isolated shack deep in the swamps, as stereotyping and poking fun at the locals. But the viewer would have to bring his own negative perspective to the film, for Pierce obviously approached the farmers and hunters of Fouke, and especially the landscape they inhabited, with a reverence stoked by nostalgia and romanticism. As the camera pans the swamps at the end of the film, the narrator intones a central tenet of the appeal of the Arkansaw image: "I'd almost like to hear that terrible cry

Movie poster, *Bootleggers*, 1974. Courtesy of Howco International Pictures.

again, just to be reminded that there is still a bit of wilderness left, and there are still mysteries that remain unsolved."[34]

Like the filmmaking of Charles B. Pierce, the music and style of Arkansas's major contribution to the 1970s southern rock genre tended to be unpolished and celebratory of the wilder side of nature, in this case mainly human nature. Nobody did Arkansaw quite like Black Oak Arkansas. Formed in the mid-1960s as The Knowbody Else by six young men from northeastern Arkansas, by the early 1970s Black Oak Arkansas (the new band name taken from lead singer James "Jim Dandy" Mangrum's hometown) had become one of the country's most popular southern rock bands. Though Black Oak Arkansas never rivaled contemporaries such as the Allman Brothers Band and Lynyrd Skynyrd on the rock 'n' roll charts, their high-energy, sexually charged concerts made them one of the world's most popular touring acts during their mid-1970s heyday. Black Oak Arkansas shared with Lynyrd Skynyrd and the Charlie Daniels Band an unapologetic, confrontational defensiveness when it came to their southern heritage. While Charlie Daniels was promising "The South's Gonna Do It Again" and Lynyrd Skynyrd was defending Alabama from the criticisms of Neil Young, Black Oak Arkansas made use of Confederate iconography and recorded their own version of "Dixie." At the same time the band helped introduce the state and region to the counterculture. And beneath the long hair and bacchanalian lifestyle boiled a class consciousness that recognized in the Arkansas hillbilly of legend a fellow commoner who "ain't had a voice in a lotta things."[35]

Perhaps more than any other southern rock band of the era, Black Oak Arkansas played up the hillbilly/redneck image of their home region and state. Jim Dandy Mangrum and his cohorts understood the stereotypes Americans held about the rural South and Arkansas in particular, argues historian Cecil Kirk Hutson, and "were able to sell themselves as a band of wild 'Arkansas hillbillies.'" Cultivating an image as working-class outlaws, to the point of exaggerating their rather benign rap sheets, Black Oak Arkansas, like many southerners and Arkansawyers, co-opted the negative images of their region and state and in so doing, according to Hutson, reinforced these same stereotypes in the minds of media and other outsiders who couldn't appreciate the band's attempts at self-caricature.[36]

Black Oak Arkansas's album covers and a few of their song titles reflected their embrace of the Arkansaw image. The band's first album, released in 1971, utilized *Beverly Hillbillies* imagery by picturing the boys in an old pickup loaded down with furniture. Two years later *High on the Hog*'s cover art featured a cartoon version of the band astraddle a hog and holding a washboard (which Mangrum actually used in concert) and a moonshine jug. The album featured one of the band's own compositions, "Moonshine

Sonata," while a later album included a song called "Wild Men from the Mountains." The cover of *Early Times* pictured the band, again in animated form, huddled around a pot-bellied stove in a mountain shack. Music critics played along. In the British weekly *Melody Maker*, Allan Jones referred to Black Oak's popular tour as a "triumph for the Arkansas hillbillies," and Jack Hiementz of *Circus* described the band members as a "hillbilly fraternity."[37]

But none of the members of Black Oak Arkansas was from the highland half of the state. Although the original band members hailed from the Delta region east of Jonesboro, notes Hutson, "the nation as a whole . . . has typecast Arkansas residents as Ozark hillbillies and that is the image the record companies wished to stress."[38] It is unclear just how much of Black Oak Arkansas's antics emanated from the band's own sense of ironic self-caricaturing and how much was dictated by their record company. But

Black Oak Arkansas's 1973 album, *High on the Hog*.
Courtesy of Atlantic Records.

it is quite clear that Mangrum, whose gravelly voice evoked guttural cotton-field blues one moment and nasally hill-country whines the next, and Black Oak's other band members cultivated a connection to their state's hillbilly image. This effort was reflected not only in album art and song lyrics but also in the band's purchase and development of a hillside compound in the Arkansas Ozarks. Like the sweaty South movies of the 1970s, Black Oak Arkansas tended to jumble their rural southern iconography and flit along the fringes of bigotry, but their embrace of the hillbilly, outlaw image (with its hippy-length hair and penchant for booze, drugs, and overt sexuality) announced the arrival of a new South, one light years removed from (at least on the surface) the seething, crew-cutted, race-baiting South of the previous decade. It signaled Black Oak's repudiation of all the things that the Arkansas hillbilly had stood in contrast to: condescending outsiders, the local elite, and the forces of progress and conformity in general. And, for our purposes, this conscious identification with the Arkansaw image represented the continuing dominance of the hillbilly motif and the common Arkansawyer's time-tested willingness to wear the image as a badge of honor.[39]

Novel Arkansas

While the history, mind, and culture of Arkansas have not received the literary scouring that, say, Mississippians have subjected their state to in the years since the southern renascence, Arkansas has not been bereft of talented writers eager to tell the world about their home. These novelists have in different ways and to varying degrees contributed to the image of Arkansas. Francis Irby Gwaltney emerged in the 1950s as the first serious novelist of the post–World War II era to locate his fictional world in Arkansas. Beginning with *The Yeller-Headed Summer* in 1954, the Arkansas native published eight novels over a twenty-year period, all of which took place in the state or involved Arkansas characters. Although his writing style is not Faulknerian, Gwaltney emulates the great novelist in his effort to craft a "fictional history of his mid-South" and in his subject matter, which tends toward such gothic southern themes as race and class. Gwaltney's is a black and white Arkansas, both literally and figuratively. Most of his characters are two dimensional; few inhabit the modernist's gaping gray divide between the white heights of heroism (figuratively speaking) and the black depths of despicability. Most often, a sort of class determinism creeps into this picture, as poor whites represent the lowest order of society in every sense and only the intelligence and integrity of the well born and bred prevent society from crumbling beneath the bigotry and self-destruction of the unwashed.

Gwaltney's 1959 novel, *The Numbers of Our Days*, reflects the author's grapplings with his state's struggles with social change and belies a paternalistic, patrician attitude that pervaded the culture of the elite in the South and contributed to the culture of defensiveness we have observed. Set in the fictional Arkansas River town of Gray's Landing, *The Numbers of Our Days* represents Gwaltney's response to the Little Rock Central crisis, as well as his tribute to the peaceful integration effort carried out earlier in his hometown, Charleston. The story centers on a decade and a half in the life of Tom Williams, a boy from the wrong side of the tracks (literally) who becomes a college football star and war hero and returns to Gray's Landing to marry the daughter of the town's wealthiest resident and eventually lift the sagging fortunes of his father-in-law's business interests through savvy investments and square dealings with black sharecroppers and laborers. But with the exception of Tom, who through some "strange alchemy of history" becomes "a man of courage and stubborn integrity," Gray County's whites of mean birth never get above their raising, while the Oak Street denizens, the local old-family elites, display a racial progressivism and tolerance befitting the author's ideals. Gwaltney's Arkansas, thus, is in essence the gothic South, a place where whites are divided by history and money and memory and where blacks, though more likely than poor whites to be portrayed sympathetically, are passive victims or recipients of respectable white paternalism or white-trash hatred.[40]

This Arkansas and South of Gwaltney's earlier novels stands in contrast to the hillbilly Arkansas that has most often dominated the literary landscape of the state, reflecting the Faubus-era dalliance with membership in the Deep South. Gwaltney himself altered this fictional Arkansas landscape a bit in his later works, most notably in his 1973 novel *Destiny's Chickens*. Although set in the same midcentury, small-town Arkansas atmosphere of *The Number of Our Days*, *Destiny's Chickens* contains little of the idealism of the earlier book. Gwaltney follows the ultimately entwined lives of two Korean War veterans who were in almost every other sense diametrically opposed: Grover Sands, scion of a prominent old family who returns to his hometown and winds up unhappily married and president of the local state university, and Orval Pierce, a redneck logtruck driver who becomes wealthy in spite of his ignorant and uncivilized ways. Ultimately, in the Arkansas of *Destiny's Chickens* we find that the redneck mindset, like W. J. Cash's "mind of the South," brings low everything in its path.[41]

Arkansas's unique location in the South and its geographical diversity challenges the would-be generalizer. A culture and landscape similar to Gwaltney's could have been found in much of the state, stretching along the major rivers and filling vast interstices between them. The state's location on the western periphery of the Confederacy, its nineteenth-century role as the last "civilized" stop before Indian Territory, rendered much of Arkansas a hybrid land. It was the meeting place of South and West. "Fort Smith ought to be in Oklahoma instead of Arkansas," opined one of the state's most famous fictional characters, Mattie Ross, and I dare say that a poll of modern Arkansawyers would back her up.[42] This Arkansas—the restless, frontier Arkansas—was, and is, no less a part of the state than the Delta or the Ozarks, though its peripheral nature, both physical and literary, has often made it seem so. This is the Arkansas reflected in the fiction of native son Charles Portis, a novelist for whom "Arkansas is always his center of consciousness," even though the action almost always takes place somewhere else. Portis's novels exude a dry wit straight out of the southwestern storytelling tradition, and like Mark Twain he has mastered the art of winking in print. He has also placed the traditionally defensive Arkansawyer on the offensive. "Portis takes the cliché of the Arkansas Traveler and stands it on its head," according to one critic, by taking "his Arkansas protagonists and set[ting] them on the move, launching them into a bewildering, and sometimes dangerous, world."[43] Whether his characters are naively self-confident (Mattie Ross in *True Grit*) or disconnected and drifting (Ray Midge in *The Dog of the South*), they "leave Arkansas and most of them come back sooner or later."[44] And even when they are as painfully ordinary as Midge, a cuckolded career student who pursues his runaway wife and his Ford Torino all the way to the jungles of Honduras, Portis portrays them in a favorable light, unlike Gwaltney, and by extension restores to the Arkansaw image the traits of independence, stubbornness, and a sort of natural decency.

The Portis novel that most forcefully reconsiders the Arkansas Traveler is also his most famous, *True Grit,* which became a bestseller after its release in 1968, even before being made into a successful and award-winning John Wayne movie. The story concerns the adventure of fourteen-year-old Mattie Ross, a Yell County farm girl who enlists the aid of a federal marshal, "Rooster" Cogburn, and a Texas ranger in her determined pursuit of her father's murderer into Indian Territory in the 1870s. It is narrated by a much older, but no less gritty, Mattie in the 1920s. Portis challenges the presuppositions of readers reared on Arkansas stereotypes by presenting Mattie as literate, articulate, self-confident, and even self-righteous, a regular Yankee schoolmarm in the making in western Arkansas. She regularly voices her low opinion of border-town Fort Smith, contrasting life there with that back home in Christian, civilized Yell County. Shrewd yet naive, bold yet vulnerable, she outdickers a horse trader, earns the admiration of her two incredulous companions, and survives a broken arm and rattlesnake bite to see justice and death meted out to a killer. "People who don't like Arkansas can go to the devil!" Portis has Mattie Ross tell a disre-

spectable Fort Smith horse trader.[45] It's a command defensive and courageous, and in Portis's world Arkansawyers have the ability to be both.

But, as we have seen, Gwaltney's and Portis's images of Arkansas were
to be nothing more than alternative visions, secondary images to the state's
traditional and persistent hillbilly persona. Gwaltney's decent if unspectac-
ular fiction flew under the radar, while Portis's highly acclaimed work
soared on the wings of *True Grit* for a time and inexplicably faded. But neither writer has left a literary imprint on the image of Arkansas as significant as that of novelist and Arkansas native Donald Harington. In a career
that has spanned more than four decades and produced more than a dozen
novels, Harington has created, populated, and examined the intentionally
fantastical yet utterly believable community of Stay More, a sort of Yokna-
patawpha County for Arkansas and the Ozarks. Inspired by the summers
he spent at his grandparents' general store in rural Madison County and
by the folklore books of Vance Randolph, Harington has crafted an Ozark
community that the old folklorist would have loved to call home, or at
least to visit every chance he got.

But before we go to Stay More, it should be noted that Harington's
own literary journey reflects an evolution that we have just witnessed. Stay
More and the Ingledews were no where to be found in the writer's first
novel, *The Cherry Pit,* a rumination that Thomas Wolfe might have penned
had he been born three decades later and in Little Rock. Published in 1965,
the memories of Little Rock Central still fresh and the city's lurching and
hesitant journey into modernity still in progress, *The Cherry Pit* deals with
the Arkansas perched on the precipice of racial and cultural transformation, the Arkansas that the world saw in the battle over Central High. But
just as the hillbilly reclaimed his dominance of the Arkansaw image with
the arrival of the folk revival and reemergence of the rube Arkansawyer in
the 1960s, Harington found his way to the Ozarks and discovered a community like no other. His next novel, 1970's *Lightning Bug,* introduced readers
to Stay More, Arkansas, and only rarely since has Harington's fiction not
involved this community or its citizens, the Stay Morons.

Harington's Arkansaw offers yet another example of the dual nature
of the Arkansaw image, the gestalt that has been fundamental to perceptions of the state and its people since the early nineteenth century. Two
different readers can come away from a Harington novel with widely diver-
gent notions of Arkansas Ozarkers and of the novelist's opinion of them.
It might seem ridiculous to claim that a novelist's loving portrait of his hill-
country characters could include ample helpings of stereotyping: moonshining, illiteracy, superstition, incest. For some readers, Harington's
overindulgence in such base stereotypes obscures any genuine fondness he
might display for his characters, and such a reader is likely to dismiss the

novelist as yet another peddler of cornpone caricature, one even more per-
fidious as a native enabler of the Arkansaw image. Literary scholar William J.
Schafer espoused just such a view. While the Arkansaw world created by
Harington reflected "his concepts of noble savagery and life-affirming earth-
iness," Schafer argued, "it is perhaps no more trustworthy or interesting
than the overtly derogatory stereotyping that filled the pages of nineteenth-
century local colorists' mountain romances or created the grotesqueries of
the comic-strip, B-movie, TV-sitcom hillbilly farces."[46]

Others would see in his copulating cousins and store-porch simpletons
the tools of Harington's not-so-subtle deconstruction of the Arkansaw
image. The overwrought manner in which he treats the taboos that would
strike the chamber of commerce with communal apoplexy underscores the
absurdity of stereotype without denying the existence of such supposedly
backwoods traits, in fictional Arkansaw or in the real Arkansas.

Beneath the hillbilly hilarity and decidedly non-Victorian sexual
exploits of Stay More runs the familiar stream of romanticism that con-
nects Harington's novels to Vance Randolph and Charles Morrow Wilson
and C. F. M. Noland and Friedrich Gerstäcker. One element of this romantic spirit must have been the nostalgic longing for home. Harington's earliest, and arguably best, evocations of a bygone Arkansaw were written, he
admits, in a state of "desperate homesickness for the state of Arkansas."
The soul-searching New England college professor and Arkansas expatriate—and thinly disguised stand-in for the author himself—in *Some Other
Place. The Right Place.* (1972) so longs for home that "even the squalid ugli-
ness of flatland eastern Arkansas will seem lovely, lovely, to him."[47] Just as
Mark Twain had met the unpleasantries of his Victorian New England life
by navigating the riverine memories of boyhood, the expatriate Harington
found solace in the creation of his own Arkansaw community.

Yet, Harington's Stay More novels are not mere escapism. For Harington,
as for Randolph before him, the Ozark region—or at least a set of anachronistic Ozarkers who captured a new generation's fancy in the 1960s and
1970s—represents everything that has been deemed backward and unprogressive by modern American society. The hill country is a last bastion
against "PROG RESS," a holdout against the old Yankee march toward the
kingdom of God on earth, a kingdom that Stay Morons regard with the
incredulity generally reserved for a revenuer. And Harington appreciates
his Stay Morons for their cussedness and nonconformity, even if this backwoods reticence might emanate as much from insecurity and provincialism as from idealism. Harington's is a nuanced romanticism, and like
Randolph he senses that the Arkansawyer's fight with modernity is doomed
to be a losing battle. Consequently, according to literary scholar Linda K.
Hughes, Harington's fiction, like that of a more widely read romantic, Sir

Novelist Donald Harington, c. 1976, Arcata Springs. Ozark Institute
Records (MC 252), box 9, file 1, number 1. Special Collections,
University of Arkansas Libraries, Fayetteville.

Walter Scott, depicts a contested space between two cultures and two eras.
Ultimately and ironically, claims Hughes, Harington utilizes the literary
techniques of the postmodernist to preserve, not deconstruct, his nostalgic vision of the Ozarks.[48]

Harington's postmodern tendencies impact the evolution of the
Arkansaw image like no other contribution we have discussed. Unlike other
writers, journalists, cartoonists, and performers who have contributed to the
image over the past two centuries, Harington reveals an awareness of
Arkansaw imagery and a willingness to confront stereotypes in his own fiction, which some would argue perpetuates them. In *The Architecture of the
Arkansas Ozarks,* the 1975 novel that serves as a brief history of Stay More
and best reflects the novelist's creative genius, Harington crafts a number
of scenes that explore Arkansaw/Ozark imagery: magazine-story-inspired
back-to-the-landers who want to live in reproduction barns but settle for
anachronistic cabins, which today "are mistaken for early settlers' houses";
city folks' fascination with Emelda Ingledew's cornhusk dolls; and the con-
gregation of idiots on the porch of Lum Ingledew's store who, through the

auspices of visiting sportsmen from Kansas City and St. Louis, provide "the origin of all of the spurious [Ozark] humor, not to mention the ridicule, that has been perpetuated ever since."[49] Harington also finds ways to use actual Arkansaw image makers in his work, such as the insertion of Faubus into *Let Us Build Us a City* and the central role of Vance Randolph as narrator in his 1996 novel *Butterfly Weed*.

In a 1975 survey of Arkansas imagery in fiction, historian Michael B. Dougan lamented Arkansas's misfortune that no pre–World War II "native son arose to do what Faulkner did for Mississippi."[50] While most scholars would argue that no writer has ever done for Arkansas what Faulkner did for Mississippi—when it gets right down to it, can any state claim such a native son who's bequeathed it with such a regionally specific yet universally profound body of literature?—Donald Harington has come close. If what you're looking for is Faulkner's South in Arkansas literature, though, you won't find it in the accounts of Stay More. This isn't the gothic South. The racial demographics skew toward lily-whiteness. Twentieth-century Stay Morons don't appear to be still fighting THE WAR, even in some existential sense—Jacob Ingledew was a Union officer and Reconstruction governor, for God's sake. Harington's fiction is sometimes pigeon-holed as Ozark or hillbilly by Arkansans, and perhaps that has contributed to the author's low profile in the state and modest sales that have never allowed him to quit his day job. (After all, *Entertainment Weekly* referred to him as "America's greatest unknown writer," practically the same title journalist Ron Rosenbaum bestowed upon Charles Portis in an *Esquire* piece.)[51] But in regards to the historic Arkansaw image, Stay More is quite a serviceable representative. As we have seen, the Arkansaw image has since the earliest days of the territory's existence been dominated by the white plebians of the backcountry, not always in the hills but increasingly so in the twentieth century. After a brief dalliance with a more Faulknerian image in the wake of Little Rock, Arkansas returned to familiar, mythical territory as a place populated by independent, resourceful, natural souls unburdened with the conventions of society, undeterred by an encroaching culture of conformity. For these hillbillies, Stay More is a pretty good place to come home to.

Bubba Clinton: In Case You Forgot We're Here

Thirty-five years after Orval Faubus and the Little Rock Nine focused the attention of the world on Little Rock, Arkansas found itself once again in the center of a media frenzy. And the spotlight beamed on the state and its people this time proved infinitely brighter and more revealing than the world's scrutiny in 1957. The man who would blow past Orval Faubus in the contest for most famous son of Arkansas was making his improbable run toward the White House, and the world couldn't get enough Arkansas. This small, sparsely populated state and its inhabitants—for generations ignored by real reporters and when noticed, more often than not, wishing that they hadn't been—were the flavor of the season and, whether farkle-berry-bitter or muscadine-sweet, everybody had to get a little taste. But as every Arkansas native understood, Bill Clinton's notoriety was bound to be a double-edged sword. Not only would Arkansas's real problems be placed under the microscope, but reporters, pundits, commentators, and enter-tainers would find this the ideal time to trot out the old Arkansaw image, an image aged yet remarkably vibrant in American popular culture.

Some defensive Arkansas people urged their governor not to throw his hat in the ring, suspecting that there was more than a grain of truth in one Beltway political consultant's proclamation that "Arkansas is guaranteed to be bashed. It's a given." Months before the kickoff of the Democratic pri-mary, Little Rock political consultant Jerry Russell warned that "'it would be embarrassing for the state for Clinton to run.'" John Robert Starr, manag-ing editor of the *Arkansas Democrat-Gazette,* echoed the fears of many Arkansans, as well as the conservative sentiments of Arkansas Republicans, when he worried that Clinton's "campaign will reinforce negative myths about our state." *Arkansas Gazette* columnist Max Brantley managed to couch his "please don't run" plea in stereotypical imagery. Commenting on Clinton's delayed but ultimately wholehearted endorsement of President George H. W. Bush's public stance on the recent coup attempt in the Soviet Union, Brantley wrote: "Why in the name of George Lindsey should we elect some Gomer Pyle whose best answer to a pressing international crisis is to solemnly intone, 'Me, too.'"[52]

The naysaying and skepticism of Arkansans might have sprung from a tradition of Clinton-hating, but it was just as likely to bubble up from the state's massive reservoir of an inferiority complex, a condition that the can-didate himself had battled, according to friends, as a Georgetown under-graduate and likely for years afterward. Many were certain that Bill Clinton, or any Arkansan so bold for that matter, would fall flat on his face and that he would bring his state down with him. Others, though, saw promise, especially economic opportunity, in a Clinton presidential bid. Marketing consultant Hugh Hart Pollard foresaw a public relations bonanza, "millions of dollars of favorable exposure," for Arkansas and a much-needed boost to economic development. So giddy was Pollard that, like a stray dog parading a bone in front of his fellow curs, he flaunted Arkansas's good for-tune in the face of her sure-to-be-envious bordering states by ending each paragraph with a lusty "Eat your heart out," followed by the name of a dif-ferent neighbor each time.[53]

Pollard and everyone else in Arkansas would get more publicity than they had ever bargained for. Once the national press became convinced that the governor of Arkansas might actually be a legitimate candidate, Arkansas, and especially Little Rock, found itself in the middle of a publicity storm that seemed to have blown in from another galaxy. For many journalists with little exposure to the South or to fly-over country in general, Arkansas possessed a certain exoticism, a land of dirt roads, big hairdos, and people who referred to the man who would be president as "Bill" not out of some exaggerated egalitarian sensibility but because they really knew William Jefferson Clinton, or had at least met him once. "Arkansas is a funny, even captivating place," wrote James M. Perry of the *Wall Street Journal*, "It is quirky and independent, and stubborn. It is full of contradictions."[54] Suddenly *real* journalists, not just travel writers, found themselves documenting the by now familiar signposts of the colorful South: hounds and plastic razorback hats, catfish fries and duck hunts, pickup trucks and corner café gossip. Just how central such things were to Clinton's background or to Arkansas's essence remained undetermined, but they served as reminders to reporters that they weren't in Manhattan anymore. Quirky Arkansiana could lend the Clinton campaign and presidency a valuable folksy, populistic aura, but reporters' other "discoveries"—such as Arkansas's perennial jostling with Mississippi for forty-ninth place in the rankings for a variety of indicators of economic and educational attainment—provided ammunition for Clinton's opponents and for commentators less inclined to find Linda Bloodworth Thomason's genteel eccentricity in the Land of Opportunity.

While former president Richard Nixon pulled no punches in criticizing the Arkansas governor as "Dogpatch," Bill Clinton's candidacy and early presidency proved a conundrum for many a journalist and Republican speechwriter. Left-of-center reporters from New York, Washington, and Los Angeles struggled to reconcile inherited cultural preconceptions and stereotypes of Arkansas with the articulate and media-savvy Rhodes Scholar–Yale Law graduate thrust suddenly before them. Ordinarily paragons of political correctness, many nonetheless found a target like Arkansas too inviting to pass up, the popular stereotypes of Arkansawyers in particular and white southerners in general too familiar to be incorrect, too accurate to be offensive. The power of the Arkansaw image produced head-scratching, unintentionally patronizing toss-offs. "As a child, Bill Clinton was gored by a boar in the Arkansas bush because he was 'too fat and slow' to get away. He's been running ever since," commented a writer for *Newsweek*. *Time*'s Margaret Carlson identified Clinton as "one of the first from [Hope] to go to college"—in spite of the fact that his family had moved to Hot Springs when he was small—and dipped into the Arkansaw

Ma and Pa salt and pepper shakers, just two of the hundreds of hillbilly and Arkansaw curios available in generations of gift shops.

image inkwell when describing Clinton's defeat for gubernatorial reelection in 1980. "In Pea Ridge and the Ozarks, the voters resented the notion that this whiz kid had returned home to put shoes on everybody and introduce them to book learning."[55]

In New York City, where provincialism is leavened with a convenient dollop of myopia, Clinton's Arkansas origins provided the starting point for a variety of putdowns. Talk radio host Don Imus dismissed the candidate as a "redneck bozo." Protesters welcomed the Arkansas governor with "Bubba Stinks" signs. Following a Clinton speech on the topic of black-Jewish relations, one incredulous audience member cracked, "'What does this bubba know from bar mitzvahs?'" By the time the Clintons pulled the jalopy into the White House drive, the Big Apple had developed its own little Bubba cottage industry to denigrate, and occasionally honor, Clinton. In early 1993 the publishers of the *Quayle Quarterly,* a magazine devoted to mocking Vice President Dan Quayle, announced that they were "celebrating the first Bubba president" with a new quarterly entitled simply *Bubba.* And a northeastern admirer (one would assume) of the Arkansas governor named a racehorse Bubba Clinton. Taking a page from the Arkansas manual of good-natured self-deprecation, Clinton made a last-minute campaign stop at a New Jersey racetrack to wish his thoroughbred namesake a good run. He had learned a thing or two about co-opting the Arkansaw image.[56]

Clinton also realized that there were benefits to an Arkansas background, especially when running on populistic economic promises against a blueblood like George H. W. Bush. He had no log cabin birth story ala Orval Faubus, but he did have a brush or two with an outhouse to tell about, and the fact that his grandparents had ranked somewhere below the middle class certainly didn't hurt his appeal to the masses.[57] But it's one thing to be able to craft an up-from-poverty narrative, regardless of the level of craftiness that might require. It's quite another thing to fend off critics arguing that Arkansas forty years later had made only modest advances beyond the outhouse era. Asked months before the primary season how he would advise a political opponent of Clinton, Jerry Russell summoned a powerful if unflattering motto: "'He'll do for America what he's done for Arkansas.'" The implication, of course, was that Clinton's detractors need look no farther than the ample statistical evidence of Arkansas's laggard economy, struggling school system, and poor climate for champions of labor and the environment.[58] It wasn't as if Clinton had inherited a state renowned for its progressivism and economic development, but if he was inclined to take credit for the good he had to answer for the bad, and his Democratic primary challengers and Republicans knew it.

In a piece for the *Los Angeles Times* in late 1991, Elaine Ciulla Kamarck gave Arkansans a taste of things to come when she referred to Arkansas as "a state that resembles, in some ways, a Third World country." In a brief jaunt through the state she discovered "mind-numbing, mostly rural, poverty" existing "alongside a handful of extremely rich people who form a small and interconnected elite." Clinton would weather such blows from the left, as well as subtler digs from primary opponents, such as Virginia governor Douglas Wilder's claim that Arkansas's comparative unimportance freed Clinton for the campaign trail and thus presented him an advantage over other hopefuls, but George H. W. Bush and Ross Perot would focus their sights on the Arkansas of poverty and illiteracy.[59]

Jerry Russell should have billed the Republican National Committee, for by the fall debates of 1992 President Bush was warning anyone who would listen that Bill Clinton would "do for the United States what he's done for Arkansas." Angering many with his description of Arkansas as the "lowest of the low," Bush and his camp took advantage of the state's statistical shortcomings. Republicans noted that Arkansas ranked in the bottom five in such crucial indexes as median household income, average annual pay, average hourly earnings, expenditures for public schools, number of doctors and dentists per capita, and Green Index environmental ranking. Clinton's Arkansas heritage was tailor-made for attack politics. At a pro-Bush rally in Ohio, actor Bruce Willis exclaimed that Arkansas was "synonymous with 'last in everything.'" One Republican television ad featured footage of Clinton with "hillbilly music playing in the background." Delegates at the Republican National Convention in Houston donned buttons dismissing Clinton as the "Failed Governor of a Small State," so small, apparently, that Bush had trouble locating it on a map. In a speech just a couple of weeks earlier, the president had referred to his opponent as "the governor of a certain state with a profitable chicken industry . . . located somewhere between Texas and Oklahoma." In a thirty-minute television spot aired a couple of nights before the election, independent candidate Ross Perot, raised just across the state line in Texarkana, took a swipe or two at the "chicken man" and his state that sat "at the bottom of everything." Generating more Arkansan protest than anything else may have been the speech of Marilyn Quayle, wife of the vice president, at the Republican National Convention, in which she asked the viewing public and convention delegates, some of whom were from Arkansas, "Do we want our country to look like Arkansas?" Her subsequent attempt to ameliorate bruised feelings in Arkansas lost a bit of its punch when it arrived at the *Arkansas Democrat-Gazette* office in an envelope addressed to "Little Rock, Arizona."[60]

Given the state's, and especially central Arkansas's, tradition of defensiveness, it is no surprise that the fallout from Marilyn Quayle's remarks lingered in Little Rock for weeks. In fact, a sensitive Arkansas press corps maintained a high-powered radar that detected insults, perceived insults, and sometimes just plain unpopular truths and diligently reported them to a readership anticipating slurs and poised to react with righteous indignation. Even though it refrained from endorsing Clinton, the right-leaning *Arkansas Democrat-Gazette* frequently found itself in the position of defending the state from criticism by the Bush camp. Arkansas Republicans also experienced divided loyalties. While other states' delegates at the Republican National Convention sported their "Failed Governor of a Small State" buttons, the Arkansans there came up with their own design, "Arkansas Pride." The path to an unbridled defense of both Clinton and the state lay open to Democrats, however. In response to President Bush's geographical gaffe, Senator David Pryor sent a stack of maps to the White House and took to the grandstand: "I want to say on behalf of the nearly two and a half million people of my state that we resent this, and we don't understand the low tone that these people are trying to set." Betsey Wright, Clinton's deputy campaign chair, fended off Republican attacks against the candidate and his state with a steady stream of rejoinders and rebuttals.[61]

Although the Bush campaign carefully avoided direct attacks on Arkansas's citizenry and the use of such inflammatory terms as Bubba and rednecks, many in Arkansas interpreted the president's debate remarks in the language of the Arkansaw image. Trolling through the southern rim of the Ozarks after the final televised debate, reporter Ronald Smothers found one farmer who claimed Bush's negative remarks about Arkansas "reminded him of the 'hillbilly put-downs' he and other Arkansans used to hear in the Army." The mayor of the tiny Van Buren County burg of Shirley agreed. "He didn't use the word 'hillbilly,' but that's what a lot of us thought about when he" called Arkansas the "lowest of the low." And it wasn't just Arkansas folks picking up on Bush's and Perot's use of thinly veiled stereotype. In a skit lampooning the presidential election debates, *Saturday Night Live* encapsulated in less than a minute's time the continuing power and cultural cache of the Arkansaw image and its intersection with Arkansas defensiveness and attack politics. In the late-night comic version of the debate, newsman and debate moderator Sam Donaldson (played by Kevin Nealon) addresses the Arkansas candidate:

> Governor Clinton, let's be frank. You're running for president, yet the main streets of your capital city, Little Rock, are something out of *Lil' Abner,* with buxom underage girls in cut-off denims prancing around in front of Jethro and Billy Bob while corn-cob-pipe-smoking, shotgun-toting grannies fire indiscriminately at runaway hogs.

Not to be outdone, Ross Perot (Dana Carvey) calls Clinton "cracker boy" and launches into his own diatribe at the expense of Arkansas.

> Why're we talking about Arkansas? Hell, everybody knows all they got down there is a bunch of ignorant, inbred crackers, peckerwoods, catch me? Now, can we talk about the deficit? While we been here jabbering, the deficit's increased by half-a-million dollars. That's enough to buy a still and a new outhouse for every family in Little Rock.[62]

An inferiority complex doesn't go away overnight. Neither does almost two centuries of imagery. But a lot of Arkansans were convinced that Bill Clinton's election as president represented the first huge step toward reversing generations of negative stereotypes. In a visit to Little Rock in the aftermath of the 1992 election, one writer for the *New York Times* found Clinton's home staters basking in the glow of the president-to-be. There was a vicarious pleasure to be had in the triumph of their governor, even if they were among the almost 60 percent of Americans who hadn't voted for Clinton, for to people in Arkansas this was the state's victory just as much as it was the governor's. It was an opportunity to prove to the nation that Arkansas was more than the hillbilly state of popular culture. An elderly barber beamed with pride over Clinton's election, assured that his presidency would "make a lot of people realize that we're not just a bunch of rednecks and hillbillies." A clothing store manager, raised a sharecropper's son, suspected, as did so many in the state, that outsiders "thought of Arkansas as hardly a state at all, just some back place where nobody lived except a few old hillbillies." "Clinton's election will make people realize Arkansas is part of the country, too," he stated in confidence, "They'll see we're the same sort of people they are, except perhaps a little more friendly." A few months later, in the early days of the Clinton presidency, an Associated Press writer found the Arkansaw image still on the minds of Little Rockers. One woman celebrated the "whole different image of Arkansas." "We're not barefoot and pregnant all the time, running in the woods." In spite of his political differences with the president, a Republican state senator could appreciate what he perceived as an improvement in the image of Arkansas. "We're not a bunch of hillbillies down here. We're just glad some of the rest of the country is beginning to realize that."[63]

While many in Arkansas were curious to see what Clinton's presidency could do for the Arkansaw image, some folks in Washington, D.C., and elsewhere around the nation wondered what an infusion of Arkansawyers would and could do for the nation's capital. As one might expect, the arrival of the Clinton team in D.C. provided sport for the locals, unaccustomed as they were to large numbers of newcomers, many of them in important positions, who didn't yet look and act like Washingtonians. The rumors that Bill and Hillary had arrived in town driving a Ford pickup, with the first-mother, Virginia Kelley, perched atop a rocker mounted on a stack of mattresses, turned out to be false. A brief period of something akin to gawking at carnies ensued. So taken with the naive attitudes and fresh faces of young Clinton staffers from Arkansas was the *Washington Post's* Joel Achenbach that he nicknamed these coat-tailers "Arkanauts," the brave few who had risked breaking one of the cherished traditions of their people: "that he or she spends virtually all of his or her life in Arkansas." Achenbach's observations revealed the survival of the dualistic Arkansaw image into the late twentieth century. Beneath his smug and probably unintentionally offensive glibness—he refers to one young staffer's shock of curly hair as "Li'l Abner-esque"—lay a genuine admiration for these unpretentious and polite Arkansans, these descendants of the natural man of Arkansaw legend. "Perhaps they'll learn to walk fast, dress severely and talk like a press release," feared Achenbach, "But maybe . . . the Arkanauts will stay the same, immutably Arkansan, and Washington will be what changes. Into something nicer."[64]

Immutably Arkansan. Achenbach's copy editor could have stricken the phrase as redundant. For generations the name Arkansas—and, more purely, Arkansaw—had been synonymous with immutability. This inability or unwillingness to change seemed part and parcel of the Arkansaw experience, fundamental to what it meant to be *Arkansaw*. This resistance or obliviousness to change could be bad or good, depending upon the context and the observer. It shone through the Stay Morons' detestation of PROG RESS. It could manifest itself in the screaming, hate-filled throngs at Central High. It was in the spring water that nourished the "deliberately unprogressive" people of Vance Randolph's Ozarks. It stunted the Arkansas economy, sapped the Arkansawyer's ambition, and sentenced him to a peasant's education. It imbued the frontiersman and hunter with a resourcefulness and independence that bode well for democracy and American achievement. It glimmered in the sheen of an Arkansas toothpick and glowered in the shadows of a violent and reckless place. Arkansas had changed in many ways by the 1990s, but in a fundamental sense the Arkansaw image remained the Janus-faced wonder that it had always been.

Conclusion

Bernie Babcock, Charles H. Brough, and Ham Moses must have been turning in their graves in the summer of 2000. Late-night comedians and political pundits must have been counting their lucky stars. The news coming out of Little Rock sounded like some sort of postmodern, ironic prank, as if Donald Harington had suddenly found himself in charge of public relations for his native state. Mike Huckabee and his family were temporarily vacating the aging governor's mansion, long overdue for renovations, and their new dwelling place? A mobile home. Well, technically a "manufactured home," as the first family and their handlers insisted, but no amount of euphemism repetition was going to keep the hounds at bay. Sure, this thing had no wheels and its underbelly was sealed up tighter than Dick's hatband, but the crucial elements of the story were indisputable—the leader of the great state of Arkansas had worn out his house and was now living in a big ole trailer.[1]

It's not that anyone with a pulse in Arkansas couldn't sense what was coming. "I know," sighed first lady Janet Huckabee, "of all the states in the world, for Arkansas to be the one with a governor living in manufactured housing—well, you can just hear the jokes already." And the jokes, wisecracks, and condescending analysis did come. Scotland's *Sunday Herald* reported the story under the headline "Possum Pie and Down-Home Hospitality for the 'Trailer Trash' Governor." Noting that Little Rock was "known less for sophistication than for big hair, hillbillies and pick-up trucks," the paper observed (correctly) that the Huckabees' new triple-wide would be larger and more valuable than most immobile homes in the state. NBC's Jay Leno, who made the story a key component of his *Tonight Show* monologues for the better part of a month, quipped that the new governor's pad might even open the Huckabees up to charges that they were putting on airs. After about three weeks of ribbing from comedians around the nation, the Huckabees agreed to appear via remote camera on the *Tonight Show*. For a few minutes Mike and Janet Huckabee went toe-to-toe with Leno, and viewers caught their first glimpse of yet another media-savvy Arkansas first family. After playing along with the host's put-downs, the governor drew the evening's biggest laugh when he promised Leno that "it's actually large enough so that we could get you and your chin inside," a reference to the comedian's most famous oversized facial feature. Like most other prominent Arkansans on whom the national or international spotlight had shone, the Huckabees had already become adept at

185

defending themselves and their state with a little self-deprecating deflection.[2]

The manufactured home episode illustrated a few things. First, although it might have lost some of its cultural relevance in the decades since World War II, the Arkansaw image would survive into the new millennium. If nothing else, it seemed that Arkansas would make sure of that. Second, the reaction of the Huckabees, a mixture of defensiveness and self-deprecation, reminded us that Arkansas people remained first and foremost cognizant of the state's place in the American consciousness and that they retained the ability to laugh at themselves. As Governor Huckabee explained it to Leno: "One of the things we want to do is to show that people in Arkansas aren't all that sensitive about people making light of us. We know who we are." Huckabee knew full well that there were a good many Arkansans who took exception to their state's reoccurring role as the butt of national jokes and that more than a few resented his decision to knowingly invite derision with his triple-wide plan. Finally, Huckabee's ultimate decision to subject his state to stereotyping and mirth-making in order to save taxpayers a few dollars reflected the old spirit of nonconformity that had inspired admiration for the natural Arkie. Speaking for defiant Arkansawyers through the generations, the governor told reporters at a Little Rock press conference, "Let the people laugh. I think the difference between an Arkansan and some uptight, wound-up northerner, is that . . . we're laughing with you, because we like the way we live." Pete Whetstone and Jacob Ingledew couldn't have said it any better.[3]

We've come a long way since Henry Rowe Schoolcraft quilled a few uncomplimentary lines about Arkansawyers the better part of two centuries ago. Or have we? In this worrisome and unfathomable thing we call time our brief experience with a place called Arkansas barely qualifies as a blip. Only the myopic mortal would wonder over the survival of a state's image. But we are what we are. This may not represent the pinnacle of enlightenment, but I would argue it beats watching the Weather Channel on a clear day or playing checkers. The fact that you've just read a book on the history of the Arkansaw image suggests that whatever it means to be from Arkansas still has some sort of cultural relevance in the twenty-first century, at least for the time being and at least for Arkansans and Arkansawyers. It also suggests that the people of Arkansas are probably more obsessed with their state's image than are the people of any other state. Even if Americans haven't reserved a special place in their hearts for good old Arkansas, we've long been convinced that they have. And perception is a powerful thing.

But we can't deny that Arkansas probably no longer occupies quite the unique position that it once held in the American consciousness, and it now seems likely that this uniqueness has probably been exaggerated over the years by our own defensiveness. The Arkansas and Arkansans offered up for public consumption over the past two decades offer a hodgepodge of images, some hewing close to the dualistic Arkansaw image we have chronicled and others venturing far afield. Prolific mystery writer and Arkansas native Joan Hess has rediscovered the backwoods Ozarks in her popular Maggody series, set in a small Arkansas town peopled by stock characters straight out of the Hollywood hillbilly instruction manual. Hess's humorous and unsophisticated books have reached an audience larger than Donald Harington's, which is unfortunate, for other than Sheriff Arly Hanks, who has returned to her hometown after seasoning in New York, most of the other characters remain one-dimensional.[4] Reporters and late-night comedians couldn't believe their luck when the Huckabees moved into that triple-wide "manufactured home" in the summer of 2000, and *The Economist*, a British news magazine, likened the Clinton Presidential Library to a trailer house. The proliferation of internet blogs has reunited discussions of Arkansas and Arkansawyers with descriptive references now infrequently found in the mainstream media—rednecks, hillbillies, white trash. And even after a full term removed from the White House, Bill Clinton was still subject to the occasional cultural putdown, such as New York representative Charles Rangel's description of the former president as "a redneck" in an interview with *New York Magazine*. When later asked on a New York radio program if he still believed Clinton was a redneck, Rangel remarked, "Of course he is. He's from Arkansas."[5]

The Clinton presidency, Arkansas's moment in the spotlight, with its peaks and valleys and sagas of triumphs and foibles, ultimately revealed a very human Bill Clinton and by extension a very American Arkansas, a place that might not be that different after all. Mass media depictions of Arkansas and Arkansas characters in recent years have often offered alternatives to the dual Arkansaw image. The 1991 feature film *Thelma and Louise*, perhaps the most recognized Arkansas-related pop-cultural product during Clinton's run for president, was a late twentieth-century feminist manifesto whose protagonists just happened to be Arkansas women. The early 1990s television sitcom *Evening Shade*, starring Burt Reynolds and produced by Clinton friends Linda Bloodworth Thomason and Arkansas native Harry Thomason, conjured an eccentric yet rather idyllic post–civil rights era portrait of a small, integrated Arkansas town. Arkansas native Billy Bob Thornton's 1996 movie, *Sling Blade*, deftly incorporated potentially one-dimensional, stereotypical characters (the "slow" man-child, the abusive, drunken redneck, and a few good old boys) into the best movie ever filmed in or set in the state. Fox Television's *The Simple Life*, a "reality" *Green Acres* that sent Hollywood socialite brats Paris Hilton and Nicole Richie to live with an Altus, Arkansas, farm family for three months, appeared to be a set-up for making fun of hicks but instead offered a striking contrast between the sheltered and callous shallowness of the stars and the "natural" decency of their hosts. It's hard to imagine *South Park*'s resident Arkansan Mr./Mrs. Garrison, a closeted homosexual-turned-transgendered lesbian, in the pre-Clinton television landscape. Come to think of it, it is difficult to imagine a character of that description period, regardless of state of origin. And Arkansas's most successful musical export of the present century has been not Tracy Lawrence, Buddy Jewell, or Joe Nichols (all popular country singers) but Grammy-winning Little Rock alternative rock band Evanescence. All of this is simply to suggest that as the twenty-first century progresses we will likely continue to encounter the old familiar Arkansaw image, for good and bad, but we may be just as likely to find representations of Arkansas that bear little resemblance to that image. As the twentieth century's most significant purveyors of the Arkansaw image (be they radio programs, plays, movies, theme parks, whatever) fade into memory and as Arkansas joins the rest of the nation in distancing itself from its rural and agricultural past, it is only natural that the Arkansaw image would begin to fade away.

The hillbilly image of Arkansas may be less evident in American popular culture today, but does that reflect real change in the state? There is not always a direct correlation between reality and perception, but even the most die-hard defender of Arkansas would have to admit that the state has historically set itself up for condemnation. What about now? Are we deserving of whatever derision we might receive? Let's take a page out of Mencken's book and analyze the statistical evidence for and against the Natural State. A survey of a variety of statistical tables ranking the fifty states reveals what just about anyone might expect—Arkansas is generally low where you want to be high and high where low might be a good thing. We rarely rank dead last, but we're generally not far behind Mississippi or whatever unfortunate state dwells in a particular cellar.

It should come as no surprise that Arkansas makes a poor showing in economic rankings. Poverty, after all, has been a hallmark of the Arkansaw image. In the oft-cited median family income category in 2004, Arkansas found itself in the "Thank God for Mississippi" position, forty-ninth out of the fifty states and a full 25 percent below the national average. Only Mississippi, Louisiana, and New Mexico reported higher percentages of poverty-stricken people in 2004, and in only three states, and none in the old Confederacy, were citizens more burdened by taxes than were those in Arkansas.[6] Despite the state's comparative poverty, only eight states reported fewer welfare recipients per capita in 2003 than did Arkansas. Perhaps there is something to the image of the independent and resourceful

Hillbilly postcards have long been a staple of the Arkansaw image, but so have more romantic postcards depicting the beauty and serenity of rural Arkansas. Courtesy of Brooks Blevins.

Arkansawyer; or maybe this statistic is more a reflection of the tradition of Jeffersonian government in Arkansas.

Arkansas's educational standing continues to mirror its economic status. Only West Virginia counted fewer college graduates per capita, and Arkansas's 79.2 percent high school graduation rate bested only Texas and Louisiana in 2004. The 6.1 percent of Arkansas residents with advanced degrees placed us in forty-ninth place, slightly ahead of South Dakota. But the Natural State's lowly rankings were not for lack of effort. Arkansas ranked fifteenth nationally in total expenditures on public education when adjusted for gross domestic product, and by the early twenty-first century Arkansas students were regularly scoring near the middle of the pack on national educational assessments. Morgan Quitno Press's "Smartest State" computations, which put less emphasis on school spending, ranked Arkansas thirty-seventh in 2005 and ahead of such states as Oregon and California.

Arkansas also fared slightly better than might be expected in Morgan Quitno's "Healthiest State" category, climbing out of the bottom ten. The state avoided the top ten of such rankings as violent crime, homicide, percentage of residents incarcerated, and Morgan Quitno's "Most Dangerous State" category. In the hands of the right spin doctor, the state's number-thirty ranking in robberies per capita could become a testament to a people unaffected by the scourge of materialism—in the wrong hands a judgment on how little of value there was to steal. Given the press the state received over the governor's triple-wide, it might come as a surprise to learn that in 2004 Arkansas failed to crack the top ten in the percentage of people living in mobile homes—though at number eleven there was every reason to believe that we could climb into that category before the decade was out. But whether or not our houses came with wheels attached, they weren't likely to be featured in *Architectural Digest,* for Arkansas finished dead last in the nation in the average value of owner-occupied abodes. Perhaps the fact that Arkansawyers had so little to come home to caused more than a few to take up roosting somewhere else; only Nevada reported a higher divorce rate than Arkansas in 2002.

We could make something of the fact that New Hampshire, Connecticut, and Rhode Island all boasted more Walmarts per capita than the state that hatched the retail behemoth, but we won't. And there are those among us who consider it an honor that Arkansas finished last in the country in the number of Starbucks coffee shops per capita. But the people at Morgan Quitno must have preferred their java anyway but black. In their "Livability" category, the granddaddy of all state rankings, more or less, and one designed to identify the best and worst states in which to live, Arkansas came in third from the bottom, thanking the Lord for Louisiana and, of course, Mississippi.

So what does this all mean? Well, for starters, it would appear that our neighbor across the big river hasn't loosened its grip on the sobriquet H. L. Mencken bestowed upon it more than three-quarters of a century ago. Statistically speaking, Mississippi remains the "worst American state." So we've got that going for us. Deflecting criticism onto others is a tried-and-true method of Arkansas defensiveness, but the past two decades have presented unique opportunities to improve the state's image and chip away at the Arkansas inferiority complex. Arkansas's most famous son lasted two full terms in the White House, besting Georgia's president and any chief executive to come out of Massachusetts or Ohio. Like any son, he found ways to make his Arkansas family proud and on occasion to embarrass us. Just weeks after the 1992 presidential election, Carol Tucker Foreman, sister of governor-elect Jim Guy Tucker, mused that "Clinton's election will help people get over their inferiority complex." After two months of the Clinton presidency, *Arkansas Democrat-Gazette* editorial page editor Paul Greenberg noted an improvement in the state's collective self-esteem but observed that "the inferiority complex is still there."[7]

The Clinton presidency did not cure our inferiority complex, nor did it wipe out 180 years of the Arkansaw image. But the nation's saturation with all things Arkansas in the early 1990s helped demystify the state and went a long way toward stripping it of its exoticism and robbing it of any perceived uniqueness. General Wesley Clark's Arkansas origins seemed to be a non-issue in the 2004 Democratic primaries, and that was probably due as much to the Clinton factor as to the fact that Clark's connection with the state was only a tenuous one after his high school graduation. By the time Mike Huckabee made his surprising run in the 2008 Republican primary, the nation had grown accustomed to voting for, or watching people vote for, articulate presidential candidates from the Natural State. The former Arkansas governor's home state remained essentially a non-factor, except insofar as it helped explain, according to some pundits, the conservative evangelicalism at the heart of his campaign. As the homogenizing and modernizing influences of the twenty-first century continue to chip away at regional and state distinctiveness and as Arkansas experiences demographic change and suburbanization, the old Arkansaw image of slovenly hillbillies and deliberately unprogressive good old boys will be less and less a reflection of reality and more and more a product of history and the folklore of popular culture. That doesn't make the Arkansaw image any less useful for many Americans. Arkansas can still serve as sitcom shorthand for a backward place, a state passed over by the forces of economic and cultural progressivism in modern America. It can also serve those romantically and nostalgically inclined or those disillusioned with the materialism and soullessness of modern society as a beacon of tin-roof, cussed nonconformity in a world of droning Babbittry.

The Arkansaw image can still be useful to Arkansawyers as well. In an essay published in the *American Mercury* in 1954, political pollster Eugene Newsom ruminated on the problems of his native state and the image issues that continued to dog Arkansawyers. In Newsom's estimation, the problem with Arkansas stemmed from its divided mind, or what we might recognize as the struggle between those for and against "progress." On the one hand were the chamber of commerce types, who defensively played down negative stereotypes while "whooping it up in a frenetic effort to bring in more industries, on the theory that industrial activity cures practically all ills." On the other were the "local yarn spinners," the folklorists, hillbilly hustlers, and champions of anachronism who fancied visiting writers "with fables involving the gowrow, the hickelsnoopus, the ringtailed tooter and its cousin, the hoo-hoo." The latter cherished and often sought to profit off of the very image that the former fought so hard to suppress, that is the "myth" of "the unshaven Arkie, the moonshiner, slow trains, malnutrition and mental debility, hookworms, hogs, the big fat lie, shoelessness, illiteracy, poverty, . . . windy politicians and hillbillies and paddlefeet who cannot seem to pronounce correctly the name of their native state."[8]

Skunk Holler Hillbilly Band, Springdale, Arkansas, 1943. *Standing, left to right:* Joe Robinson, "Doc" Boone, D. D. Deaver, Scott Price. *Sitting, left to right:* Yvonne Ballew, Rogers Sanders. Howard Clark, photographer. Courtesy of the Shiloh Museum of Ozark History / Caroline Price Clark Collection (S-2002-72-1214B).

"The brutal truth is, Arkansawyers are poor folks," wrote Newsom. "They just don't realize it." And no amount of manufacturer tax breaks and new shoe factories would make this untrue, he suspected. But Newsom had a plan, one at least partially tongue-in-cheek and not likely to earn endorsement at the Arkansas Industrial Development Commission or the state chamber of commerce.

> I say, breed up a race of razorbacks, as the Texans are doing with their longhorns; fire the old caplock muzzle-loader at the neighbors once a week. Give the inquiring stranger directions to Possum Trot or Goose Ankle, and give him a sample of Uncle Rafe's last run of corn squeezings. . . . If Arkansas is ever going to amount to anything, she's got to advertise the very characteristics she's been shushing for a hundred years. . . . What Arkansas needs to do is not look, dress, talk and think like and be indistinguishable from the other states. She needs to uncurl her little finger from the teacup and proclaim her known and recognized orneriness to the whole wide world.[9]

Newsom's vision, as we know more than half a century later, was not as far-fetched as it may have seemed and as he may have believed. His was a blueprint for heritage tourism, albeit a crasser version than the Rotary Club might approve of. Within a generation of the publication of his essay, Arkansas would boast tourism establishments capitalizing on the positive aspects of the Arkansaw image (Ozark Folk Center) as well as the negative (Dogpatch, U.S.A.).

Even if Eugene Newsom didn't completely comprehend the dual nature of the Arkansaw image, he recognized the constituencies within Arkansas's populace who drew from the image differing conclusions—progressive v. unprogressive, urban v. rural, better sort v. commoner, defensive v. apathetic. And unlike many other educated, ambitious Arkies, he was willing to admit that the Arkansaw image wasn't necessarily a bad thing. It depended on how you looked at it. It always has and it still does.

Within Arkansas the Vance Randolphs have struggled against the Charles H. Broughs for control of the Arkansaw image, one group exaggerating those characteristics that have kept Arkansawyers out of the American mainstream, the other overstating Arkansans' progressive tendencies and accomplishments. The real Arkansas has always resided somewhere between. Outside of Arkansas, writers, social commentators, cartoonists, and filmmakers have gazed upon Arkansaw and have tended toward one of two polarized images as well: a land of backward and most often buffoonish hillbillies whose very existence underscores the superiority of the Puritan-Progressive strand of American society or the habitat of the unpretentious, hearty natural man whose very survival amid the homogenizing influences of a materialistic and hyper-civilized society offers a glimmer of hope for those still harboring alternative visions of life in America, an antithesis to the American myth.

These often-contradictory bundles of characteristics, leavened with generous portions of defensiveness and provincialism and paranoia, constitute the surprisingly complex image of our state, this land of Arkansaw. More akin to one part of the Christian trinity than to some sort of doppelgängerish bizarro Arkansas, Arkansaw *is* Arkansas, only not exactly. As the frequency of scholarly treatments on the subject and the existence of this book attest, Arkansaw is a key element of our story. In the American popular culture universe, it has been *the* key element of our story. Arkansaw, not Arkansas, has been most conducive to lively fiction and exotic nonfiction. Arkansaw, not Arkansas, has shaped the notions of generations of Americans. It is Arkansaw that makes us defensive or proud, and defiant either way. Without Arkansaw, what would Arkansas be? A mid-South version of South Dakota? New Mexico with humidity and hickories? Maine with less grating accents? To paraphrase a former student who fessed up to a certain appreciation for his state's place in the American consciousness: "Let them say whatever they want about us; it doesn't bother me. At least they know we're here." And in this age of "reality" television, blogs, and general media narcissism, anonymity would seem the worst fate of all.

Admit it. We need Arkansaw. It's part of our heritage as Arkansawyers or Arkansans, maybe the most crucial part. To be sure, it gives us an excuse to feel sorry for ourselves, a balm we all need in this age of victimization, and a quick one-liner to explain our inability to navigate a subway system or order from the menu. But more important, it teaches us to laugh at ourselves, instills in us a sense of humility regardless of how far above our raising we may get, reminds us that name-calling really doesn't break bones, that try as we might there are things that are out of our control and can't be fixed, that life isn't always fair, that admitting our limitations isn't proof of weakness but of common sense, and that it ain't what you want that makes you fat—it's what you get. All valuable lessons, ones that too often go unlearned in localities too insistent on American exceptionalism and among populations too unaccustomed to being made fun of. My advice? To the Arkansawyer, keep on doing whatever it is you're doing, unless what you're doing is illegal, in which case I'll take no responsibility for advice offered. To the Arkansan, embrace your inner Arkansawyer, relinquish your uncalled for resentment of Bob Burns, and get over yourself. Don't get so bent out of shape over a joke or two, and, next time you find yourself telling someone, "Yes, I wear these shoes back home, too," or repeating the phrase "I'm fixing to call it a night" for a rapt cocktail crowd, just remind yourself that they don't know any better. And remember that there is a positive side to the Arkansaw image. It's all in how you look at it. But what do I know? I'm from Arkansas.

Notes

INTRODUCTION

1. Eugene Newsom, "What's Wrong with Arkansas?" *American Mercury,* May 1954, 41; Neal R. Peirce and Jerry Hagstrom, *The Book of America: Inside 50 States Today* (New York: W. W. Norton & Company, 1983), 478.

2. "Prejudice and Pride," *Time,* 27 July 1942.

3. In his study of Branson, Missouri, Aaron K. Ketchell notes this duality in the Ozark/hillbilly image and argues that "the characterization of the word has more often been affirmative than negative." Ketchell, *Holy Hills of the Ozarks: Religion and Tourism in Branson, Missouri* (Baltimore: Johns Hopkins University Press, 2007), 174.

4. C. Vann Woodward, "The Irony of Southern History," in *The Burden of Southern History,* rev. ed. (Baton Rouge: Louisiana State University Press, 1968), 190, 191.

5. The term "cotton snobs" comes from Daniel R. Hundley's *Social Relations in Our Southern States,* edited with an introduction by William J. Cooper Jr. (1860; Baton Rouge: Louisiana State University Press, 1979). See chapter 4.

6. James C. Cobb, *Away Down South: A History of Southern Identity* (New York: Oxford University Press, 2005), 5.

7. This statement emanates from a series of unscientific internet searches I conducted in March and June of 2007. I did exact phrase searches on Google.com for four different phrases: "STATE hillbilly," "STATE hillbillies," "hillbilly from STATE," and "hillbillies from STATE." The searches covered all southern states, a number of other rural nonsouthern states such as Kansas, Indiana, South Dakota, and Idaho, and the states of California and New York. Arkansas received more "hits" than any other state, almost 20 percent more than second-place Texas. When adjusted per capita, Arkansas was even more clearly the "hillbilliest" state, with almost 50 percent more hits than West Virginia and more than two and a half times as many hits as third-place Kentucky. Google searches conducted 20 March 2007 and 15 June 2007.

CHAPTER ONE

1. Henry Rowe Schoolcraft, *Rude Pursuits and Rugged Peaks: Schoolcraft's Ozark Journal, 1818–1819,* with introduction, map, and appendix by Milton D. Rafferty (Fayetteville: University of Arkansas Press, 1996), 63.

2. Ibid., 52.

3. See James A. Brown, *Prehistoric Southern Ozark Marginality: A Myth Exposed,* Missouri Archaeological Society Special Publications, No. 6 (Columbia: Missouri Archaeological Society, 1984). See also George Sabo III, Ann M. Early, Jerome C. Rose, Barbara A. Burnett, Louis Vogele Jr., and James P. Harcourt, *Human Adaptation in the Ozark and Ouachita Mountains,* Arkansas Archeological Survey Research Series, No. 31 (Fayetteville: Arkansas Archeological Survey, 1990).

4. Morris S. Arnold, "The Significance of Arkansas's Colonial Experience," in Jeannie Whayne, ed., *Cultural Encounters in the Early South: Indians and Europeans in Arkansas* (Fayetteville: University of Arkansas Press, 1995), 137.

5. Both sources quoted in Arnold, "Significance of Arkansas's Colonial Experience," 138.

6. Ibid.

7. Schoolcraft, *Rude Pursuits and Rugged Peaks,* 52, 53, 55, 56.

8. Ibid., 60.

9. Ibid., 63.

10. Ibid., 72–73.

11. Ibid., 74, 109 (quote).

12. Ibid., 74.

13. Ibid.

14. Thomas Nuttall, *A Journal of Travels into the Arkansas Territory During the Year 1819,* edited by Savoie Lottinville (1821; Norman: University of Oklahoma Press, 1980), 128.

15. Quoted in S. Charles Bolton, *Arkansas, 1800–1860: Remote and Restless* (Fayetteville: University of Arkansas Press, 1998), 33.

16. George William Featherstonhaugh, *Excursion Through the Slave States, from Washington on the Potomac to the Gulf of Mexico* (1844; New York: Negro Universities Press, 1968), 89, 92, 104, 114. See also Robert B. Cochran, "'Low, Degrading Scoundrels': George W. Featherstonhaugh's Contribution to the Bad Name of Arkansas," *Arkansas Historical Quarterly* 48 (Spring 1989): 3–16.

17. Henry Merrell, *The Autobiography of Henry Merrell: Industrial Missionary to the South,* edited by James L. Skinner (Athens: University of Georgia Press, 1991), 249–51.

18. Featherstonhaugh, *Excursion Through the Slave States,* 81, 109, 114.

19. Ibid., 111, 114.

20. Merrell, *Autobiography of Henry Merrell,* 274–75.

21. Ibid., 250.

22. Featherstonhaugh, *Excursion Through the Slave States,* 81, 104.

23. Friedrich Gerstäcker, *Wild Sports in the Far West: The Narrative of a German Wanderer Beyond the Mississippi, 1837–1843,* introduction and notes by Edna L. Steeves and Harrison R. Steeves (1854; Durham, N.C.: Duke University Press, 1968), 164.

24. Quoted in Bolton, *Remote and Restless,* 34; John Francis McDermott,

editor and annotator, *The Western Journals of Washington Irving* (Norman: University of Oklahoma Press, 1944), 165, 157; Charles Joseph Latrobe, *The Rambler in North America* (1836; New York: Johnson Reprint Corp., 1960), quoted in James R. Masterson, *Arkansas Folklore: The Arkansas Traveler, Davey Crockett, and Other Legends* (1942; Little Rock: Rose Publishing Co., 1974), 4; Frederick Marryat, *A Diary in America, with Remarks on Its Institutions* (London: Longman, Orme, Brown, Green & Longmans, 1839), quoted in Masterson, *Arkansas Folklore*, 4.

25. Quoted in Jane Louise Mesick, *The English Traveler in America, 1785–1835* (1922; Westport, Conn.: Greenwood Press, 1970), 42.

26. Featherstonhaugh, *Excursion Through the Slave States*, 97, 100, 136.

27. Merrell, *Autobiography of Henry Merrell*, 237.

28. Gerstäcker, *Wild Sports in the Far West*, 171.

29. Ibid., 171.

30. Ibid., 95, 242, 283, 374.

31. "The Creole Village: A Sketch from a Steamboat," in McDermott, ed. and ann., *The Western Journals of Washington Irving*, 173, 175, 179.

32. Herman Melville, *Moby-Dick*, with introduction and notes by Carl F. Hovde (1851; New York: Barnes & Noble Classics, 2005), 226.

33. John Q. Anderson, *With the Bark On: Popular Humor of the Old South* (Nashville, Tenn.: Vanderbilt University Press, 1967), 3.

34. Leonard Williams, ed., *Cavorting on the Devil's Fork: The Pete Whetstone Letters of C. F. M. Noland* (Memphis, Tenn.: Memphis State University Press, 1979), 122. See also Sarah Brown, *"The Arkansas Traveller:* Southwest Humor on Canvas," *Arkansas Historical Quarterly* 46 (Winter 1987): 348–75.

35. Ibid., 126.

36. Milton Rickels, *Thomas Bangs Thorpe: Humorist of the Old Southwest* (Baton Rouge: Louisiana State University Press, 1962), 51.

37. Ibid., 58, 59 (quote); J. A. Leo Lemay, "The Text, Tradition, and Themes of 'The Big Bear of Arkansas,'" *American Literature* 47 (November 1975): 335.

38. Michael B. Dougan, *Arkansas Odyssey: The Saga of Arkansas from Prehistoric Times to Present* (Little Rock: Rose Publishing Co., 1994), 537–38; Anderson, *With the Bark On*, 176, 239.

39. David Rattlehead, *The Life and Adventures of an Arkansaw Doctor*, edited by W. K. McNeil (Fayetteville: University of Arkansas Press, 1989), ix (first quote), x, 86–87 (second quote), 140, 141. Both James R. Masterson and W. K. McNeil expressed doubt that there was ever a Raccoon Bayou, Arkansas. There is, however, a small stream by that name in Poinsett County. It is unclear if the Raccoon Bayou that Byrn wrote about was in this vicinity.

40. Williams, *Cavorting on the Devil's Fork*, 210.

41. H. C. Mercer, "On the Track of 'The Arkansas Traveler,'" *Century*, March 1896, 709; Clyde Brion Davis, *The Arkansas*, Rivers of America Series (New York: Rinehart & Company, 1940), 254.

42. Terry Turner, "Arkansas Travelers [Baseball Team]," *Encyclopedia of Arkansas History & Culture,* http://www.encyclopediaofarkansas.net (accessed 8 August 2007).

43. Vance Randolph, *Ozark Folksongs,* vol. 3 (1946; Columbia: University of Missouri Press, 1980), 22–25.

44. Mercer, "On the Track of the Arkansas Traveler," 710, 711. For the most complete analysis of the Arkansas Traveler legend, see chapter 14 of Masterson, *Arkansas Folklore.*

45. Albert Pike, "Letters From Arkansas," *American Monthly Magazine,* 1836, 25.

46. Ibid., 26.

47. W. K. McNeil, "'By the Ozark Trail': The Image of the Ozarks in Popular and Folk Songs," *JEMF Quarterly* (Spring–Summer 1985): 21.

48. Mercer, "On the Track of the Arkansas Traveler," 707; Brown, "*The Arkansas Traveller,*" 349, 370. See also Walter Blair, "Inquisitive Yankee Descendants in Arkansas," *American Speech* 14 (February 1939): 11–22.

49. See Brooks Blevins, *Hill Folks: A History of Arkansas Ozarkers and Their Image* (Chapel Hill: University of North Carolina Press, 2002), 261–62.

50. Pike, "Letters From Arkansas," 26.

51. All quotations from letters quoted in William L. Shea, "A Semi-Savage State: The Image of Arkansas in the Civil War," in *Civil War Arkansas: Beyond Battles and Leaders,* edited by Anne J. Bailey and Daniel E. Sutherland (Fayetteville: University of Arkansas Press, 2000), 88.

52. Ibid., 89.

53. Ibid., 90.

54. Ibid.

55. Ibid., 89.

FIRST INTERLUDE

1. James R. Masterson, *Arkansas Folklore: The Arkansas Traveler, Davey Crockett, and Other Legends* (1942; Little Rock: Rose Publishing Co., 1974), 1.

2. Bob Lancaster, *Arkansas Democrat,* 5 December 1976, quoted in Friedlander, 70.

3. Foy Lisenby, "Talking Arkansas Up: The Wonder State in the Twentieth Century," *Mid-South Folklore* 6 (Winter 1978): 87–88 (quote); Morris S. Arnold, "The Significance of Arkansas's Colonial Experience," in Jeannie Whayne, ed., *Cultural Encounters in the Early South: Indians and Europeans in Arkansas* (Fayetteville: University of Arkansas Press, 1995), 135; S. Charles Bolton, *Territorial Ambition: Land and Society in Arkansas, 1800–1840* (Fayetteville: University of Arkansas Press, 1993), 37 (second quote). See also Foy Lisenby, "A Survey of Arkansas's Image Problem," *Arkansas Historical Quarterly* 30 (Spring 1971): 60–71, and Stephen A. Smith, "The Rhetorical Images of the Ozark Hillbilly," *Journal of Communication Studies* 4, no. 2 (1986): 1–7. See also W. C. Jameson, "The Image of

Arkansas: The View from at Home and Beyond," *Mid-America Folklore* 15 (Spring 1987): 54–62.

4. Lisenby, "Talking Arkansas Up," 85; S. Charles Bolton, "Slavery and the Defining of Arkansas," *Arkansas Historical Quarterly* 58 (Spring 1999): 22.

5. Michael B. Dougan, "Bumpkins and Bigots: The Arkansas Image in Fiction," *Publications of the Arkansas Philological Association* 1 (Summer 1975): 5–15; Lisenby, "Talking Arkansas Up," 87; Lee A. Dew, "'On a Slow Train Through Arkansaw'—The Negative Image of Arkansas in the Early Twentieth Century," *Arkansas Historical Quarterly* 39 (Summer 1980): 126.

6. E. E. Dale, "Arkansas: The Myth and the State," *Arkansas Historical Quarterly* 12 (1953): 22. Even before the impact of this millpond effect, in the first quarter of the nineteenth century Arkansas had served as an Indian territory in its own right, serving as a temporary abode of the Cherokee, Choctaws, and other eastern nations before their final relocation to present-day Oklahoma. Bob Lancaster, *The Jungles of Arkansas: A Personal History of the Wonder State* (Fayetteville: University of Arkansas Press, 1989), 40.

7. C. Fred Williams, "The Bear State Image: Arkansas in the Nineteenth Century," *Arkansas Historical Quarterly* 34 (Summer 1980): 99 (quote), 101, 102.

8. Ibid., 99, 100.

9. Ibid., 101. See also Malcolm J. Rohrbough, *Trans-Appalachian Frontier: People, Societies, and Institutions, 1775–1850,* 3rd ed. (Bloomington: Indiana University Press, 2008), 389–90.

10. Quoted in Williams, "Bear State Image," 101.

11. Elmo Howell, "Mark Twain's Arkansas," *Arkansas Historical Quarterly* 29 (Autumn 1970): 195.

12. *The WPA Guide to 1930s Arkansas,* with a new introduction by Elliott West (Lawrence: University Press of Kansas, 1987), 4.

CHAPTER TWO

1. Robert L. Morris, *Opie Read: American Humorist* (New York: Helios Books, 1965), 14, 15, 52, 57, 61, 68, 76, 95, 96, 97, 105, 106. See also Michael B. Dougan, "Opie Pope Read," *The Encyclopedia of Arkansas History & Culture,* http://www.encyclopediaofarkansas.net (accessed 9 March 2009).

2. Thomas W. Jackson, *On a Slow Train Through Arkansaw,* edited with an introduction by W. K. McNeil (Lexington: University Press of Kentucky, 1985), 3, 4, 5; Thomas W. Jackson, *On a Slow Train Through Arkansaw,* introduction by Harlan Daniel (Forrest City, Ark.: M. Vance, 1982), iii. See also Linda Lovell, "*On a Slow Train Through Arkansaw* [Book]," *Encyclopedia of Arkansas History & Culture,* http://www.encyclopediaofarkansas.net (accessed 9 March 2009).

3. Edward King, "The Great South: Down the Mississippi—The Labor Question—Arkansas," *Scribner's Monthly,* October 1874, 662.

4. Rev. D. A. Quinn, *Heroes and Heroines of Memphis, on Reminiscences of the Yellow Fever Epidemics That Afflicted the City of Memphis During the Autumn Months of 1873, 1878, and 1879* (Providence, R.I.: E. L. Freeman & Son, 1887), 248, 272, 273.

5. King, "The Great South," 662.

6. Mark Twain, *Roughing It,* Vol. 1 (1871; New York: Harper & Brothers, 1913), 213.

7. Mark Twain, *The Adventures of Huckleberry Finn* (1884; New York: Harper & Brothers, 1923), 199 (first quote), 198 (second quote), 200–201 (third quote).

8. Robert Hunting, "Mark Twain's Arkansaw Yahoos," *Modern Language Notes* 73 (April 1958): 265.

9. Elmo Howell, "Mark Twain's Arkansas," *Arkansas Historical Quarterly* 29 (Autumn 1970): 206.

10. Ibid., 207.

11. The Arkansaw image also made an occasional appearance in the dime novels and serials produced for a mass audience in the late nineteenth century. Characters linked to this image were often protagonists, though their uncouth ways and penchant for violence continued to separate them from polite society. See T. C. Harbaugh, "Arkansaw, The Man with the Knife; or, The Queen of Fate's Revenge," *Beadle's Half Dime Library,* 10 May 1881; Edward Willett, "Ozark Alf, King of the Mountain; or, Featherweight Among the Outlaws," *Beadle's Half Dime Library,* 1 November 1881; Harry Hazard, "Arkansaw Jack, of the Man-Hunters; or, The Scourge of the Mines," *Beadle's Half Dime Library,* 2 October 1883.

12. Ethel C. Simpson, "Octave Thanet," *Encyclopedia of Arkansas History & Culture,* http://www.encyclopediaofarkansas.net (accessed 9 March 2009). See also Michael B. Dougan, "Bumpkins and Bigots: The Arkansas Image in Fiction," *Publications of the Arkansas Philological Association* 1 (Summer 1975): 5–15.

13. Another book from this era that is set in Arkansas is George H. Briscoe, *Angels of Commerce: Or, Thirty Days with the Drummers of Arkansas* (New York: Publishers' Printing Co., 1891). A work of fiction based on the author's real-life experiences as a traveling salesman, or drummer, the book is primarily concerned with the humorous exploits of a group of drummers. Briscoe occasionally dabbles in Arkansaw imagery, as when his drummers come upon a poor hill family on their journey from Batesville to Sugar Loaf Springs (Heber Springs). The family of nine resides in a "miserable log" shanty, the breakfast served the drummers is "horrible in its simplicity and filthiness," and the father, according to one drummer, "'looks like a moonshiner in disguise'" (144, 148).

14. Morris, *Opie Read,* 60, 117.

15. Ibid., 105, 181; Dougan, "Opie Pope Read"; *Arkansas Traveler,* 11 June 1882, 4, 5; Clyde Brion Davis, *The Arkansas,* Rivers of America Series (New York: Rinehart & Company, 1940), 301.

16. Morris, *Opie Read,* 169.

17. Brook Pierce, "Happy Hollow," *Encyclopedia of Arkansas History & Culture,* http://www.encyclopediaofarkansas.net (accessed 9 March 2009). Coney Island, in fact, featured an attraction called "In the Ozarks" by the early twentieth century ("Great New Dreamland at Coney Island This Year," *New York Times,* 23 April 1905, 18).

18. James R. Masterson, *Arkansas Folklore: The Arkansas Traveler, Davey Crockett, and Other Legends* (1942; Little Rock: Rose Publishing Co., 1974), 240–54.

19. Ibid., 253.

20. W. K. McNeil, "'By the Ozark Trail': The Image of the Ozarks in Popular and Folk Songs," *JEMF Quarterly* (Spring–Summer 1985): 20.

21. Charles Wolfe and Mark Wilson, Album notes for Gid Tanner and His Skillet Lickers, *The Kickapoo Medicine Show,* Rounder Records 1028, page 6 (first quote); Erika Brady, Song notes for Jimmie Davis, "In Arkansas," in Richard K. Spottswood, ed., *Songs of Local History & Events,* Folk Music of America Series, vol. 12 (Washington, D.C.: Library of Congress Music Division Recording Laboratory, 1978), 6 (second quote).

22. Masterson, *Arkansas Folklore,* 220–32; McNeil, "'By the Ozark Trail,'" 22. The authorship of the Traveler dialogue has also been attributed to Sandy Faulkner and Edward P. Washbourne.

23. Ibid., 255.

24. W. P. Detherow, "The State of Arkansas (The Arkansas Traveler)," recorded 25 June 1952, John Quincy Wolf Folklore Collection, Lyon College, Batesville, Arkansas. One of the most popular humorous songs of Arkansas in the early twentieth century was "Down in the Arkansas," written in 1913 by blackface minstrel performer George "Honey Boy" Evans. Typical of many of the era's Tin Pan Alley ditties, it is composed primarily of nonsense lyrics and contains little that ties it to the state other than the oft-repeated title.

25. Wolfe and Wilson, Album notes, 7.

26. Brady, Song notes, 5–6.

27. Patrick J. Huber, "The Riddle of the Horny Hillbilly," in *Dixie Emporium: Tourism, Foodways, and Consumer Culture in the American South,* edited by Anthony Stanonis (Athens: University of Georgia Press, 2008).

28. Julian Hawthorne, "Mountain Votes Spoil Huntington's Revenge," New York *Journal,* 23 April 1900, 2.

29. Charles H. Hibler, *Down in Arkansas* (New York: Abbey Press, 1902), 32, 40, 44, 65.

30. Ibid., 32, 33, 35.

31. Jackson, *Slow Train,* introduction by W. K. McNeil, 7.

32. Marion Hughes, *Three Years in Arkansaw* (Chicago: M. A. Donohue & Company, 1904), 34, 76.

33. Ibid., 112–13.

34. Other humorous books from the era are Press Woodruff's *A Backwoods Philosopher from Arkansaw* (Chicago: Thompson & Thomas, 1901) and George D. Beason's *I Blew in from Arkansaw* (Chicago: George D.

Beason, 1908). Woodruff's book is no more about Arkansas, per se, than it is about Oregon, Minnesota, or Michigan, but Woodruff was an Arkansas native who referred to himself as "The Arkansaw Humorist." The book also contains one of the better lines concerning Arkansas's reputation: "Some folks say that Arkansaw was made on Saturday night after all the rest of the universe had been finished" (23). Beason's book, subtitled "Funny Railroad Stories, Darky and Hoosier Sayings. The Latest Jokes and Yarns of the Day," was purely a rip-off of *On a Slow Train,* with a liberal sampling of ethnic and racial jokes and perhaps more jabs at Indiana than Arkansaw humor.

35. Herb Lewis, *Eb Peechcrap and Wife at the Fair* (New York: Neale Publishing Company, 1906), 22, 7.

36. See T. J. Jackson Lears, *No Place of Grace: Antimodernism and the Transformation of American Culture, 1880–1920* (New York: Pantheon Books, 1981).

37. Roderick Nash, *The Nervous Generation: American Thought, 1917–1930* (Chicago: Rand McNally and Co., 1970), 139.

38. Lynn Morrow and Linda Myers-Phinney, *Shepherd of the Hills Country: Tourism Transforms the Ozarks, 1880–1930s* (Fayetteville: University of Arkansas Press, 1999), 28; Lawrence V. Tagg, *Harold Bell Wright: Storyteller to America* (Tucson, Ariz.: Westernlore Press, 1986), 32, 33; Aaron K. Ketchell, *Holy Hills of the Ozarks: Religion and Tourism in Branson, Missouri* (Baltimore: Johns Hopkins University Press, 2007), 8, 9.

39. I am not suggesting here that *The Shepherd of the Hills* was the first novel to utilize an Ozark setting, only that it was the most popular and thus most influential in shaping perceptions of the region. Among earlier novels featuring Ozark settings or Ozark natives, all set in Missouri, were John Monteith, *Parson Brooks* (1884), James Newton Baskett, *At You-all's House* (1899), J. Gabriel Woerner, *The Rebel's Daughter* (1899), and Rose Emmet Young, *Sally of Missouri* (1903). For a critique of these and other writers' often-miserable attempts to put the Ozark dialect on paper, see Vance Randolph, "The Ozark Dialect in Fiction," *American Speech* 2 (March 1927): 283–89.

40. Michael B. Dougan, *Arkansas Odyssey: The Saga of Arkansas from Prehistoric Times to Present* (Little Rock: Rose Publishing Co., 1994), 543; J. Breckinridge Ellis, "Arkansans Who Have Made Good," *The Arkansas Writer,* November 1921, 21. See Ethel C. Simpson, ed., *Simpkinsville and Vicinity: Arkansas Stories by Ruth McEnery Stuart* (Fayetteville: University of Arkansas Press, 1999).

41. Lyrics from "My Happy Little Home in Arkansas" come from recording of Mrs. W. L. Deal, Heber Springs, Arkansas, 16 July 1953, John Quincy Wolf Folklore Collection, Lyon College, Batesville, Arkansas, http://www.lyon.edu/wolfcollection/songs/dealmy1234.html; James White, "'Way Down in Arkansaw" (Chicago: Forster Music Publisher, 1915), sheet music collection, Ozark Cultural Resource Center, Ozark Folk Center, Mountain View, Arkansas; Eva Ware Barnett and Will M. Ramsey, "Arkansas" (Central Music Co., 1916), #59, Mary D. Hudgins Arkansas Music Collection, University of Arkansas Special Collections, Fayetteville.

Among the other sentimental Arkansas songs to appear between the Civil War and World War I were Franz Dierich's "Arkansaw, Our Arkansaw!" (Hudgins Collection #151); G. W. Slater's "Way Down in Dear Old Arkansaw" (#490); Alice McGuigan and Douglass Bancroft's "Arkansaw" (#53) written to raise money for Hot Springs's Louisiana Purchase Exposition fund; and Will J. Harris and Milton Ager's "If You Saw All That I Saw in Arkansas" (#252). John T. Rutledge's "Gwine Back to Dear Old Arkinsaw" (#469) is an example of a post-Reconstruction minstrel song depicting the freedman's supposed nostalgia for the Old South and as such is somewhat less farcical, though perhaps no less stereotypical and racist, than George "Honey Boy" Evans's better-known 1913 song, "Down in Arkansaw" (#186).

SECOND INTERLUDE

1. My apologies to Gordon D. Morgan. See his *Black Hillbillies of the Arkansas Ozarks* (Fayetteville: University of Arkansas Department of Sociology, 1973).

2. *The WPA Guide to 1930s Arkansas,* with a new introduction by Elliott West (Lawrence: University Press of Kansas, 1987), ix.

3. This phrase was coined by Berea College president William Goodell Frost in the late nineteenth century. See Frost, "Our Contemporary Ancestors in the Southern Mountains," *Atlantic Monthly,* March 1899, 311–19.

4. James C. Klotter, "The Black South and White Appalachia," *Journal of American History* 66 (March 1980): 832.

5. Anthony Harkins, *Hillbilly: A Cultural History of an American Icon* (New York: Oxford University Press, 2004), 29, 33.

6. David E. Whisnant, *All That Is Native and Fine: The Politics of Culture in an American Region* (Chapel Hill: University of North Carolina Press, 1983), 239. See also Henry D. Shapiro, *Appalachia on Our Mind: The Southern Mountains and Mountaineers in the American Consciousness, 1870–1920* (Chapel Hill: University of North Carolina Press, 1978); David E. Whisnant, *Modernizing the Mountaineer: People, Power, and Planning in Appalachia* (1980; Knoxville: University of Tennessee Press, 1994); John Higham, *Strangers in the Land: Patterns of American Nativism, 1860–1925* (1955; New Brunswick, N.J.: Rutgers University Press, 1988); Allen W. Batteau, *The Invention of Appalachia* (Tucson: University of Arizona Press, 1990); David C. Hsiung, *Two Worlds in the Tennessee Mountains: Exploring the Origins of Appalachian Stereotypes* (Lexington: University Press of Kentucky, 1997).

CHAPTER THREE

1. Ronald L. Smith, *Who's Who in Comedy* (New York: Facts on File, 1992), 78; John Dunning, *On the Air: The Encyclopedia of Old-Time Radio* (New York: Oxford University Press, 1998), 102, 103; Van Buren *Press-Argus,*

31 July 1936, 6, 7; 7 February 1936, 1; *Newsweek,* 14 December 1935, 29.

2. Ronald L. Smith, *Who's Who in Comedy* (New York: Facts on File, 1992), 78; Dunning, *On the Air,* 102, 103; Van Buren *Press-Argus,* 31 July 1936, 6, 7, 14.

3. Anthony Harkins, *Hillbilly: A Cultural History of an American Icon* (New York: Oxford University Press, 2004), 9.

4. Charles J. Finger, "Utopia in Arkansas," *Century,* June 1923, 278.

5. H. L. Mencken, "The Sahara of the Bozart," in Mencken, *Prejudices: Second Series* (New York, 1920); "The South Begins to Mutter," *The Smart Set,* August 1921, 141; E. J. Friedlander, "'The Miasmatic Jungles': Reactions to H. L. Mencken's 1921 Attack on Arkansas," *Arkansas Historical Quarterly* 38 (Spring 1979): 63, 64.

6. H. L. Mencken, "Famine," Baltimore *Evening Sun,* 19 January 1931. Mencken also wrote a series of essays for the *American Mercury* in the fall of 1931 in an attempt to identify the "worst American state." Based on statistics for wealth, health, education, and public order, Mencken ranked Arkansas forty-fourth out of forty-eight states, ahead of the Deep South states Georgia, South Carolina, Alabama, and Mississippi. See "The Worst American State, Part III," *American Mercury,* November 1931, 356.

7. H. L. Mencken, "The Case of Arkansas," Baltimore *Evening Sun,* 16 February 1931; Mencken, "How to Improve Arkansas," Baltimore *Evening Sun,* 9 March 1931.

8. Travis Y. Oliver, "Hell's Fire—Arkansas," *Vanity Fair,* September 1933, 14, 57.

9. Elmer J. Bouher writing in *Brick Church Life,* Newsletter of Brick Presbyterian Church, Rochester, New York, June 1922, 115, in Folder 1, Box 1, Kingston, Arkansas Collection, University of Arkansas Special Collections, Fayetteville; Finger, "Utopia in Arkansas," 278.

10. C. L. Edson, "Arkansas: A Native Proletariat," *Nation,* 2 May 1923, 515, 516. This essay was reprinted in Ernest Gruening, ed., *These United States: A Symposium* (New York: Boni and Liveright, 1923), 355–72.

11. Clay Fulks, "Arkansas," *American Mercury,* July 1926, 292. Jukes and Kallikak were synonyms of families who were the subjects of once-famous studies of the relationship between genetics and crime and/or antisocial behavior. Both studies were linked to the eugenics movement of the late nineteenth and early twentieth centuries. See J. David Smith, *Minds Made Feeble: The Myth and Legacy of the Kallikaks* (Rockville, Md.: Aspen Systems Corp., 1985); R. L. Dugdale, *"The Jukes": A Study in Crime, Pauperism, Disease, and Heredity* (1895; New York: AMS Press, 1975); and Matt Wray and Annalee Newitz, eds., *White Trash: Race and Class in America* (New York: Routledge, 1996).

12. Fulks, "Arkansas," 293 (first quote), 294 (second quote), 295 (third quote). Historian James C. Cobb notes that Mencken had a "significant following among young southern journalists" who shared his displeasure with the region's cultural and intellectual backwardness. Fulks seems to

have been Arkansas's most notable contribution to this cadre. See Cobb, *Away Down South: A History of Southern Identity* (New York: Oxford University Press, 2005), 109–10.

13. Ibid., 295.

14. Edson, "Arkansas: A Native Proletariat," 517, 516.

15. Ibid., 515.

16. Rev. Warren Wilson, "Work of Mr. Bouher Commended," *Brick Church Life*, Newsletter of Brick Presbyterian Church, Rochester, New York, August 1921, 156, in Folder 1, Box 1, Kingston, Arkansas Collection, University of Arkansas Special Collections, Fayetteville; Lawrence F. Abbott, "An Arkansas Traveler," *Outlook*, 1 June 1927, 147, 148; Charles Phelps Cushing, "The Ozarks, The Highlands of the Middle West," *Mentor*, July 1927, 23, 27.

17. Edward Larocque Tinker, "New Editions, Fine & Otherwise," *New York Times*, 10 November 1940, 120; Dorothy Scarborough, "Where the Eighteenth Century Lives On," *New York Times*, 27 December 1931, 54; "Book Notes," *New York Times*, 25 September 1931, 33; Thomas Benton, "America's Yesterday," *Travel*, July 1934, 8; Typescript of address before the National Council of Teachers of English, Memphis, Tennessee, 26 November 1932, Box 16, Folder 29, Charles H. Brough Papers; Charles Morrow Wilson, "Elizabethan America," *Atlantic Monthly*, August 1929, 238; Otto Ernest Rayburn, *Ozark Country* (New York: Duell, Sloan & Pearce, 1941); see chapter 2.

18. "Thirsty from Dry States Flocking to the Ozarks," *New York Times*, 6 May 1934, E7.

19. Louis La Coss, "Ozarkians Ready for Tourist Season," *New York Times*, 24 May 1931, E8. Some of the writers quoted in this section, including La Coss, wrote almost exclusively of the Missouri Ozarks. Their observations are included here because they differ little from the comments about the Arkansas Ozarks and because the Ozark image—irrespective of state boundaries—became during this era virtually indistinguishable from the older Arkansaw image.

20. William R. Draper, "The Ozarks Go Native," *Outlook*, 10 September 1930, 60; "From Khabarousk and Macao to Opobo and the Ozarks," *New York Times*, 29 December 1929, XX2; W. R. Draper, "Motoring into the Ozarks," *New York Times*, 20 July 1930, XX7; Dorothy Scarborough, "Where the Eighteenth Century Lives On," *New York Times*, 27 December 1931, 54; Laura Knickerbocker, "The New Deal Dazes the Ozark Hillman," *New York Times*, 21 July 1935, SM10.

21. Charles Morrow Wilson, "Backwoods Morality," *Outlook and Independent*, 9 January 1929, 65.

22. Ellen Compton, "Charles Morrow Wilson," *The Encyclopedia of Arkansas History & Culture*, http://www.encyclopediaofarkansas.net (accessed 9 March 2009).

23. Draper, "Motoring into the Ozarks," XX7; "Thirsty from Dry States," E7.

24. Charles Morrow Wilson, "Moonshiners," *Outlook and Independent*, 19

December 1928, 1351 (first quote), 1350 (second and third quotes); Charles Morrow Wilson, *Backwoods America* (Chapel Hill: University of North Carolina Press, 1935), 153, 158 (fourth and fifth quotes); Charles Morrow Wilson, "Moonshining Booms as Spring Arrives," *New York Times,* 20 April 1930, 51 (final quote.)

25. Ben F. Johnson III, *John Barleycorn Must Die: The War against Drink in Arkansas* (Fayetteville: University of Arkansas Press, 2005), 28–29; Vance Randolph, *The Ozarks: An American Survival of Primitive Society* (New York: Vanguard Press, 1931), 239.

26. Brooks Blevins, *Hill Folks: A History of Arkansas Ozarkers and Their Image* (Chapel Hill: University of North Carolina Press, 2002), 135–36; Randolph, *The Ozarks,* 21–22.

27. Cushing, "The Ozarks," 28; Louis La Coss, "Century-Old Town Bows to Progress," *New York Times,* 15 September 1929, E2; "Natives of Ozark Mountains Resist Electric Power Plan," *New York Times,* 22 June 1930, XX2; "Ozarks Plan Festival for Native-Born Folk," *New York Times,* 18 March 1934, E6; Tinker, "New Editions," 120.

28. Cushing, "The Ozarks," 24; Louis La Coss, "The Ozarks Emerge from Somnolence," *New York Times,* 3 March 1929, E1; Charles Morrow Wilson, "Backhill Culture," *Nation,* 17 July 1929, 65; "Ozark Tourists Demand Modern Improvements," *New York Times,* 16 July 1933, E6; Knickerbocker, "New Deal Dazes," SM10.

29. Wilson, "Backhill Culture," 64; Draper, "Ozarks Go Native," 60; Randolph, *The Ozarks,* 53 (first quote), 105 (second quote).

30. Catherine S. Barker, *Yesterday Today: Life in the Ozarks* (Caldwell, Id.: Caxton Printers, 1941), 23, 9.

31. Benton, "America's Yesterday," 8.

32. Blevins, *Hill Folks,* 142–43.

33. Rayburn, *Ozark Country,* 32 (first two quotes), 54 (last quote).

34. F. M. Van Natter, "Highlands of the Ozarks," *National Republic,* June 1930, 6; Tinker, "New Editions," 120; Charles Morrow Wilson, "Friendly Days in the Ozarks," *Travel,* March 1933, 19; Charles Morrow Wilson, "On an Ozark Store-Porch," *American Magazine,* October 1929, 494.

35. Wilson, "Backhill Culture," 63 (first quote); Wilson, "Backwoods Morality," 65 (second and third quotes), 66 (sixth quote); Charles Morrow Wilson, "Ozarkadia," *American Magazine,* January 1934, 112 (fourth quote); Wilson, "Friendly Days," 20 (fifth quote); Wilson, "Elizabethan America," 241 (seventh quote); Van Natter, "Highlands of the Ozarks," 5 (final quote); Benton, "America's Yesterday," 10.

36. "Natives of Ozark Mountains," XX2; Knickerbocker, "New Deal Dazes Ozark Hillman," SM10; Wilson, "Backhill Culture," 65; Charles Morrow Wilson, "Hemmed-In Holler," *Review of Reviews and World's Work,* August 1935, 58.

37. Vince Staten, *Ol' Diz: A Biography of Dizzy Dean* (New York: HarperCollins, 1992), 26, 71.

38. Ibid., 109, 154, 164. See also Curt Smith, *America's Dizzy Dean* (St.

Louis: Bethany Press, 1978); Robert Gregory, *Diz: Dizzy Dean and Baseball During the Great Depression* (New York: Viking, 1992); Doug Feldmann, *Dizzy and the Gas House Gang: The 1934 St. Louis Cardinals and Depression-era Baseball* (Jefferson, N.C.: McFarland & Co., 2000).

39. Staten, *Ol' Diz*, 264; W. K. McNeil, "'By the Ozark Trail': The Image of the Ozarks in Popular and Folk Songs," *JEMF Quarterly* (Spring–Summer 1985): 20, 27.

40. *Hard Time Come Again No More, Vol. 2: Early American Songs of Hard Times and Hardships,* Yazoo 2037.

41. W. K. McNeil, Liner notes for *Somewhere in Arkansas: Early Commercial Country Music Recordings from Arkansas, 1928–1932* (Fayetteville: Center for Arkansas and Regional Studies, University of Arkansas, 1997), 31–32.

42. Al Bernard and Russel Robinson, "Blue-Eyed Sally" (New York: Henry Waterson, Inc., 1924), Sheet Music Collection, Ozark Cultural Resource Center, Ozark Folk Center, Mountain View, Arkansas.

43. Herbert R. Cushman and Lee Browne, "The Foothills of the Ozarks" (Chicago: M. M. Cole Publishing Co., 1942), Sheet Music Collection, Ozark Cultural Resource Center; McNeil, "'By the Ozark Trail,'" 26; McNeil, Liner notes for *Somewhere in Arkansas,* 30; James Braswell, "In the Land of a Million Smiles" (Jasper, Ark.: James Braswell, 1925), Mary D. Hudgins Arkansas Music Collection, #91, University of Arkansas Special Collections, Fayetteville.

44. McNeil, Liner notes for *Somewhere in Arkansas,* 27, 29; Maude Bethel Lewis, "Arkansas I Love You" (Little Rock: Central Music Co., 1922), Hudgins Collection, #315.

45. A. M. Haswell, *A Daughter of the Ozarks* (Boston: Cornhill Publishing Co., 1921); A. M. Haswell, *A Drama of the Hills* (Boston: Cornhill Publishing Co., 1923); Rose Wilder Lane, *Hill-Billy* (New York: Harper & Brothers, 1926). See also review of *Hill-Billy* in "Ozark Mountaineers," *New York Times,* 13 June 1926, BR9.

46. Louise Platt Hauck, *Wild Grape* (Philadelphia: Penn Publishing Co., 1931); Louise Platt Hauck, *Rainbow Glory* (Philadelphia: Penn Publishing Co., 1935). Quote taken from advertisement for *Wild Grape* in *New York Times,* 15 March 1931, 66. See also Harold Bell Wright, *Ms. Cinderella* (New York: Harper & Brothers, 1932); Helen Todd, *So Free We Seem* (New York: Reynal & Hitchcock, 1936); Ruth Hesse Artist, *Salt Pork* (Aurora, Mo.: Burney Brothers Publishing Co., 1938); Elizabeth Seifert, *Hillbilly Doctor* (New York: Dodd, Mead & Co., 1940); Frances Grinstead, *The High Road* (New York: Doubleday, Doran, 1945).

47. On the stage version of the novel, see Zoe Lund Schiller, "Acres of Sky: A Dramatic Musical," Typescript of Musical Play, 1950, University of Arkansas Special Collections, Fayetteville.

48. Charles Morrow Wilson, *Acres of Sky* (New York: G. P. Putnam's Sons, 1930), 52, 151.

49. Thames Williamson, *The Woods Colt: A Novel of the Ozark Hills* (New York: Harcourt, Brace and Company, 1933), 69.

50. "Ozarks," *Time,* 9 October 1933, 67; Williamson, *The Woods Colt,* 287–88.

51. Harkins, *Hillbilly,* 103, 104.

52. Ibid., 112.

53. Ibid., 117, 119.

54. Ibid., 123, 127.

55. Ibid., 125, 127, 128, 131, 132 (quote).

56. Ibid., 132 (first quote), 132–33 (second quote), 131 (third quote), 135 (fourth quote).

57. Randal L. Hall, *Lum and Abner: Rural America and the Golden Age of Radio* (Lexington: University Press of Kentucky, 2007), 8–13; John Dunning, *On the Air: The Encyclopedia of Old-Time Radio* (New York: Oxford University Press, 1998), 412, 414; Kathryn Moore Stucker, *"Lum and Abner," The Encyclopedia of Arkansas History & Culture,* http://www.encyclopediaofarkansas.net (accessed 9 March 2009); Kathryn Moore Stucker, "Chet Lauck," *The Encyclopedia of Arkansas History & Culture,* http://www.encyclopediaofarkansas.net (accessed 9 March 2009); Kathryn Moore Stucker, "'Tuffy' Goff," *The Encyclopedia of Arkansas History & Culture,* http://www.encyclopediaofarkansas.net (accessed 9 March 2009); Obituary of Norris Goff, *Time,* 19 June 1978, 87; "Lum and Abner Come to Town," *New York Times,* 19 November 1933, X11.

58. Hall, *Lum and Abner,* 13–14. On the fifth anniversary of the show in April 1936, the citizens of Waters officially changed their town's name to Pine Ridge. Stucker, *"Lum and Abner."*

59. Stucker, *"Lum and Abner."*

60. "Lum and Abner Come to Town," X11 (first quote); Dunning, *On the Air,* 414.

61. Stucker, "Chet Lauck"; Stucker, "'Tuffy Goff"; Hall, *Lum and Abner,* 4.

62. Dunning, *On the Air,* 414. By the time of its last syndicated broadcast on 7 May 1954, *Lum and Abner* had appeared on five networks—the big three plus Mutual Broadcasting and the Blue Network—under the sponsorship of a variety of companies, including Ford Motors, Horlick's Malted Milk, Alka-Seltzer, and Frigidaire. With the exception of a period of time between 1948 and 1950 when CBS converted it to a standard thirty-minute, once-weekly sitcom format, *Lum and Abner* aired four to six days a week as a fifteen-minute sketch.

63. Ronald L. Smith, *Who's Who in Comedy* (New York: Facts on File, 1992), 78; Idwal Jones, "How to Overcome an Education," *New York Times,* 19 March 1939, 136; "Bob Burns Has as Much Fun as His Fans Here," *Arkansas Gazette,* 28 July 1936, 1, 9; "Just 'Being Myself' Credited by Bob Burns with Achieving Radio and Movie Fame for Him," *Arkansas Gazette,* 28 July 1936, 1, 9; Dunning, *On the Air,* 102, 103.

64. Ronald L. Smith, *Who's Who in Comedy* (New York: Facts on File, 1992), 78; Gary Giddins, *Bing Crosby: A Pocketful of Dreams, the Early Years 1903–1940* (New York: Little, Brown and Company, 2001), 398, 399; Idwal Jones, "How to Overcome an Education," *New York Times,* 19 March 1939, 136; Dunning, *On the Air,* 102, 103 (quote), 386, 90, 592.

65. "The Bob Burns Show," 6 May 1943; Dunning, *On the Air,* 102.

66. Van Buren *Press-Argus,* 31 July 1936, 6; "Scratch a Hillbilly," *New York Times,* 15 May 1938, 152 (first two quotes); "Doin' O.K., Pardner," *New York Times,* 18 January 1942, X10 (third quote); Jones, "How to Overcome an Education," 136 (fourth quote); Dunning, *On the Air,* 102 (final quote).

67. *The WPA Guide to 1930s Arkansas,* with a new introduction by Elliott West (Lawrence: University Press of Kansas, 1987), 253; Ben F. Johnson III, *Arkansas in Modern America, 1930–1999,* Arkansas in Modern America Series (Fayetteville: University of Arkansas Press, 2000), 40; Hall, *Lum and Abner,* 42; Bob Lancaster, *The Jungles of Arkansas: A Personal History of the Wonder State* (Fayetteville: University of Arkansas Press, 1989), 139. His humor resonated throughout rural America, according to one *New York Times* reporter who found in his survey of Wetzel County, West Virginia, that "Bob Burns's Arkansas Traveler is said to be considered virtually a neighbor by set-owners in the countryside." John K. Hutchens, "Field Report," *New York Times,* 9 August 1942, X8. See also Wade Austin, "The Real Beverly Hillbillies," *Southern Quarterly* 19 (Spring–Summer 1981): 85, 86.

68. "Bob Burns Has as Much Fun," 1; "Just 'Being Myself,'" 9; Lancaster, *Jungles of Arkansas,* 139; *Arkansas Gazette,* 8 February 1936, 4; 11 February 1936, 4; 12 February 1936, 4; 14 February 1936, 4; 16 February 1936, II-4; 18 February 1936, 4; 23 February 1936, II-4.

69. Lancaster, *Jungles of Arkansas,* 139.

70. Wayne Glenn, *The Ozarks' Greatest Hits: A Photo History of Music in the Ozarks* (N.P., 2005), 106 (first quote), 107 (second quote), 156.

71. One example of the era's Arkansaw humor, Vaudeville style, is "An Arkansaw Swap," a fifteen-minute "comedy rural sketch." A dialogue between two characters, a country storekeeper and a backwoods farmer, in fictional Tinker's Dam, Arkansas, it's typical, Vaudeville wordplay and banter rendered in hillbilly dialect. The publisher, T. S. Denison & Company of Chicago, offered a number of other sketch comedies and dialogues, many of them rooted in the humor of racial, ethnic, and regional stereotypes. Larry E. Johnson, *An Arkansaw Swap* (Chicago: T. S. Denison & Company, 1923).

72. "This New Vaudeville," *New York Times,* 28 October 1928, 118; "Gossip of the Rialto," *New York Times,* 27 September 1936, X1; "The Theatre," *Wall Street Journal,* 20 October 1936, 13; Edwin Bronner, *The Encyclopedia of the American Theatre, 1900–1975* (San Diego, Calif.: A. S. Barnes, 1980), 459; Tony Thomas, *The Films of Ronald Reagan* (Secaucus, N.J.: Citadel Press, 1980), 37, 38; Clifford McCarty, *Bogey: The Films of Humphrey Bogart* (New York: Citadel Press, 1965), 53.

73. "Producer at 19: His Debut Tonight," *New York Times,* 28 April 1943, 20; Bronner, *Encyclopedia of the American Theatre,* 159 (first quote); "'Maid in Ozarks' Arrives Tonight," *New York Times,* 15 July 1946, 20 (second and fifth quotes); Lloyd Lewis, "Revenge on Chicago," *New York Times,* 14 March 1943, X1 (third, fourth, sixth, and seventh quotes).

74. Lewis, "Revenge on Chicago," X1; Lloyd Lewis, "A Chicago Letter," *New York Times,* 28 November 1943, X1; "The Play," *New York Times,* 16 July 1946, 20; Bronner, *Encyclopedia of the American Theatre,* 291.

75. Among the other early films set in the Arkansas or Missouri Ozarks were *That Houn' Dawg* (1912), *Cinderella of the Hills* (1921), *Human Hearts* (1922), *Wolf Law* (1922), and *Souls Aflame* (1928). Source: Jerry Wayne Williamson, "Southern Mountaineers Filmography," W. L. Eury Appalachian Collection, Appalachian State University, http://www.library. appstate.edu/appcoll/filmography.html.

76. *Girl of the Ozarks* (1936, Paramount); "The Screen," *New York Times,* 13 July 1933, 17; "If You Have Tears," *New York Times,* 16 July 1933, X3; Douglas W. Churchill, "Sweetness and Light," *New York Times,* 31 May 1936, X3.

77. *I'm From Arkansas* (1944, PRC).

78. Austin, "The Real Beverly Hillbillies," 87, 88. Unless otherwise stated, all information on synopses of films comes from author's viewing or from one of two internet resources: *The Internet Movie Database* (http://imdb.com [accessed 9 March 2009]) and *allmovie* (http://www.allmovie.com [accessed 9 March 2009]).

79. "Lum and Abner Pleased by Reception," *Arkansas Gazette,* 5 September 1940, 15; "Lum 'n' Abner Tell Jokes and Rotary Abandons Dignity," *Arkansas Gazette,* 6 September 1940, 10 (quotes).

80. Bosley Crowther, "The Screen," *New York Times,* 14 May 1940, 31; Frank S. Nugent, "The Screen," *New York Times,* 23 March 1939, 31; Frank S. Nugent, "The Screen," *New York Times,* 17 November 1938, 29.

81. "New Pictures," *Time,* 31 October 1938, 26; Frank S. Nugent, "The Screen," *New York Times,* 17 November 1938, 29; "Premiere of Bob Burns' Movie Tonight," *Arkansas Gazette,* 6 October 1938, 13; "Movie Fans Have Holiday at Premiere," *Arkansas Gazette,* 7 October 1938, 24;

82. Frank S. Nugent, "The Screen," *New York Times,* 17 November 1938, 29; "New Pictures," *Time,* 31 October 1938, 26; *Time,* 8 December 1941, 76.

THIRD INTERLUDE

1. Timothy P. Donovan, Willard B. Gatewood Jr., and Jeannie M. Whayne, eds., *The Governors of Arkansas: Essays in Political Biography,* 2nd ed. (Fayetteville: University of Arkansas Press, 1995), 150, 151.

2. Ibid., 152; Charles Orson Cook, "Boosterism and Babbittry: Charles Hillman Brough and the 'Selling' of Arkansas," *Arkansas Historical Quarterly* 37 (Spring 1978): 76 (quote).

3. Quoted in Harry S. Ashmore, *Arkansas: A Bicentennial History* (New York: W. W. Norton & Co., 1978), 141.

4. James P. Henry, *Resources of the State of Arkansas, With Description of Counties, Railroads, Mines, and the City of Little Rock* (Little Rock: Price & McClure, 1872), 133 (first quote), 10 (second quote).

5. James P. Henry, *The Arkansas Gazetteer for 1873: An Emigrant's Guide to Arkansas* (Little Rock: Price & McClure, 1873), 29 (first and third quotes); Henry, *Resources of the State of Arkansas,* 10 (second quote), 125 (fourth quote).

6. T. B. Mills & Co., *The New Arkansas Travelers: A History of the Northwestern Editorial Excursion to Arkansas, A Short Sketch of its Inception and the Routes Traveled over, the Manner in which the Editors were Received, the Resolutions Adopted and Speeches Made at Various Points, the View of the Editorial Visitors to Arkansas as Expressed in their Papers* (Little Rock: T. B. Mills & Co., 1876), 1 (italics added), 2.

7. George W. Donaghey, "Arkansas: The Only State That Produces Diamonds," *Collier's,* January 1910, 19.

8. George W. Donaghey, *Autobiography of George W. Donaghey, Governor of Arkansas, 1909–1913* (Benton, Ark.: L. B. White Printing Company, 1939), 245, 246, 247.

9. Charles Hillman Brough, "Are Paving the Wilderness," *The Sample Case,* July 1919, 9, 10, 12 (quote); Robert Frost, "New Hampshire," in *New Hampshire* (New York: H. Holt and Co., 1923), 3.

10. Charles H. Brough, "Dr. Brough Proclaims Wonders of 'Wonder State' in Talk to Radio Fans of United States," *Arkansas Democrat,* 10 March 1929, 10.

11. "Abstract of Address of Former Governor Charles Hillman Brough of Arkansas, before the Ozark Writers' Guild, West Plains, Missouri, Nov. 21st, 1930," Folder 26, Box 15, Charles Hillman Brough Papers, University of Arkansas Special Collections, Fayetteville; "Noon Luncheon Address Before the National Council of Teachers of English, Memphis, Tennessee, November 26th, 1932, By Former Governor Charles Hillman Brough of Arkansas," Folder 29, Box 16, Brough Papers.

12. "Brough Asks Collier's to Correct Story," unidentified newspaper clipping, c. December 1930, Folder 2, Box 18, Brough Papers.

13. H. L. Mencken, "The Case of Arkansas," Baltimore *Evening Sun,* 16 February 1931; Charles Hillman Brough to H. L. Mencken, 24 February 1931, Folder 163, Box 10, Brough Papers; H. L. Mencken, "How to Improve Arkansas," Baltimore *Evening Sun,* 116–20; "Brough Composes Still Another Paean to Arkansas' Glories," Baltimore *Evening Sun,* 24 April 1931, clipping, Folder 2, Box 18, Brough Papers.

14. H. L. Mencken, "How to Improve Arkansas," Baltimore *Evening Sun,* 9 March 1931, reprinted in *The Impossible H. L. Mencken: A Selection of His Best Newspaper Stories,* edited by Marion Elizabeth Rodgers (New York: Doubleday, 1991), 116–20; "Brough Composes Still Another Paean to Arkansas' Glories," Baltimore *Evening Sun,* 24 April 1931, clipping, Folder 2, Box 18, Brough Papers.

15. "Roasting the South," *Little Rock Daily News,* 10 August 1921, 4; Fred C. Hobson Jr., *Serpent in Eden: H. L. Mencken and the South* (Chapel Hill: University of North Carolina Press, 1974), 26.

16. Clio Harper, "Menace of Herr Mencken," *The Arkansas Writer,* July–August 1921, 6, 7; J. Breckinridge Ellis, "Arkansans Who Have Made Good," *The Arkansas Writer,* November 1921, 21; Anita Thompson, "Telling the North About the Successful Writers of Arkansas," *The Arkansas Writer,* November 1921, 22; M. E. Dunaway, "The Philosophy of an Arkansas Farmer," *The Arkansas Writer,* November 1921, 2–5.

17. "How Writers May Serve," *The Arkansas Writer,* July–August 1921, 7, 8; David M. Tucker, *Arkansas: A People and Their Reputation* (Memphis, Tenn.: Memphis State University Press, 1985), 69; block quote from *The Arkansas Advancement Association,* pamphlet (1921), University of Arkansas Archives, Little Rock, reprinted in part in *A Documentary History of Arkansas,* edited by C. Fred Williams, S. Charles Bolton, Carl H. Moneyhon, and LeRoy T. Williams (Fayetteville: University of Arkansas Press, 1984), 190–91.

18. "To Ask Congress to Probe Rantings Against South by N.Y. Magazine," *Arkansas Democrat,* 3 August 1921, 10; "The South and Mr. Mencken," *Arkansas Democrat,* 5 August 1921, 8.

19. Marcia Camp, "Bernie Babcock," *Encyclopedia of Arkansas,* http://www.encyclopediaofarkansas.net (first quote); Bernie Babcock, *The Man Who Lied on Arkansas and What It Got Him* (Little Rock: Sketch Book Publishing Co., 1909), 1 (second quote), 23 (third quote), 11 (fourth quote). See also Marcia Camp, "The Soul of Bernie Babcock," *Pulaski County Historical Review* 36 (Fall 1988): 50–62.

20. Alexander Johnson, "Notes of an Arkansas Traveler," *The Survey,* 19 February 1916, 618; Sherman Rogers, "A Defense of Arkansas," *Outlook,* 26 October 1921, 294–98; Lawrence F. Abbott, "An Arkansas Traveler," *Outlook,* 1 June 1927, 147; W. G. Clugston, "The State of Arkansas," in W. G. Clugston and Others, *Facts You Should Know About Arkansas,* Little Blue Book No. 1297 (Girard, Kan.: Haldeman-Julius Publications, 1928), 6; Frederick Simpich, "Arkansas Rolls Up Its Sleeves," *National Geographic,* September 1946, 273.

21. Avantus Green, *With This We Challenge* (Little Rock: n.p., 1945), 45.

22. Ibid., 44 (first quote), 5 (second quote); Avantus Green, *The Arkansas Challenge: A Bragging, Boasting, Swaggering, Toasting Handbook on the Wonder State* (Little Rock: n.p., 1966), 63 (third quote), 62 (fourth quote), 5 (fifth quote).

23. Shannon Roe, "Henry Karr Shannon," *Encyclopedia of Arkansas History & Culture,* http://www.encyclopediaofarkansas.net (accessed 9 March 2009); "Shannon's a Versatile Man," *Arkansas Democrat,* 8 September 1940, Sunday Magazine Section, 3.

24. C. Hamilton Moses, foreword to Karr Shannon, *On a Fast Train Through Arkansas* (Little Rock: Democrat Printing & Lithographing, 1948), 5; Shannon, *On a Fast Train,* 16, 19.

25. Richard Allin, "Our Town," *Arkansas Gazette,* undated newspaper clipping in File 8, Series 3, Box 4, Jimmy Driftwood Collection, University of Central Arkansas Archives, Conway.

26. *Arkansas Gazette,* 9 January 1976, 25A; House Resolution 79, 70th General Assembly, State of Arkansas, 16 January 1976; Bill Lewis, "Little Rock Is 'Incredible,' and D-A-Y Wants to Prove It," *Arkansas Gazette,* 17 January 1976.

CHAPTER FOUR

1. John Dunning, *On the Air: The Encyclopedia of Old-Time Radio* (New York: Oxford University Press, 1998), 415 (quote); Ronald L. Smith, *Who's Who in Comedy* (New York: Facts on File, 1992), 88.

2. Anthony Harkins, *Hillbilly: A Cultural History of an American Icon* (New York: Oxford University Press, 2004), 168.

3. Ibid., 174.

4. The more nuanced, even revisionist, take on Faubus's role in the Little Rock crisis presented here is largely informed by Elizabeth Jacoway's *Turn Away Thy Son: Little Rock, the Crisis that Shocked the Nation* (New York: Free Press, 2007) and Roy Reed's *Faubus: The Life and Times of an American Prodigal* (Fayetteville: University of Arkansas Press, 1997). As Jacoway observes, Harry S. Ashmore was primarily responsible for crafting the version of events that lay blame squarely on Faubus's shoulders. See Ashmore's *An Epitaph for Dixie* (New York: W. W. Norton & Co., 1958) and *Civil Rights and Wrongs: A Memoir of Race and Politics, 1944–1994* (New York: Pantheon Books, 1994). A good example of an academic historian's recapitulation of this widely accepted version appears in the chapter aptly titled "The Faubus Detour" in David M. Tucker, *Arkansas: A People and Their Reputation* (Memphis, Tenn.: Memphis State University Press, 1985), 87–96.

5. Michael B. Dougan, "Bumpkins and Bigots: The Arkansas Image in Fiction," *Publications of the Arkansas Philological Association* 1 (Summer 1975): 8.

6. Richard Schickel, *Elia Kazan: A Biography* (New York: HarperCollins, 2005), 336; Stephen Michael Shearer, *Patricia Neal: An Unquiet Life* (Lexington: University Press of Kentucky, 2006), 185. In Schulberg's short story, "Your Arkansas Traveler," Rhodes, a native of fictional Riddle, Arkansas, begins his odyssey in Wyoming before getting his own show, "Your Arkansas Traveler," in Chicago and eventually New York. While in Chicago, Rhodes signs on with a cartoonist for a comic strip about a folk singer named Hill-Bilious Harry. Budd Schulberg, *Some Faces in the Crowd: Short Stories* (New York: Random House, 1953).

7. "Hell in Arkansas," *Time,* 9 February 1968, 18; Thomas O. Murton and Joe Hyams, *Accomplices to the Crime* (1969; New York: Grove Press, 1970). Tucker Telephone was the nickname given to a device used to punish prisoners by administering electric shocks to their body through the big toe and genitals. See Guy Lancaster, "Tucker Telephone," *Encyclopedia of Arkansas History & Culture,* http://www.encyclopediaofarkansas (accessed 6 July 2008).

8. Roy Reed, *Faubus: The Life and Times of an American Prodigal* (Fayetteville: University of Arkansas Press, 1997), 154, 196.

9. Jacoway, *Turn Away Thy Son,* 154; *Time,* 23 September 1957, 12, 13; Robert Sherrill, *Gothic Politics in the Deep South: Stars of the New Confederacy* (New York: Grossman, 1968), 76–77.

10. Editorial cartoon by Alexander, *Philadelphia Evening Bulletin,*

reproduced in *New York Times,* 3 August 1958, E10; editorial cartoon by Hutton, *Philadelphia Inquirer,* reproduced in *New York Times,* 3 August 1958, E10.

11. Brooks Blevins, *Hill Folks: A History of Arkansas Ozarkers and Their Image* (Chapel Hill: University of North Carolina Press, 2002), 249, 251.

12. Peter Braestrup, "Ozarks First to Get Depressed-Area Aid," *New York Times,* 24 July 1961, 1, 13.

13. James C. Tanner, "Echoes of Appalachia: Poverty-Ridden Ozarks See a Brighter Future if U.S. Aid Materializes," *Wall Street Journal,* 13 November 1965, 1, 12. See also James P. Sterba, "Ava, Mo., a Small Town in the Ozarks, Is Winning Poverty Battle," *New York Times,* 14 April 1969, 40.

14. John Gunther, *Inside U.S.A.* (New York: Harper & Brothers, 1947), 342, 762; Neal R. Peirce and Jerry Hagstrom, *The Book of America: Inside 50 States Today* (New York: W. W. Norton & Company, 1983), 478.

15. Peirce and Hagstrom, *The Book of America,* 478.

16. Virginia Schone, "Peaceful Ozarks," *New York Times,* 11 July 1948, X17; Henry N. Ferguson, "The Once-Remote Ozarks Are Now Accessible," *New York Times,* 11 December 1960, XX13; Richard Rhodes, "Home to the Ozarks," *Reader's Digest,* November 1981, 156; Roger Minick and Bob Minick, *Hills of Home: The Rural Ozarks of Arkansas* (San Francisco: Scrimshaw Press, 1975; reprinted with the title *Hills of Home: The Rural Ozarks,* New York: Ballantine Books, 1976); Brooks Blevins, *Hill Folks: A History of Arkansas Ozarkers and Their Image* (Chapel Hill: University of North Carolina Press, 2002), 269.

17. C. W. Gusewelle, "'A Continuity of Place and Blood': The Seasons of Man in the Ozarks," *American Heritage,* December 1977, 108.

18. Faubus letter quoted in Reed, *Faubus,* 328.

19. State of Arkansas, Act 1352, 1995.

20. Harkins, *Hillbilly,* 187, 188.

21. Quoted in Arnold Hano, "The G.A.P. Loves the 'Hillbillies,'" *New York Times,* 17 November 1963, SM120.

22. Ibid., SM16; "Review," *Variety,* 3 October 1962, 35, quoted in Harkins, *Hillbilly,* 190.

23. All information on Hanna-Barbera cartoons from Don Markstein, *Don Markstein's Toonopedia,* http://www.toonopedia.com/ (accessed 2 May 2007).

24. Mark Evanier, "Li'l Abner in Hollywood," POV Online, http://povonline.com/Abner2 (accessed 11 March 2009), originally published in *Li'l Abner,* v. 25. Rodger Brown, "Dogpatch, USA: The Road to Hokum," *Southern Changes* 15 (1993): 22; *Time,* 1 September 1967, 2.

25. Rodger Brown, "In Arkansas, a Dogpatch Way Past Its Prime," *Atlanta Journal-Constitution,* 11 July 1993, M6; Rodger Brown, "Dogpatch, USA," 24, 25. Though Dogpatch's mountain music and crafts may have been influenced by Silver Dollar City, it would appear that the latter and older theme park reacted to Dogpatch as well. The historian of Silver Dollar City notes: "In 1968, a permanent 'entertainment troupe' of 18 performers was

hired to roam the park doing hillbilly vaudeville, hillbilly slapstick." Crystal Payton, *The Story of Silver Dollar City: A Pictorial History of Branson's Famous Ozark Mountain Theme Park* (Branson: Silver Dollar City, 1997), 70.

26. Donald Harington, *Let Us Build Us a City: Eleven Lost Towns* (New York: Harcourt Brace & Company, 1986), 109, 110, 126, 108.

27. Harington, *Let Us Build Us a City,* 130; Reed, *Faubus,* 329.

28. *Arkansas Gazette,* 10 January 1967, 6A, 6 January 1967, 1B, 7 January 1967, 6A.

29. *Arkansas Gazette,* 23 February 1967, B1, 19 May 1968, G7.

30. *Arkansas Gazette,* 10 January 1967, 6A.

31. Fred C. Hobson, *Tell About the South: The Southern Rage to Explain* (Baton Rouge: Louisiana State University Press, 1983), 352 (first quote); James C. Cobb, *Away Down South: A History of Southern Identity* (New York: Oxford University Press, 2005), 237.

32. Jack Temple Kirby, *Media-Made Dixie* (Baton Rouge: Louisiana State University Press, 1978), 153; John Shelton Reed, *Southern Folk, Plain & Fancy: Native White Social Types,* Lamar Memorial Lectures No. 29 (Athens: University of Georgia Press, 1986), 35.

33. As with most B movies, *Bootleggers's* cast consisted of relatively unknown actors, with the exception of Slim Pickens in the role of the patriarch of the Pruitt clan. The film featured the debut of Jaclyn Smith, later of *Charlie's Angels* fame.

34. In addition to *The Legend of Boggy Creek* and *Bootleggers,* Pierce made a third Arkansas-set movie in the 1970s: *The Town That Dreaded Sundown* (1976). Based on a series of ultimately unsolved murders in and around Texarkana, this otherwise poor film was redeemed somewhat by the appearance of veteran character actor Ben Johnson as a gruff Texas ranger. Unfortunately, Johnson nor anyone else with any discernable talent was around to redeem *Boggy Creek II,* a film so unintentionally funny that it received the *Mystery Science Theater 3000* treatment in 1999.

35. Cecil Kirk Hutson, "Cotton Pickin', Hillbillies and Rednecks: An Analysis of Black Oak Arkansas and the Perpetual Stereotyping of the Rural South," *Popular Music and Society* 17 (1993), 53; James "Jim Dandy" Mangrum quoted in Cecil Kirk Hutson, "Hot 'N' Nasty: Black Oak Arkansas and Its Effect on Rural Southern Culture," *Arkansas Historical Quarterly* 54 (Summer 1995): 185.

36. Hutson, "Cotton Pickin'," 47.

37. Ibid., 50, 51, 52, 53. Music critics quoted in Hutson.

38. Ibid., 56.

39. Southwestern Missouri's Ozark Mountain Daredevils was the Ozark region's contribution to southern rock. Like Black Oak Arkansas, the Daredevils made use of Ozark iconography—with albums featuring a quilt, an elderly woman, a log cabin, and two men with mules—but the Daredevils avoided the more blatant self-caricaturing practiced by Black Oak. For an analysis of the sociocultural implications of southern rock, see

Mark Kemp, *Dixie Lullaby: A Story of Music, Race, and New Beginnings in a New South* (New York: Free Press, 2004).

40. Francis Irby Gwaltney, *The Numbers of Our Days* (New York: Random House, 1959), 305. For a brief analysis of Gwaltney's body of work, see Lyman B. Hagen, "Francis Irby Gwaltney," Arkansas Authors series (Jonesboro, Ark.: Craighead County and Jonesboro Public Library, 1980).

41. Francis Irby Gwaltney, *Destiny's Chickens* (Indianapolis: Bobbs-Merrill, 1973).

42. Charles Portis, *True Grit* (New York: Simon & Schuster, 1968), 17.

43. "Charles Portis," Frank N. Magill, ed., *Magill's Survey of American Literature,* Vol. 5 (New York: Marshall Cavendish Corp., 1991), 1667.

44. Charles Portis, *The Dog of the South* (New York: Alfred A. Knopf, 1979), 245.

45. Portis, *True Grit,* 35.

46. William J. Schafer, "All God's Chillun Got Wings (And Six Legs, Carapaces, Rube Accents)," *Appalachian Journal* (Spring 1990): 281.

47. Gene Hyde, "'The Southern Highlands as Literary Landscape': An Interview with Fred Chappell and Donald Harington," *Southern Quarterly* 40 (Winter 2002): 90; Donald Harington, *Some Other Place. The Right Place.* (New York: Harcourt Brace Jovanovich, 1972), 363.

48. Linda K. Hughes, "Harington's Highlanders: Donald Harington's Ozarks and the Mapping of Cultures," *Southern Quarterly* 40 (Winter 2002): 40, 44.

49. Donald Harington, *The Architecture of the Arkansas Ozarks* (1975; New York: Harvest/Harcourt Brace Jovanovich, 1987), 233, 202.

50. Dougan, "Bumpkins and Bigots," 8.

51. Stephen Koch, "Donald Harington," *Encyclopedia of Arkansas History & Culture,* http://www.encyclopediaofarkansas.net (accessed 9 May 2007); Ron Rosenbaum, "Our Least-Known Great Novelist," *Esquire,* January 1998, 30.

52. Randy Lilleston, "Arkansas-bashing Back in Fashion," *Arkansas Democrat-Gazette,* 29 March 1992, 1A; Mark Oswald and Max Parker, "Strategists Scrutinize Clinton Past," *Arkansas Gazette,* 1 September 1991, 1A; John R. Starr, "Clinton Bid Will Strengthen Negative Myths," *Arkansas Democrat-Gazette,* 28 December 1991, 9B; Max Brantley, "Rise Above Gooberdom, Governor," *Arkansas Gazette,* 23 August 1991, 1B.

53. Hugh Hart Pollard, "Clinton Bid Could Boost Arkansas," *Arkansas Gazette,* 23 June 1991, 1F. For a discussion of Clinton's inferiority complex, see Donald Baer and Seven V. Roberts, "The Making of Bill Clinton," *U.S. News and World Report,* 30 March 1992, 28.

54. James M. Perry, "Clinton's Home, Arkansas, Is Foreign to a Lot of Americans," *Wall Street Journal,* 4 June 1992, reprinted in *Arkansas Democrat-Gazette,* 7 June 1992, 18A.

55. Bonnie Angelo, "Her Master's Voice," *Time,* 12 August 1996, 65; *Newsweek,* 14 October 1991, 24; Margaret Carlson, "Bill Clinton: Front Runner by Default," *Time,* 30 December 1991, 19.

56. Bill Clinton, *My Life* (New York: Alfred A. Knopf, 2004), 405; Robin Toner, "Clinton's Roots Trip Him in New York," *New York Times,* 1 April 1992, A20; Deborah Sontag, "Clinton on Blacks and Jews, and Himself," *New York Times,* 28 March 1992, 8; Michael Kelly, "A Magazine Will Tell All About Bubba," *New York Times,* 4 February 1993, A20; B. Drummond Ayres Jr., "After Months of Running, Advice for a Winner Named Clinton," *New York Times,* 3 November 1992, A14.

57. John R. Starr, "A Lesson Clinton Didn't Learn," *Arkansas Democrat-Gazette,* 26 July 1992, 5J.

58. Oswald and Parker, "Strategists Scrutinize," 1A.

59. John R. Starr, "LA Writer Insults Arkansas with Uninformed Comments," *Arkansas Democrat-Gazette,* 5 April 1992, 5J; *Arkansas Democrat-Gazette,* 6 December 1991, 1B.

60. Don Johnson, "How Low Does State Really Go?" *Arkansas Democrat-Gazette,* 30 October 1992, 1A, 16A; Jane Fullerton, "Bush Keeps Low Arkansas Statistics in Spotlight," *Arkansas Democrat-Gazette,* 2 November 1992, 9A; Richard L. Berkes, "Bush Ad Strikes, but Problems Loom," *New York Times,* 25 September 1992, A19; Noel Oman, "Republicans Defend State, Bash Governor at Convention," *Arkansas Democrat-Gazette,* 11A; *Arkansas Democrat-Gazette,* 8 August 1992, 1A; Evan Ramstad, "Perot Turns TV Guns on Clinton," *Arkansas Democrat-Gazette,* 2 November 1992, 1A; Ron Fournier, "Delegates Grin, Bear Blasts at State," *Arkansas Democrat-Gazette,* 21 August 1992, 16A; Terry Lemons, "Marilyn Quayle Explains Comments," *Arkansas Democrat-Gazette,* 1 October 1992, 14A.

61. Oman, "Republicans Defend State," 11A; *Arkansas Democrat-Gazette,* 8 August 1992, 1A; Donald M. Rothberg, "Wright Counterattacks, Defends State Rankings," *Arkansas Democrat-Gazette,* 20 August 1992, 14A.

62. *Saturday Night Live,* 10 October 1992.

63. Michael Kelly, "Little Rock Hopes Clinton Presidency Will Put Its Dogpatch Image to Rest," *New York Times,* 27 November 1992, A20; Sharon Cohen, "Clinton Helps State Lift Image from Hillbilly to High-Profile," *Arkansas Democrat-Gazette,* 22 March 1993, 5B.

64. Joel Achenbach, "Spotlight on Arkansas," *Washington Post,* n.d., reprinted in *Arkansas Democrat-Gazette,* 14 January 1993, 1F.

CONCLUSION

1. David Firestone, "Governor's Mansion is a Triple-Wide," *New York Times,* 19 July 2000, A16; "Arkansas Governor, Family to Move into 'Triplewide,'" Associated Press release, 19 July 2000, CNN.com (http://edition.cnn.com [accessed 23 May 2007]).

2. Firestone, "Governor's Mansion," A16; Ros Davidson, "Possum Pie and Down-Home Hospitality for the 'Trailer Trash' Governor," *Sunday Herald,* 13 August 2000; James Jefferson, "Ark. Governor Laughs with Leno Over Triplewide," Associated Press release, CNN.com, 11 August 2000 (http://archives.cnn.com/ [accessed 23 May 2007]).

3. "Arkansas Governor, Family to Move"; Jefferson, "Ark. Governor Laughs."

4. Hess's Maggody Series began with *Malice in Maggody* (New York: St. Martin's, 1987) and to date includes more than a dozen titles. Hess is also the author of the Claire Malloy series of mysteries, set in the fictional Arkansas college town of Farberville. Not as consciously Arkansaw as the Maggody-Arly Hanks mysteries, the Claire Malloy series illustrates the important town-rural divide long evident in the Arkansaw image.

5. "Rangel Blasts Clinton as 'a Redneck,'" NewsMax.com, 15 February 2005, http://www.newsmax.com/ (accessed 10 May 2007).

6. Tax burden here refers to total taxes paid as a percentage of a state's gross domestic product. These and all other statistics in succeeding paragraphs from StateMaster.com, http://www.statemaster.com/ (accessed 22 May 2007).

7. Marian Burros, "Little Rock, Big Time," *New York Times*, 29 November 1992, V1; Sharon Cohen, "Clinton Helps State Lift Image from Hillbilly to High-Profile," *Arkansas Democrat-Gazette*, 22 March 1993, 5B.

8. Eugene Newsom, "What's Wrong with Arkansas?" *American Mercury*, May 1954, 43, 41.

9. Ibid., 42, 44.

Bibliography

MANUSCRIPT COLLECTIONS

Charles H. Brough Papers. University of Arkansas Special Collections. Fayetteville.

Hudgins, Mary D., Arkansas Music Collection, University of Arkansas Special Collections. Fayetteville.

Kingston, Arkansas Collection. University of Arkansas Special Collections. Fayetteville.

Sheet music collection. Ozark Cultural Resource Center. See Arkansas History Commission, Little Rock, Arkansas.

John Quincy Wolf Folklore Collection. Lyon College. Batesville, Arkansas.

BOOKS

Anderson, John Q. *With the Bark On: Popular Humor of the Old South.* Nashville, Tenn.: Vanderbilt University Press, 1967.

———. *An Epitaph for Dixie.* New York: W. W. Norton & Co., 1958.

Ashmore, Harry S. *Arkansas: A Bicentennial History.* New York: W. W. Norton & Co., 1978.

———. *Civil Rights and Wrongs: A Memoir of Race and Politics, 1944–1994.* New York: Pantheon Books, 1994.

Babcock, Bernie. *The Man Who Lied on Arkansas and What It Got Him.* Little Rock: Sketch Book Publishing Co., 1909.

Barker, Catherine S. *Yesterday Today: Life in the Ozarks.* Caldwell, Id.: Caxton Printers, 1941.

Batteau, Allen W. *The Invention of Appalachia.* Tucson: University of Arizona Press, 1990.

Blevins, Brooks. *Hill Folks: A History of Arkansas Ozarkers and Their Image.* Chapel Hill: University of North Carolina Press, 2002.

Bolton, S. Charles. *Arkansas, 1800–1860: Remote and Restless.* Fayetteville: University of Arkansas Press, 1998.

———. *Territorial Ambition: Land and Society in Arkansas, 1800–1840.* Fayetteville: University of Arkansas Press, 1993.

Briscoe, George H. *Angels of Commerce: Or, Thirty Days with the Drummers of Arkansas.* New York: Publishers' Printing Co., 1891.

Bronner, Edwin. *The Encyclopedia of the American Theatre, 1900–1975*. San Diego, Calif.: A. S. Barnes, 1980.

Brown, James A. *Prehistoric Southern Ozark Marginality: A Myth Exposed*, Missouri Archaeological Society Special Publications, No. 6. Columbia: Missouri Archaeological Society, 1984.

Clinton, Bill. *My Life*. New York: Alfred A. Knopf, 2004.

Clugston, W. G., and Others. *Facts You Should Know About Arkansas*, Little Blue Book No. 1297. Girard, Kan.: Haldeman-Julius Publications, 1928.

Cobb, James C. *Away Down South: A History of Southern Identity*. New York: Oxford University Press, 2005.

Donaghey, George W. *Autobiography of George W. Donaghey, Governor of Arkansas, 1909–1913*. Benton, Ark.: L. B. White Printing Company, 1939.

Donovan, Timothy P., Willard B. Gatewood Jr., and Jeannie M. Whayne, eds. *The Governors of Arkansas: Essays in Political Biography*, 2nd ed. Fayetteville: University of Arkansas Press, 1995.

Dougan, Michael B. *Arkansas Odyssey: The Saga of Arkansas from Prehistoric Times to Present*. Little Rock: Rose Publishing Co., 1994.

Dugdale, R. L. *"The Jukes": A Study in Crime, Pauperism, Disease, and Heredity*. 1895. New York: AMS Press, 1975.

Dunning, John. *On the Air: The Encyclopedia of Old-Time Radio*. New York: Oxford University Press, 1998.

Featherstonhaugh, George William. *Excursion Through the Slave States, from Washington on the Potomac to the Gulf of Mexico*. 1844. New York: Negro Universities Press, 1968.

Feldmann, Doug. *Dizzy and the Gas House Gang: The 1934 St. Louis Cardinals and Depression-era Baseball*. Jefferson, N.C.: McFarland & Co., 2000.

Gerstäcker, Friedrich. *Wild Sports in the Far West: The Narrative of a German Wanderer Beyond the Mississippi, 1837–1843*. Introduction and notes by Edna L. Steeves and Harrison R. Steeves. 1854. Durham, N.C.: Duke University Press, 1968.

Glenn, Wayne. *The Ozarks' Greatest Hits: A Photo History of Music in the Ozarks*. N.P., 2005.

Green, Avantus. *The Arkansas Challenge: A Bragging, Boasting, Swaggering, Toasting Handbook on the Wonder State*. Little Rock: n.p., 1966.

Green, Avantus. *With This We Challenge*. Little Rock: n.p., 1945.

Gregory, Robert. *Diz: Dizzy Dean and Baseball During the Great Depression*. New York: Viking, 1992.

Gunther, John. *Inside U.S.A.* New York: Harper & Brothers, 1947.

Gwaltney, Francis Irby. *The Numbers of Our Days*. New York: Random House, 1959.

———. *Destiny's Chickens*. Indianapolis: Bobbs-Merrill, 1973.

Harington, Donald. *The Architecture of the Arkansas Ozarks*. 1975. New York: Harvest/Harcourt Brace Jovanovich, 1987.

———. *Let Us Build Us a City: Eleven Lost Towns*. New York: Harcourt Brace & Company, 1986.

Harkins, Anthony. *Hillbilly: A Cultural History of an American Icon*. New York: Oxford University Press, 2004.

Hauck, Louise Platt. *Wild Grape*. Philadelphia: Penn Publishing Co., 1931.

Henry, James P. *The Arkansas Gazetteer for 1873: An Emigrant's Guide to Arkansas*. Little Rock: Price & McClure, 1873.

———. *Resources of the State of Arkansas, With Description of Counties, Railroads, Mines, and the City of Little Rock*. Little Rock: Price & McClure, 1872.

Hess, Joan. *Malice in Maggody*. New York: St. Martin's, 1987.

Hibler, Charles H. *Down in Arkansas*. New York: Abbey Press, 1902.

Higham, John. *Strangers in the Land: Patterns of American Nativism, 1860–1925*. 1955. New Brunswick, N.J.: Rutgers University Press, 1988.

Hobson, Fred C., Jr. *Serpent in Eden: H. L. Mencken and the South*. Chapel Hill: University of North Carolina Press, 1974.

———. *Tell About the South: The Southern Rage to Explain*. Baton Rouge: Louisiana State University Press, 1983.

Hsiung, David C. *Two Worlds in the Tennessee Mountains: Exploring the Origins of Appalachian Stereotypes*. Lexington: University Press of Kentucky, 1997.

Hughes, Marion. *Three Years in Arkansaw*. Chicago: M. A. Donohue & Company, 1904.

Hundley, Daniel R. *Social Relations in Our Southern States*. Edited with an introduction by William J. Cooper Jr. 1860. Baton Rouge: Louisiana State University Press, 1979.

Jackson, Thomas W. *On a Slow Train Through Arkansaw*. Introduction by Harlan Daniel. Forrest City, Ark.: M. Vance, 1982.

———. *On a Slow Train Through Arkansaw*. Edited with an introduction by W. K. McNeil. 1903. Lexington: University Press of Kentucky, 1985.

Jacoway, Elizabeth. *Turn Away Thy Son: Little Rock, the Crisis that Shocked the Nation*. New York: Free Press, 2007.

Johnson, Ben F., III. *John Barleycorn Must Die: The War against Drink in Arkansas*. Fayetteville: University of Arkansas Press, 2005.

Johnson, Larry E. *An Arkansaw Swap*. Chicago: T. S. Denison & Company, 1923.

Kirby, Jack Temple. *Media-Made Dixie*. Baton Rouge: Louisiana State University Press, 1978.

Latrobe, Charles Joseph. *The Rambler in North America*. 1836. New York: Johnson Reprint Corp., 1970.

Lancaster, Bob. *The Jungles of Arkansas: A Personal History of the Wonder State*. Fayetteville: University of Arkansas Press, 1989.

Lane, Rose Wilder. *Hill-Billy*. New York: Harper & Brothers, 1926.

Lears, T. J. Jackson. *No Place of Grace: Antimodernism and the Transformation of American Culture, 1880–1920*. New York: Pantheon Books, 1981.

Lewis, Herb. *Eb Peechcrap and Wife at the Fair*. New York: Neale Publishing Company, 1906.

Magill, Frank N., ed. *Magill's Survey of American Literature*. Vol. 5. New York: Marshall Cavendish Corp., 1991.

Masterson, James R. *Arkansas Folklore: The Arkansas Traveler, Davey Crockett, and Other Legends*. Published as *Tall Tales of Arkansaw*, 1942. Little Rock: Rose Publishing Co., 1974.

McCarty, Clifford. *Bogey: The Films of Humphrey Bogart*. New York: Citadel Press, 1965.

Melville, Herman. *Moby-Dick*. Introduction and notes by Carol F. Hovde. 1851. New York: Barnes & Noble Classics, 2005.

Merrell, Henry. *The Autobiography of Henry Merrell: Industrial Missionary to the South*. Edited by James L. Skinner. Athens: University of Georgia Press, 1991.

Mesick, Jane Louise. *The English Traveler in America, 1785–1835*. 1922. Westport, Conn.: Greenwood Press, 1970.

Mills, T. B., & Co. *The New Arkansas Travelers: A History of the North-western Editorial Excursion to Arkansas, A Short Sketch of its Inception and the Routes Traveled over, the Manner in which the Editors were Received, the Resolutions Adopted and Speeches Made at Various Points, the View of the Editorial Visitors to Arkansas as Expressed in their Papers*. Little Rock: T. B. Mills & Co., 1876.

Minick, Roger, and Bob Minick. *Hills of Home: The Rural Ozarks*. 1975. New York: Ballantine Books, 1976.

Morgan, Gordon D. *Black Hillbillies of the Arkansas Ozarks*. Fayetteville: University of Arkansas Department of Sociology, 1973.

Morris, Robert L. *Opie Read: American Humorist*. New York: Helios Books, 1965.

Morrow, Lynn, and Linda Myers-Phinney. *Shepherd of the Hills Country: Tourism Transforms the Ozarks, 1880–1930s*. Fayetteville: University of Arkansas Press, 1999.

Murton, Thomas O., and Joe Hyams. *Accomplices to the Crime*. 1969. New York: Grove Press, 1970.

Nash, Roderick. *The Nervous Generation: American Thought, 1917–1930*. Chicago: Rand McNally and Co., 1970.

Nuttall, Thomas. *A Journal of Travels into the Arkansas Territory During the Year 1819*. Edited by Savoie Lottinville. 1821. Norman: University of Oklahoma Press, 1980.

Payton, Crystal. *The Story of Silver Dollar City: A Pictorial History of Branson's Famous Ozark Mountain Theme Park*. Branson, Mo.: Silver Dollar City, 1997.

Peirce, Neal R., and Jerry Hagstrom. *The Book of America: Inside 50 States Today*. New York: W. W. Norton & Company, 1983.

Portis, Charles. *The Dog of the South*. New York: Alfred A. Knopf, 1979.

———. *True Grit*. New York: Simon & Schuster, 1968.

Quinn, Rev. D. A. *Heroes and Heroines of Memphis, on Reminiscences of the Yellow Fever Epidemics That Afflicted the City of Memphis During the Autumn Months of 1873, 1878, and 1879*. Providence, R.I.: E. L. Freeman & Son, 1887.

Randolph, Vance. *Ozark Folksongs,* Revised edition. 4 volumes. 1946.
　　Columbia: University of Missouri Press, 1980.
———. *The Ozarks: An American Survival of Primitive Society.* New York:
　　Vanguard Press, 1931.
Rayburn, Otto Ernest. *Ozark Country.* New York: Duell, Sloan & Pearce, 1941.
Rattlehead, David. *The Life and Adventures of an Arkansaw Doctor.* Edited by
　　W. K. McNeil. Fayetteville: University of Arkansas Press, 1989.
Reed, John Shelton. *Southern Folk, Plain & Fancy: Native White Social Types.*
　　Lamar Memorial Lectures No. 29. Athens: University of Georgia Press,
　　1986.
Reed, Roy. *Faubus: The Life and Times of an American Prodigal.* Fayetteville:
　　University of Arkansas Press, 1997.
Rickels, Milton. *Thomas Bangs Thorpe: Humorist of the Old Southwest.* Baton
　　Rouge: Louisiana State University Press, 1962.
Rodgers, Marion Elizabeth. *The Impossible H. L. Mencken: A Selection of His
　　Best Newspaper Stories.* New York: Doubleday, 1991.
Rohrbough, Malcolm J. *Trans-Appalachian Frontier: People, Societies, and
　　Institutions, 1775–1850,* 3rd ed. Bloomington: Indiana University Press,
　　2008.
Sabo, George, III, Ann M. Early, Jerome C. Rose, Barbara A. Burnett, Louis
　　Vogele Jr., and James P. Harcourt. *Human Adaptation in the Ozark and
　　Ouachita Mountains.* Arkansas Archeological Survey Research Series No.
　　31. Fayetteville: Arkansas Archeological Survey, 1990.
Schickel, Richard. *Elia Kazan: A Biography.* New York: HarperCollins, 2005.
Schiller, Zoe Lund. "Acres of Sky: A Dramatic Musical." Typescript of
　　Musical Play, 1950, University of Arkansas Special Collections,
　　Fayetteville.
Schoolcraft, Henry Rowe. *Rude Pursuits and Rugged Peaks: Schoolcraft's Ozark
　　Journal, 1818–1819.* Introduction, maps, and appendix by Milton D.
　　Rafferty. Fayetteville: University of Arkansas Press, 1996.
Schulberg, Budd. *Some Faces in the Crowd: Short Stories.* New York: Random
　　House, 1953.
Shannon, Karr. *On a Fast Train Through Arkansas.* Little Rock: Democrat
　　Printing & Lithographing, 1948.
Shapiro, Henry D. *Appalachia on Our Mind: The Southern Mountains and
　　Mountaineers in the American Consciousness, 1870–1920.* Chapel Hill:
　　University of North Carolina Press, 1978.
Shearer, Stephen Michael. *Patricia Neal: An Unquiet Life.* Lexington:
　　University Press of Kentucky, 2006.
Sherrill, Robert. *Gothic Politics in the Deep South: Stars of the New Confederacy.*
　　New York: Grossman, 1968.
Simpson, Ethel C., ed. *Simpkinsville and Vicinity: Arkansas Stories by Ruth
　　McEnery Stuart.* Fayetteville: University of Arkansas Press, 1999.
Smith, Curt. *America's Dizzy Dean.* St. Louis: Bethany Press, 1978.
Smith, J. David. *Minds Made Feeble: The Myth and Legacy of the Kallikaks.*
　　Rockville, Md.: Aspen Systems Corp., 1985.

Smith, Ronald L. *Who's Who in Comedy.* New York: Facts on File, 1992.

Staten, Vince. *Ol' Diz: A Biography of Dizzy Dean.* New York: HarperCollins, 1992.

Tagg, Lawrence V. *Harold Bell Wright: Storyteller to America.* Tucson, Ariz.: Westernlore Press, 1986.

Thomas, Tony. *The Films of Ronald Reagan.* Secaucus, N.J.: Citadel Press, 1980.

Tucker, David M. *Arkansas: A People and Their Reputation.* Memphis, Tenn.: Memphis State University Press, 1985.

Twain, Mark. *The Adventures of Huckleberry Finn.* 1884. New York: Harper & Brothers, 1923.

———. *Roughing It,* Vol. 1. 1871. New York: Harper & Brothers, 1913.

Whayne, Jeannie, ed. *Cultural Encounters in the Early South: Indians and Europeans in Arkansas.* Fayetteville: University of Arkansas, 1995.

Whisnant, David E. *All That Is Native and Fine: The Politics of Culture in an American Region.* Chapel Hill: University of North Carolina Press, 1983.

———. *Modernizing the Mountaineer: People, Power, and Planning in Appalachia.* 1980. Knoxville: University of Tennessee Press, 1994.

Williams, C. Fred, S. Charles Bolton, Carl H. Moneyhon, and LeRoy T. Williams, eds. *A Documentary History of Arkansas.* Fayetteville: University of Arkansas Press, 1984.

Williams, Leonard, ed. *Cavorting on the Devil's Fork: The Pete Whetstone Letters of C. F. M. Noland.* Memphis, Tenn.: Memphis State University Press, 1979.

Williamson, Thames. *The Woods Colt: A Novel of the Ozark Hills.* New York: Harcourt, Brace and Company, 1933.

Wilson, Charles Morrow. *Acres of Sky.* New York: G. P. Putnam's Sons, 1930.

———. *Backwoods America.* Chapel Hill: University of North Carolina Press, 1935.

Woodruff, Press. *A Backwoods Philosopher from Arkansaw.* Chicago: Thompson & Thomas, 1901.

ARTICLES

Bolton, S. Charles. "Slavery and the Defining of Arkansas." *Arkansas Historical Quarterly* 58 (Spring 1999): 1–23.

Brady, Erika. Song notes for Jimmie Davis, "In Arkansas." In Richard K. Spottswood, ed., *Songs of Local History & Events.* Folk Music of America Series, vol. 12. Washington, D.C.: Library of Congress Music Division Recording Laboratory, 1978.

Brown, Rodger. "Dogpatch, USA: The Road to Hokum." *Southern Changes* 15 (1993): 18–26.

Brown, Sarah. "*The Arkansas Traveller:* Southwest Humor on Canvas." *Arkansas Historical Quarterly* 46 (Winter 1987): 348–75.

Camp, Marcia. "Bernie Babcock." *The Encyclopedia of Arkansas History & Culture.* http://www.encyclopediaofarkansas.net.

Cochran, Robert B. "'Low, Degrading Scoundrels': George W. Featherstonhaugh's Contribution to the Bad Name of Arkansas." *Arkansas Historical Quarterly* 48 (Spring 1989): 3–16.

Compton, Ellen. "Charles Morrow Wilson." *The Encyclopedia of Arkansas History & Culture.* http://www.encyclopediaofarkansas.net.

Cook, Charles Orson. "Boosterism and Babbittry: Charles Hillman Brough and the 'Selling' of Arkansas." *Arkansas Historical Quarterly* 37 (Spring 1978): 74–83.

Dale, E. E. "Arkansas: The Myth and the State." *Arkansas Historical Quarterly* 12 (1953): 8–29.

Dew, Lee A. "'On a Slow Train Through Arkansaw'—The Negative Image of Arkansas in the Early Twentieth Century." *Arkansas Historical Quarterly* 39 (Summer 1980): 125–35.

Dougan, Michael B. "Bumpkins and Bigots: The Arkansas Image in Fiction." *Publications of the Arkansas Philological Association* 1 (Summer 1975): 5–15.

———. "Opie Pope Read." *Encyclopedia of Arkansas History & Culture.* http://www.encyclopediaofarkansas.net.

Edson, C. L. "Arkansas: A Native Proletariat." *Nation,* 2 May 1923, 515–17.

Finger, Charles J. "Utopia in Arkansas." *Century,* June 1923, 273–78.

Friedlander, E. J. "'The Miasmatic Jungles': Reactions to H. L. Mencken's 1921 Attack on Arkansas." *Arkansas Historical Quarterly* 38 (Spring 1979): 63–71.

Fulks, Clay. "Arkansas." *American Mercury,* July 1926, 290–95.

Gusewelle, C. W. "'A Continuity of Place and Blood': The Seasons of Man in the Ozarks." *American Heritage,* December 1977, 96–109.

Hagen, Lyman B. "Francis Irby Gwaltney." Arkansas Authors Series. Jonesboro, Ark.: Craighead County and Jonesboro Public Library, 1980.

Howell, Elmo. "Mark Twain's Arkansas." *Arkansas Historical Quarterly* 29 (Autumn 1970): 195–208.

Hughes, Linda K. "Harington's Highlanders: Donald Harington's Ozarks and the Mapping of Cultures." *Southern Quarterly* 40 (Winter 2002): 39–50.

Hunting, Robert. "Mark Twain's Arkansaw Yahoos." *Modern Language Notes* 73 (April 1958): 264–68.

Hutson, Cecil Kirk. "Cotton Pickin', Hillbillies and Rednecks: An Analysis of Black Oak Arkansas and the Perpetual Stereotyping of the Rural South." *Popular Music and Society* 17 (1993): 47–62.

———. "Hot 'N' Nasty: Black Oak Arkansas and Its Effect on Rural Southern Culture." *Arkansas Historical Quarterly* 54 (Summer 1995): 185–211.

Hyde, Gene. "'The Southern Highlands as Literary Landscape': An Interview with Fred Chappell and Donald Harington." *Southern Quarterly* 40 (Winter 2002): 86–98.

King, Edward. "The Great South: Down the Mississippi—The Labor Question—Arkansas." *Scribner's Monthly,* October 1874, 641–69.

Klotter, James C. "The Black South and White Appalachia." *Journal of American History* 66 (March 1980): 832–49.

Koch, Stephen. "Donald Harington." *Encyclopedia of Arkansas History & Culture.* http://www.encyclopediaofarkansas.net.

Lisenby, Foy. "Talking Arkansas Up: The Wonder State in the Twentieth Century." *Mid-South Folklore* 6 (Winter 1978): 85–91.

Lovell, Linda. *"On a Slow Train Through Arkansaw." Encyclopedia of Arkansas History & Culture.* http://www.encyclopediaofarkansas.net.

McNeil, W. K. "'By the Ozark Trail': The Image of the Ozarks in Popular and Folk Songs." *JEMF Quarterly* (Spring–Summer 1985): 20–30.

———. Liner notes for *Somewhere in Arkansas: Early Commercial Country Music Recordings from Arkansas, 1928–1932.* Fayetteville: Center for Arkansas and Regional Studies, University of Arkansas, 1997.

Mencken, H. L. *Prejudices: Second Series.* New York: Alfred A. Knopf, 1920.

———. "The South Begins to Mutter." *The Smart Set,* August 1921, 138–44.

———. "The Worst American State, Part III." *American Mercury,* November 1931, 355–72.

Mercer, H. C. "On the Track of 'The Arkansas Traveler.'" *Century,* March 1896, 707–12.

Newsom, Eugene. "What's Wrong with Arkansas?" *American Mercury,* May 1954, 41–44.

Pierce, Brook. "Happy Hollow." *Encyclopedia of Arkansas History & Culture.* http://www.encyclopediaofarkansas.net.

Pike, Albert. "Letters From Arkansas." *American Monthly Magazine,* 1836, 25–32.

Randolph, Vance. "The Ozark Dialect in Fiction." *American Speech* 2 (March 1927): 283–89.

Roe, Shannon. "Henry Karr Shannon." *Encyclopedia of Arkansas History & Culture.* http://www.encyclopediaofarkansas.net.

Schafer, William J. "All God's Chillun Got Wings (And Six Legs, Carapaces, Rube Accents)." *Appalachian Journal* (Spring 1990): 276–84.

Shea, William L. "A Semi-Savage State: The Image of Arkansas in the Civil War." In *Civil War Arkansas: Beyond Battles and Leaders,* edited by Anne J. Bailey and Daniel E. Sutherland, 85–99. Fayetteville: University of Arkansas Press, 2000.

Simpich, Frederick. "Arkansas Rolls Up Its Sleeves." *National Geographic,* September 1946, 275–304.

Simpson, Ethel C. "Octave Thanet." *Encyclopedia of Arkansas History & Culture.* http://www.encyclopediaofarkansas.net.

Stucker, Kathryn Moore. "Chet Lauck." *Encyclopedia of Arkansas History & Culture.* http://www.encyclopediaofarkansas.net.

———. *"Lum and Abner." Encyclopedia of Arkansas History & Culture.* http://www.encyclopediaofarkansas.net.

———. "'Tuffy' Goff." *Encyclopedia of Arkansas History & Culture.* http://www.encyclopediaofarkansas.net.

Turner, Terry. "Arkansas Travelers [Baseball Team]." *Encyclopedia of Arkansas History & Culture.* http://www.encyclopediaofarkansas.net.
Williams, C. Fred. "The Bear State Image: Arkansas in the Nineteenth Century." *Arkansas Historical Quarterly* 34 (Summer 1980): 99–111.
Wolfe, Charles, and Mark Wilson. Album notes for Gid Tanner and His Skillet Lickers, *The Kickapoo Medicine Show.* Rounder Records 1028.

NEWSPAPERS AND MAGAZINES

American Magazine
American Mercury
Arkansas Democrat
Arkansas Democrat-Gazette
Arkansas Gazette
American Heritage
Arkansas Traveler
The Arkansas Writer
Atlanta Journal-Constitution
Atlantic Monthly
Baltimore *Evening Sun*
Beadle's Half Dime Library
Brick Church Life
Collier's
Esquire
Little Rock Daily News
Mentor
Nation
National Republic
New York *Journal*
New York Times
Newsweek
Outlook
Outlook and Independent
Philadelphia Evening Bulletin
Philadelphia Inquirer
Review of Reviews and World's Work
The Sample Case
Sunday Herald
The Survey
Time
Travel
U.S. News and World Report
Van Buren *Press-Argus*
Variety
Wall Street Journal
Washington Post

ONLINE AND MISCELLANEOUS

Allmovie. http://www.allmovie.com.

CNN.com. http://edition.cnn.com.

Various Artists. *Hard Time Come Again No More, Vol. 2: Early American Songs of Hard Times and Hardships.* Yazoo 2037.

Internet Movie Database. http://imdb.com.

Markstein, Don. *Don Markstein's Toonopedia.* http://www.toonopedia.com/.

NewsMax.com. 15 February 2005. http://www.newsmax.com/.

StateMaster.com. http://www.statemaster.com/.

Williamson, Jerry Wayne. "Southern Mountaineers Filmography." W. L. Eury Appalachian Collection. Appalachian State University. http://www.library.appstate.edu/appcoll/filmography.html.

Index

An Arkansaw native and graduate of Lyon College in Batesville, Brooks Blevins is the Endowed Associate Professor of Ozarks Studies at Missouri State University. He is the author of *Hill Folks: A History of Arkansas Ozarkers and Their Image* and *Lyon College: The Perseverance and Promise of an Arkansas College* and the coeditor of John Quincy Wolf's *Life in the Leatherwoods*, the latter two books published by the University of Arkansas Press.